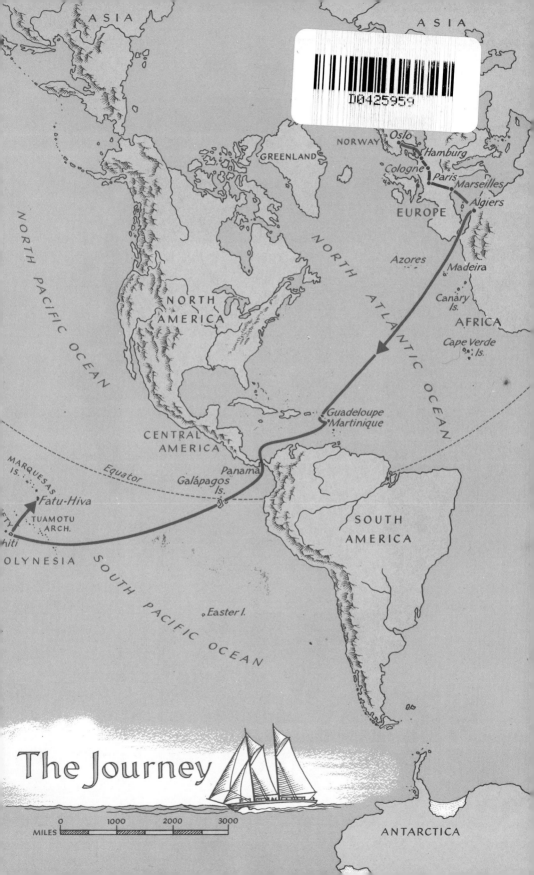

The Journey

ASIA

ASIA

D042595g

NORWAY • Oslo
• Hamburg
• Cologne
Paris •
Marseilles
EUROPE
• Algiers

GREENLAND

NORTH ATLANTIC OCEAN

NORTH
AMERICA

Azores

Madeira

Canary
Is.

AFRICA

Cape Verde
Is.

NORTH PACIFIC OCEAN

Guadeloupe
Martinique

CENTRAL
AMERICA

MARQUESAS
IS.

Fatu-Hiva

TUAMOTU
ARCH.

hiti

Equator

Galápagos
Is.

Panama

OLYNESIA

SOUTH
AMERICA

SOUTH PACIFIC OCEAN

Easter I.

MILES 0   1000   2000   3000

ANTARCTICA

PHOTO BY WALTER LEONARDI

Dr. Heyerdahl needs no introduction. His books *Kon-Tiki, Aku-Aku,* and *The Ra Expeditions* are landmarks in twentieth-century culture. In addition, he has published seven scientific books; he has received awards and honors throughout Europe and the Americas.

By Thor Heyerdahl

THE KON-TIKI EXPEDITION

AKU-AKU

THE RA EXPEDITIONS

AMERICAN INDIANS IN THE PACIFIC

SEA ROUTES TO POLYNESIA

THE ART OF EASTER ISLAND

With Edwin N. Ferdon, Jr.

Reports of the Norwegian Archaeological Expedition
to Easter Island and the East Pacific

VOL. I: THE ARCHAEOLOGY OF EASTER ISLAND

VOL. II: MISCELLANEOUS PAPERS

FATU-HIVA

Back to Nature

THOR HEYERDAHL

Doubleday & Company, Inc.
Garden City, New York
1975

Library of Congress Cataloging in Publication Data

Heyerdahl, Thor
Fatu-Hiva: back to nature.

Includes bibliographical references.
1. Fatu-Hiva Island—Description and travel.
2. Heyerdahl, Thor   I. Title.
DU701.F3H47   1975   919.6′31   [B]
ISBN 0-385-08921-X
Library of Congress Catalog Card Number 74-33646

First American Edition

Contents

	LIST OF ILLUSTRATIONS	vii
1.	FAREWELL TO CIVILIZATION	1
2.	BACK TO NATURE	25
3.	WHITE MEN, DARK SHADOWS	59
4.	EXODUS	85
5.	TABOO	101
6.	OCEAN ESCAPE	123
7.	ON HIVAOA	151
8.	ISLAND OF ILL OMEN	185
9.	IN THE CANNIBAL VALLEY	193
10.	CAVE DWELLERS	237
	INDEX	271

Illustrations

FOLLOWING
PAGE:

Tahiti, arrival by steamer   38
Chief Teriieroo and his wife   "
Author and wife in Tahitian dress   "
The chief's children; tropical fruits; climbing a coconut palm   "
Author and wife on a copra schooner; coral atolls
   in the Tuamotu group   "
The Marquesas Islands from the sea; a shark and a moray eel   "
Palm valley in the Marquesas Islands   "
Landing on Fatu-Hiva   "
Our first shelter in the jungle   62
Clearing an overgrown site   "
Our first home, of plaited bamboo   "
Mountain stream below the bamboo hut   "
Sugar cane; papaya; bananas   "
Pantry in the breadfruit tree; the royal trail into the interior   "
Homeward bound with food; petroglyphs in the forest   "
Ancient Marquesan art   "
Pakeekee; Father Victorin; Tioti; Paho   86
Feeling like a king   "
Liv's bathing pool   "
Haii, a sufferer from elephantiasis   "
On the mountain trail   "
Paho with piglet; Liv with stallion; camp on the high plateau   "
Liv cooking in the highlands   "
Resting under a mango tree; wild horses; the sure-footed
   Tuiveta   "
Above the Hanavave Valley; on the island hills   110
Above the Omoa Valley   "
Tuiveta and Liv on the shelf; back to the jungle cabin   "
At an old burial ground; human craniums   "
The cabin at night   "
Exploring taboo ground   "

Sacred jungle trees; the Tauaouoho Mountain Ridge;
  climbing a taboo pinnacle   110
Exploring a taboo cave; embarking on the sacred lake;
  on the sacred lake   "
The Puamau Valley, on Hivaoa   158
Stone giant in the Puamau Valley; stone giant
  in South America; prone statue in South America   "
Prone statue in the Puamau Valley   "
Headless giant on a pedestal   "
Stone head; prone statue; faceless statue; headless statue   "
Henry Lie and family; Captain Brander and Théodore;
  fellow schooner passengers; Gauguin's gun   "
Back to Fatu-Hiva   "
Veo; his wife; a *poipoi* bowl; umbrella leaves;
  Hanavave Valley   "
The cabin on our return to Fatu-Hiva   182
The Tauaouoho Mountain Range; crossing the Omoa River;
  ferns and fern trees   "
The cliffs above the Ouia Valley   "
Tei Tetua   "
Tahia-Momo   "
Our pole cabin on the Ouia beach   "
Playing a bamboo nose flute   "
Tei Tetua carrying fruit; Ouia oranges; Tei Tetua
  gnawing a bone   206
Our Ouia home   "
Our wild goat   "
Tei Tetua roasting a breadfruit   "
Liv and Tahia-Momo collecting sea food   "
The open side of our pole cabin   "
Wild boars beside our cabin   "
Tei Tetua beside his own tomb; our cabin ladder;
  Liv and Tahia-Momo   230
Veo and his team of dogs   "
Fishing for octopus; Veo shares his booty with his dogs;
  octopus caught by children   "
A gay eating party   "
Liv resting with the piglet   "
Refugees on Tahaoa beach   "
Cave dwellers waiting for a ship   "

Fatu-Hiva

1. FAREWELL TO CIVILIZATION

Back to nature? Farewell to civilization? It is one thing to dream of it and another to do it. I tried it. Tried to return to nature. Crushed my watch between two stones and let my hair and beard grow wild. Climbed the palms for food. Cut all the chains that bound me to the modern world. I tried to enter the wilderness empty-handed and barefoot, as a man at one with nature.

Today I would have been labeled "hippie," for my hair hung down to my shoulders and my beard was so long that my mustache could be seen from behind. I ran away from bureaucracy, technology, and the grip of twentieth-century civilization. My only garment, if any at all, was a flowery loincloth, and my home was of plaited yellow bamboo. I drew no salary, for I had no expenses; my world was free for birds and beasts and barefoot men to help themselves to what they needed, one day at a time.

This experience was indeed a hippie's dream, a trip deep into an utterly different existence. But a trip without drugs. For this journey was carefully planned and a solid reality.

I was still a high school boy in Norway when I began to prepare myself for this wild adventure. My home was a white-painted wooden house, covered with ivy, in a little coastal town at the mouth of the Oslo Fjord. No smog, no pollution. No stress, nothing, apparently, to escape from. No hippies. The largest buildings in the town were a wooden church and my father's brick-walled brewery. The air was pure and the river clean. It was safe to drink from any running stream.

In the harbor the water was crystal clear, and little boys with long bamboo rods would sit in rows on the wooden pier watching shoals of fish wriggling up to nibble at their bait. There was nothing to see at the bottom but smooth boulders and gently waving seaweed. Farther out lay large whaling ships at anchor, with thousands of tons of blubber from marine giants which still roamed the southern seas in endless numbers. The little city of Larvik throve on its wealth of timber and its successful whaling fleet.

But there was something in the air. Modern whaling techniques had made the giant whales such an easy catch that there were real fortunes in the whaling industry. This called for caution. The ocean was endless; it ran on with no beginning and no end, reaching beyond both poles. But man, too, was everywhere. Could he, with his technical progress, one day bring an end to nature's eternal supply of whales? No. That was unthinkable then. The world of the whales was endless. The blue ocean was as infinite as the blue sky, one merging into the other, and both being part of the boundless universe.

At that time, the unrestricted air space had just begun to interest adults. Fairy tales came alive in the minds of little boys. Grown men had already begun to lift themselves above the earth like witches on broomsticks or wizards on flying carpets. With the children in the street, I climbed the wobbly tiles of our house to wave and yell as we heard the drone of a single-engined airplane which passed as a speck on the horizon. We even ran to the garden fence to watch the first driver who dared to force his automobile up the steep street past my home. How exciting! But what a choking, sickening smell it left behind compared with that of a horse.

The traffic in Larvik was still dominated by the rhythmic clacking of horses' hoofs and the rumbling of wheels over cobblestones. In the winter, however, the streets were white-padded and silent, although the merry tooting of klaxons had now begun to mingle with the familiar jingle of sleigh bells. My father enjoyed his morning walk to his office, and he enjoyed the walk back for a peaceful family lunch and a long afternoon nap. The days were never rushed, and watches were big, with ample space between the hours.

Before dusk my father and I often walked down to the piers to gaze at the fishermen's catch. Their boxes were filled with lobsters, crabs, shrimps, and an endless variety of fish and other marine creatures, flipping, wriggling, and crawling around and over each other in a fresh odor of seaweed and salt sea. Sea food was a real delicacy for those of us who could afford to get it to the kitchen alive. If delivered dead on ice, it was no longer for the gourmet.

From my two bedroom windows, upstairs, I had a splendid view of the fjord below and beyond the center of the town, which lay in terraces below us: white gables and red roofs, partly hidden among garden trees where cocks crowed from the back yards. The old seaport of Larvik was like a large and tidy village, climbing from the fjord in a pattern of terraces and ramps up the sides of low, forested hills—a verdant landscape of huge pines, firs, oaks, birches, and even Norway's only large beech forest. I could see it all by sneaking out of my bed. In the winter, my parents left my bedroom window ajar at night, and I would take only a quick look at the many city lights and the falling flakes of snow before I huddled under my warm eiderdown. But, on bright summer nights, they would leave both windows wide open, and when they thought I was sleeping, I could sit and dream on the window sill. I would rush to the window at the distant sound of a ship's bell announcing its departure. My soul went with it as it slid toward the open mouth of the fjord, perhaps to tropical dreamlands hidden from sight far beyond the hilly headlands that marked the gateway to the open ocean. Beyond that gate was the boundless, endless world which man was still exploring.

Part of it was unknown. Our compatriot Amundsen had reached the South Pole just before I was born, and now he and others were competing to reach the North Pole by air, since Nansen's drift with the *Fram* across the polar sea had shown that the top of our planet was all floating ice. In the warmer areas, other expeditions were struggling on foot, as in the days of Cortez and Pizarro, to fill in empty spaces on the world map. Search parties were trying to enter unknown areas of Brazil, where Colonel Fawcett had just been lost among mysterious head-hunters. Africa and Asia were not only different continents, but literally different worlds, where strange people were living, with manners and beliefs utterly alien to us.

What an enormous world man lived in then! The children in the nearest house below us were emigrating to America with their parents. Weeks of travel beyond the horizon. They were seen off by the rest of us like departing astronauts. Certainly, nobody would ever hear of them again.

An explorer. That was what I wanted to become. To penetrate on foot, by horse, or by camel, unknown parts of our vast world. Planet Earth had not yet started to shrivel seriously in dimension. Certainly, with steamships, America was only a quarter of the distance away compared with what it was in Columbus' time, but even that was far. It took me three days to travel with my parents from the port of Larvik to our mountain holiday cottage in the Norwegian midlands, partly by train and partly by pony and trap. I was amazed beyond description when some friends showed me what they called a "radio," a square battery box with holes into which we plugged our earphones and eagerly discussed whether or not we heard distant music.

A new era was vaguely in the making. My parents received it with pride and excitement. My father trusted the human brain, because it was the gift of God. My mother put all her faith in Darwin and was confident that man was gaining in intelligence and changing his planet into something ever better. The great World War, which had been raging when I was born, would never be repeated. With science and technology, man was marching on toward moral rectitude and peace.

Sharing my father's love for nature and my mother's passion for zoology and "primitive" tribes, I could not understand their enthusiasm for modern man's determination to sever all his ties with nature. What was it they wanted to run away from? Were they scared by the ape man Darwin had painted behind them? They were ready to welcome any change from the world of their own parents by calling it "progress," no matter what the change might be. "Progress" was synonymous with distance from nature. The adults, who set the pace of progress from nature, were so absorbed by their own ability to invent and to alter the existing world, that they hurried headlong, with no design for the ultimate structure. A man-made environment was the obvious goal, but who was the responsible architect? No one in my country. Not even the king of Great Britain or the president of America. Each inventor and producer who worked on building tomorrow's world just threw in a brick or a cogwheel wherever he cared to, and it was up to us of the next generation to find out what the result would be.

They taught us in school about the human brain. They taught us that it stopped growing at about the age of twelve. Yet now, at the age of sixteen, we were all still treated as if we had only half a brain. How could adults believe that people of my age would think more clearly, once our freshly developed minds had been pressed through the education machine and filled to capacity with the doctrines of the elders? It was now, while we were still young, that we had to think; it was now that we had to hurry and judge, if we were not to be drugged into accepting blindly the seats offered to us on the engineless train of the elders.

In school, the topic of progress was dealt with in a directly dishonest way. We were taught to believe in progress from Paradise. Our teachers seemed to me to be walking a tightrope, juggling with the Bible in one hand and Science in the other. They had succeeded in balancing so far down the line that their arrival at the other end was lost to sight. We were told that God had figured out how to create man. Darwin had discovered how he had done it, making monkeys first. We were also told that God created the world with all living species in six days, but the Bible also said that to God one day was a thousand years and a thousand years one day. Einstein agreed that time was relative, so thus far the adults agreed among themselves. Natural science had even come to the same conclusion as that written in Genesis thousands of years ago: life on earth began in the ocean and not on land. Only when the salt seas were swarming with life, and the air was filled with the winged species, did the day come when creeping things and all the beasts of the earth began to move on dry land. The unknown sages who wrote the Book of Genesis were even supported in their claim that man was the last of all to come into existence in a ready-made world of plants and beasts. Everything rotated and ticked, everything functioned, before man (not through any effort of his own) got his lungs, his heart, his senses, and his brain.

No errors had been committed in the complex design of Paradise. Even here, the Bible and Science agreed. God was completely satisfied with the world he had created. He found it very good, so perfect, in fact, that, on the seventh day, he stopped his work and went to rest, abandoning man naked in the bush. Naked, but well provided for, like any bird or beast before him. According to the Bible, God was merciful and would not let the human species he had created starve. According to science, man could not have evolved from any beasts if nature had not favored him and provided amply for his survival. So far, there was full agreement.

But this was just where we lost touch with our teachers. This was also where the conflict began. Conflict between the Creator and the created, and conflict between the right and the left hand of our juggling teachers. For, whereas God was pleased with his job, man was not. God was sure he had given man a perfect environment, an earthly Paradise. Man did not agree. While God rested, man took over. Man wanted progress. Progress from Paradise.

Man, too, worked six days, and thought he pleased God if he rested on the seventh. Men quarreled among themselves about whether they were to rest on Sundays, on Saturdays, or on Fridays. But whether Christians, Jews, or Moslems, they hurried back to work again on the eighth day and continued their struggle to make a better world. For centuries and millenniums. God rested while man invented wheelbarrows and cars. God had not thought of inventing dynamite. Did he realize his own shortcomings when he saw what we could do? Did he approve of our remodeling of everything he had done? Religious adults seemed to believe that God guided our brains to ensure that any step we took meant progress. Yet we were taught that God had left us responsible for our own planet, with ability and freedom to build and destroy, to advance and retreat, to rejoice and suffer, guided purely by the intelligence, intuition, and conscience we had been given. Surely, this had to be correct if it was true that the Creator would reward or punish us in afterlife according to our behavior. What really bothered me was that adults said that God had created nature, yet they acted as if the devil was on their heels unless they severed all their ties with nature. Even atheists, who argued that nature itself had produced man, acted as if nature was man's old and innate enemy.

At about the age of sixteen, I began to feel uneasy. My confidence in adults began to be shaken. They were not smarter than us kids. They just had fixed ideas and stuck to them even if they disagreed among themselves. They were dragging us along a road to an unknown destination; they had no goal, just something to escape from: nature. A terrible war had just raged. Now they were inventing new types of arms, worse than ever before. Disagreements in politics, in morals, in philosophy, in religion. Who could feel safe in following in the footsteps of such a generation? It was better to begin to look for a safer, side track. I began to feel like a prisoner calmly preparing to jump off a train that was on a wrong track.

This was about 1930. There were no hippies then. Nobody with respect for himself would revolt against parents or school and, for a boy, any resemblance to a girl would be a fatal degradation. My interests in natural history increased. I began to see not only the beauty, but the superintelligence behind the build-up of the world man had inherited. I took to the forests, the mountains, and the open seashore whenever I could, and became skeptical toward the trend of a civilization designed to take man away from this environment. Were we doing something mad?

Finally, I had to share my growing distrust with someone of my own age. One day, while the class was busy in the changing rooms after gymnastics, I was deep in my own thoughts.

"I don't like machinery," I blurted out to the boy next to me, who was struggling with his shirt.

"You don't say?" He merely grinned back with such an overbearing look of surprise that I felt like creeping into the shoe I was putting on and knotting the laces over my head. I had said something completely ridiculous to others. Not a word more came from my lips.

There was one boy in the class, however, to whom I gradually felt I could confide my secret. A huge fellow who did not care for sports like the rest, and who did not roam in the woods like me. He read books, wrote poetry, and liked to stroll deep into philosophical dreamlands. To Arnold, I gradually dared to open my mind. He listened with big eyes. I told him I was going to leave everything. Everything. I was going to return to nature. Somewhere in the tropics, where food could be picked from the trees. I was not going to spend my adult life in Europe, where disaster was lurking around the corner. Our twentieth-century tower of Babel was either going to collapse or to lead man into another, horrible, universal war. Better to stay far away. From now on, I had a confidant.

How could the dream be turned into reality? Careful preparations were needed. First of all, I had to build up my body and improve a rather shaky physique. There was hardship ahead. I had another friend, Erik, a huge, husky chap who for a while after junior high school had left us to go to sea. Life at sea for two years had given him the kind of muscles I needed. Erik, too, was skeptical about modern progress. He romanced about building an ideal community in the heart of Africa or in the unexplored plateau of the Mato Grosso, in Brazil. My ambitions were not that big. I wanted only to find a girl who would share the experiment with me. With Erik and his local gang, I took for the first time to sport. Cross-country running in the forest, and skiing when snow fell. On our winter vacations, we started something scarcely known in Norway in those days: we pulled ski sledges behind us with tent and provisions, and slept in the wild mountains. Weeks away from people. Soon we left with no tent, and with warm reindeer sleeping bags bought from Lapps in the far north, we dug ourselves snug and sheltered caves in hard-packed snow, or sliced it into blocks to build igloos, in Eskimo style. The cost of these trips was covered by illustrated articles about our adventures. Our mountain expeditions got longer and wilder when I obtained a huge Eskimo dog from a Norwegian sportsman, Martin Mehren, just back from crossing the then unknown center of Greenland with dog sledge and skis. With the dog, Kazan, pulling our food, Erik and I would build igloos to sleep in during the winter, sometimes even on the highest peaks and glaciers of Norway, in Rondane and Jotunheimen. Breath-taking views of the world below us at sunset or at moonrise through the door of our igloo. These holidays, during which I was exposed to all the elements and at intimate grips with nature, combined with reading about natural history and primitive cultures in my mother's well-stocked library, had a greater appeal to me than the school textbooks. High school marks became neither good nor bad. Medium. I did not care. I merely wanted to know how to get on friendly terms with nature, how men and animals could once have thrived in the environment of which we were all a product.

Girls. I was desperately interested, but too shy to approach them. Since my parents forced me through three terms of dancing school as a tiny boy, I had never dared to mingle with the other sex. They were fairies, not real human beings, and I did not know how to talk to them intelligently. Yet I should never return to nature before choosing one of that enticing species for company.

Only during holidays in the wilderness did I really feel myself. Under the blue sky, high above tree level, I felt literally on top of the world, and up there I overcame the sex barrier when I met a beautiful, sun-tanned fairy crossing the lofty plateau on skis for sport and fun. A country girl, daughter of the sheriff in the large valley below. By an open fireplace in a mountain refuge, we talked all night. Yes, she would return to nature with me, after school. She came to study in the capital and straight away fell prey to the city. Lipstick, shops, and entertainment. How stupid to have looked for a country girl. I needed a city girl who was already fed up with civilization. A gipsy-looking ballet dancer from Oslo National Theater waggled onto my mountain trail one summer evening and was introduced by mutual friends. Trout-fishing from rowboats. Dancing around campfires. Would she leave the city and come with me back to nature? Indeed! Enthusiasm! I had found my companion. Until some weeks later, when she asked me to hurry up and get the tickets, since she was just dying for the moment when I would make her queen of a South Sea island. For me, she sank into the asphalt as if with the wave of a magic wand. No girl seemed to understand my ideas.

It was at a graduation ball that I met Liv. Everyone was happy. School days were over. Everyone was dancing. But not I. I was sitting alone at an open window, watching the reflection of the moon tremble in the wake of small boats as they passed to and fro on the black waters of the fjord. Suddenly I found myself in the company of a friend who parked an unknown girl from another town beside me. Bushy blond hair, laughing blue eyes. Sorry, don't dance. But what about a walk? No? Then let's chat. OK. Words and words. From jokes to philosophy. Damned intelligent eyes. Worth taking a chance.

"What do you think about turning back to nature?" I asked out of the blue.

"Then it would have to be all the way," she answered firmly and without hesitation.

That did it; she had grasped the point.

She was to share in my experiment. Her name was Liv, and we were to meet again as soon as we had both moved to Oslo, where we were to begin our university education: I, of my own choice, zoology and geography, she, pushed by her father, and to my horror, economics.

The choice of zoology as a main subject was to follow up my childhood love of nature. The choice of geography was to prepare myself for the experiment, to learn where it could best be conducted. My interests in aboriginal tribes and foreign cultures had not diminished. Attention was now focused on Polynesia: on the stone-age people who had settled in the far-flung islands of the East Pacific. But if I were to study anthropology at any university, the courses and textbooks would devote only a few hours to all Polynesia. By good fortune, I was granted a better solution. The world's largest private collection of books and papers on Polynesia happened to belong to a wealthy Norwegian wine merchant in Oslo. Bjarne Kroepelien had as a young man spent the happiest year of his life in the home of the great Polynesian chief Teriieroo, on Tahiti, and on his return to Europe he began to collect anything published on Polynesia and the Polynesians, no matter where and when it was printed. Kroepelien was intrigued when informed of our secret plans. He let me use his important library as if I were a son in his house. Thus it happened that, whereas my formal training was in zoology, every spare moment, and more and more of my efforts, went into the world of books in Kroepelien's extraordinary library on Polynesia and its people.[1]

My animal studies never became quite what I had hoped for. We hardly heard of wild beasts and the way they lived in the wilderness. We sliced up intestines and looked at them under the microscope.

[1] Many years later, Oslo University Library purchased this unique book collection from Bjarne Kroepelien's heirs for permanent incorporation in the Kon-Tiki Museum research department.

We transplanted feet from the belly to the back of salamanders. We checked Mendel's law by breeding thousands of small banana flies in bottles and counting the inheritable number of hairs on their backs. We went on excursions to haul in dragnets seething with the queerest wonders from the sea bed, but their life and function in the environment was ignored in favor of their Latin names. Our approach to the environment was deep but partial, microscopic, and schematic. Was our knowledge of nature superior to, or only different from, that of the eagle-eyed Polynesian islanders, who specialized in appraising nature the way it could best benefit man? I had to think as a scientist now. Not as a Polynesian yet. Knowledge was to be sought independently of its purpose.

Liv moved to Oslo to start university one year after me. She still wanted to share in my attempt to return to nature. But there were great practical problems to solve, and year followed year as we trod on separate university steps, heavily laden with books on utterly different academic subjects.

Only my father could help with a loan for a journey all the way to the tropics. Only my mother could convince him to do so. Only my university professors could make her feel that this was a sensible thing to do. Only a scholarly project could encourage my professors to sponsor a field trip involving a cruise to the opposite side of the planet in those preairline days. I had to secure an academic training that would qualify me for graduate work in some special problem in the remote area I was going to choose for my experiment. This education was needed, not only to get there, but also to come back capable of supporting a wife if, against all our expectations, we should be forced to return to civilization.

After seven terms and consultations with experts in Berlin, a project was developed and sponsored by my zoology professors, Kristine Bonnevie and Hjalmar Broch. I was to visit some isolated Pacific island group and study how the local animals had found their way there. How had the fauna developed on truly oceanic islands that had never been attached to the continents but were known to have risen, sterile, from the bottom of the sea as smoking flows of molten lava. When the lava cooled off, the various living creatures must have arrived by swimming, flying, drifting, being blown, or perhaps by getting a lift from human voyagers. Winds and ocean currents were obviously major factors in the transfer, and geography as a side topic was especially useful.

Thus it happened, in the fourth year, that my professors persuaded my mother, and my mother my father, to grant me a loan big enough for the necessary ticket. I wanted nothing to cover living costs at our destination, since, according to the fundamental nature of our project, there would be nothing for us to buy or rent.

As the barriers seemed to collapse around me, Liv's turn came; she was still mentally chained to her parents, who lived in a small town south of Larvik. So far, her sufferings had been restricted to the tender soles of her feet. As contribution to a common cause, I had insisted that she take her shoes off whenever we had a Sunday hike in the forest, for our soft skin had to be prepared for the jungle floor that awaited our bare feet. But now the time had come for her to throw into the waste basket all her own studies in economics, on which she had spent so much of her own time and her father's money. We had to get her parents' consent. She was not yet of age. My own mother had approved. She was genuinely delighted at the idea of my taking with me a girl she adored rather than going alone to a place famed for its hula-hula girls. My father's less romantic reasoning brought him to quite the opposite conclusion. But he finally and reluctantly yielded to my mother's pressure and Liv's charm. The hardest moment came when Liv had to write a letter to inform her own very respectable parents. Embalmed in a thousand fine phrases, the naked words were: No more economics, no more civilization. Marrying and leaving for the Marquesas Islands. Horrified, Liv's mother had read the letter aloud. Slowly, Liv's father had raised his powerful self from the easy chair and headed for the bookshelf. The encyclopedia. M for Marquesas. Good God, in the mid-Pacific! And the old text spelled out that the islands were renowned for cannibalism and fornication.

Mental dynamite had been detonated, and it took time, more letters, and the calming interference of my own father, before the infuriated father-in-law-to-be felt at ease and had agreed to let his only child be carried away to the Marquesas by a young stranger.

Liv was only twenty and I was twenty-two when we suddenly felt ourselves free from all ties. The green light was everywhere. Nothing to stop us from launching the project of our dreams. Farewell to civilization. Destination: Nature.

Our final choice of destination was described two years later in a book recording our adventures, published in Norway just before Europe tumbled into the Second World War, the one we had feared and anticipated.[2] I then wrote:

[2] T. Heyerdahl, *Paa Jakt efter Paradiset* (Oslo, 1938). The Second World War prevented translations, thereafter rendered obsolete by *The Kon-Tiki Expedition*.

"For the thousandth time, we pored over the colorful map of the South Seas. For the thousandth time, we sailed around on the vast ocean, our eyes scanning the blue paper, hoping to find a little speck suitable for us. A single virgin speck among the thousands of islands and atolls. A speck which the world had overlooked. A tiny free port of refuge from the iron grip of civilization.

"But every tempting little speck was already swept off the map with a little, penciled cross. It didn't suit us. That could be learned from heavy volumes of geographical literature.

"Rarotonga crossed out. A motor road encircled the island.

"Moorea crossed out. Hotels and tourists.

"Motane crossed out. No drinking water.

"Hututu crossed out. Barren of fruit trees.

"This one crossed out, a naval base, and that one crossed out, too small and overpopulated. Soon the map was speckled with small crosses. It began to resemble a celestial map of no use to us.

"To live with bare hands like early man demands a lot from an environment. It would have to be fertile and luxuriant, and unclaimed by others. But wherever there was fertile land it was densely inhabited. Wherever it was uninhabited, the environment was too poor to sustain man unaided by some degree of culture. So we had crossed out the large continents one by one. Bit by bit, land by land. Now the net was drawn around the South Sea Islands, tighter and tighter, cross after cross.

"Just below the equator, where the mild trade winds flowed westward across the map like red arrows, lay the thirteen islands of the Marquesas group. They had already become thirteen crosses. But we returned to these alluring islands with an eraser when the entire map was filled with crosses and every single island rejected.

"Nuku-Hiva, Hivaoa and Fatu-Hiva were the largest. Fatu-Hiva, the most beautiful and verdant island in the South Seas. Over and over again, we brought out the sparse pictures and information available on Fatu-Hiva. Once upon a time, a hundred thousand Polynesians were supposed to have lived in the Marquesas group. Today, a mere 2,000 were left, with only a handful of white men. The Polynesian islanders were dying out at a tremendous rate. And Fatu-Hiva was the most luxuriant island in the South Seas. If 98,000 had disappeared, there had to be enough room for the two of us. There had to be a peaceful spot among the abandoned ruins. A spot remote from all diseases. A spot where civilization had not taken root, but where fruit abounded in overgrown, abandoned gardens.

Maybe we could find a deserted valley, a lonely plateau, or a small, fertile bay. There we could build a little home. From sticks and leaves. There we could toil for our living in the forest. Live on fruit and fish and eggs. At one with nature. Among palms and foliage. Among birds and game. Sun and rain.

"There we could make our experiment. Go back to the forests. Abandon modern times. The culture. The civilization. Leap thousands of years into the past. To the way of life of early man. To life itself in its fullest and simplest form.

"Would it work? Yes, in theory. That didn't interest us. We wanted to experience it. We wanted to see if the two of us, man and woman, could resume the life abandoned by our first ancestors. If we could tear ourselves away from our artificial life. Completely and utterly. Be independent. Independent of the least aid of civilization. Independent of everything except nature.

"The island of Fatu-Hiva became our choice. Mountainous and lonely. Rich in sunshine, fruit, and drinking water. Few natives and no white men. We drew a firm ring around Fatu-Hiva.

"Outside, the winter fog was stealing in upon the city.

"Thus it happened that, in a biting wind on a Christmas morning, we left for Fatu-Hiva on our honeymoon."

* * *

Tahiti rose above the horizon. We could smell a tropical aroma, a warm fragrance of spiced greenery, before we saw the hazy blue peaks of jagged mountains above the western horizon. Six weeks with nothing but the familiar smell of steam engine and salt sea made passengers from nineteen countries line the railing, sniffing the mild air and trying to see land below the peaks. Six weeks by a huge ocean liner from the French port of Marseilles. It was the only way of reaching Tahiti at that time, except by a small Norwegian cargo vessel from San Francisco, which called at long intervals. Tahiti was the road's end. World's end. The Marquesas were even farther away, never heard of by travel agencies. We had to point to our map with the circle around Fatu-Hiva, and by combined efforts found that Tahiti would be the closest we could get with any ticket. From there on, we had to hope for some local copra schooner.

The large island now rose from the sea, as if dripping wet with white surf pouring from its coral reef. Mountains wilder than sharks' teeth bit into the trade-wind clouds of the blue sky. The famous Diadem and the mountain Orohena, first climbed by Kroepelien and Chief Teriieroo, soared among green hills seven thousand feet above the palm-lined beach. Gauguin, Melville, and Hollywood had not exaggerated. Nature itself had exaggerated. Something so beautiful seemed impossible.

We began to sing Tahiti's national hymn, tender and peaceful, composed by some former island king: "*E maururu a vau* [Happy am I]." Poets and painters, businessmen and colonial clerks, tourists and adventurers, we all felt that we were approaching our lost Garden of Eden, lost in the middle of the sea. Here it came, unspoiled, toward us. Verdant as a huge flower basket sailing on the sea.

Finally we heard the surf. Soon we saw a red church spire piercing the compact roof of the tropical foliage. More houses. Papeete, the capital of French Oceania. The engine slowed down. We slid through an opening in the coral reef, the surf frothing around us. A little, calm harbor. A huge warehouse with a metal roof and a wharf packed with people. No one was wearing a loincloth. All were dressed like us. An exhilarating atmosphere of jubilation and song among the multinational passengers on board. We wanted to show them that we were an informal breed of mankind, uncomplicated and free, like them. A few hats were lifted and a few hands waved back from the unperturbed crowd ashore, while customs and immigration officers in white uniforms saluted as they came up the gangway. A sweet, too sweet, smell of copra from the warehouse filled the warm air. Thousands of sacks were waiting for the ship. This was what it had come for.

About twenty thousand people lived on Tahiti at that time, mostly of pure or mixed Polynesian blood. The little capital of Papeete was dominated by Chinese merchants, who owned all the little stores and a couple of tiny restaurants, besides countless carts selling sweets and other merchandise in the streets. The Governor's palace, a post office, a handful of French stores and colonial offices, a bamboo cinema, churches, two very primitive hotels, and a few rows of wooden bungalows made up the rest of the town. Beyond, forests and fern-clad hills quickly rose toward the central spires of the Diadem, and on both sides of the town a narrow belt of flat lowland, covered with coconut palms, banana plants, giant breadfruit trees, citrus fruits, mango, and papaya, extended in a ring all around the island, with small native homes scattered between the trees. We were longing to get into this exotic world, away from the little town.

After a couple of nights in the local hotel, where neighbors on each side could look down on us by standing in their beds and peeping over the partition walls, we decided to take off for a brief visit to the country. No schooner was yet scheduled for the long voyage to the distant Marquesas. An open bus, with more people, pigs, chickens, and bananas hanging outside or on the roof than were piled inside on the wooden benches, bumped along on a dirt road following the calm lagoon surrounding part of the island. On each side of the town, this road ended in the bush, as there was not yet a road all around Tahiti. Ten miles eastward, on the north coast, was the valley of Papenoo, running steeply down from fern-clad mountains to the level coast, where a little river emptied into the sea. The protective coral reef was broken here, and ocean swells thundered against the rattling pebbles. A lush, wild garden; Tahiti at its best. Here was the home of the supreme chief of Tahiti's seventeen chiefs, Teriieroo a Teriierooiterai, Kroepelien's friend. This was where the spark had been struck that started the library I knew so well. This was where Kroepelien had met Tuimata, Teriieroo's daughter. He himself had buried her when thousands of healthy Tahitians had died of the Spanish flu that swept the island after the Great War. Kroepelien had helped to carry away wagonloads of dead islanders. His own book on Tahiti ended at Tuimata's tomb. There, he wrote, his own heart lay buried. He never wanted to go back to the island. But he had sent with us a parcel of personal gifts to his old friend Teriieroo.

Chief Teriieroo met us at the steps of his bungalow, huge and friendly, strong and well fed. His new wife, who clearly provided well for both of them, followed two paces behind with an equally hospitable smile. Both came barefoot and each had a brightly colored *pareu* wrapped around the body, he from the waist down, she from above the breasts. We felt welcome already as they approached us, before they knew our mission.

Bjarne Kroepelien! *Biarne!* Were we friends of Biarne? There was no end to the rejoicing. We were almost carried up the stairs, and it was no longer possible to get back to the bus or Papeete. We were literally kidnaped in the Papenoo Valley. This was to be our first home together. Teriieroo's friends in Papeete would send word by the bus when some schooner captain had decided to set sail for the Marquesas. Perhaps next month. Perhaps later. Nobody went to the backward Marquesas except when a schooner captain felt he could profit by fetching a boatload of copra. The natives up there, near to the equator, were not renowned for their urge to work, and it would be too costly for a captain to undertake the long journey without finding enough copra—enough coconuts ready split and sun-dried.

We came to look upon Teriieroo as a sort of island king, strong, noble, and righteous, and thus he was generally regarded by the other islanders, although all real power was delegated through the French governor in Papeete. Teriieroo had won the *Légion d'Honneur* for his loyalty to France, but he had no personal ambitions beyond bringing joy and justice to his own surroundings and to friends of friends. A not unimportant procedure was to invite guests and entertain them with the most sumptuous Polynesian repasts, affording equal pleasure both to the palate and to the mind. Everything served was picked or caught by Teriieroo's own hands and those of his sons and made into palatable, flower-ornamented dishes by his wife, Faufau Taahitue.

In Papenoo, we had a genuine introduction to the Polynesian way of life. There was no idleness, no boredom, no rush, and no waste. The soil, sea, and river provided what the little community needed, and no effort was made to exhaust the resources in exchange for wealth. Wealth in Papenoo was not measured, as among us, by counting what we have; what counted there was how one felt. In my new friends, I recalled what I had read: in Polynesia, both pleasure and prestige were obtained by those who gave away the maximum of material possessions. Polynesians were loosely attached to personal property.

Teriieroo was not only a great personality but also an outstanding speaker. During feasts, he was a real orator in both French and Polynesian. For me he became a new teacher, a specialist in all the practical details I had not learned from the books. As a pure-blooded Polynesian of the clearly vanishing type, he was one of the few I was ever to meet who took pride in his ancestral culture. He was not convinced that the European way of life had brought only blessings to his island. Our own plan to try man's original way of life intrigued the middle-aged chief. He told his wife he would have joined us on our voyage to the Marquesas had he been a few years younger. The islands up there were reputed to be something special. He had a friend who had been there. Up to a hundred coconuts on a single palm. Wild fruits abounded in the valleys. Particularly on Fatu-Hiva, the island farthest south. Oranges grew in the forests, and there was no need of mountain climbing to find them, as on Tahiti. Even Teriieroo's favorite food, *fei*, the red mountain banana, grew in the valley bottoms. Here in Tahiti, mountain climbers, with their big toes set apart like monkeys', had to fetch the *fei* from almost inaccessible precipices, to sell them for money at the market in Papeete. And the brown rat from Europe had not reached the Marquesas, so there was no need to nail sheets of tinplate around the palm trunks to stop these rascals from robbing the coconuts. The chief was convinced that up there life was still as it used to be down here, for even in Tahiti, *fei* and other rare bananas had formerly grown in the valleys. Today they die from diseases as soon as anyone tries to plant them.

At meals, Teriieroo and Faufau were taciturn, and so were those of his children who shared with us the daily meals. It was good manners to taste the food and not distract others by talking. A belch or two at the end of the meal was healthy and even a gentle way of telling the hosts that the food had been delicious! Talking began afterward. The first day, there were forks and spoons in front of us, and we all used them. But when the chief heard of our plans, he swept all metal off the table and showed us his fingertips. Clean. For good etiquette involved washing our hands just as we sat down to a meal. With the tips of two fingers and a thumb he broke off a piece of baked breadfruit and dipped it into a thick white coconut sauce, sucking the mixture deep into his palate and rolling his tongue. This is how to enjoy good flavor, he explained. You people, he argued, are so used to putting metal into your mouths that you do not realize that it upsets the flavor. Soon we all sat with the three permissible fingertips in our food and began to think that putting metal into our mouths was barbaric.

While my young bride was sweating with sticks and branches over hot stones in Faufau's open earth oven, learning how to make unpalatable or even inedible Polynesian roots and fruits eatable and really tasty, the chief took me upstream or along the seashore to show me how to gather the raw material. There were prawns to be caught with bamboo traps in the mountain stream, and in the lagoon a vast variety of fish and crustaceans, besides octopus and mollusks of various kinds to be caught with a net, hook, spear, or with bare hands. Edible roots had to be recognized by their visible leaves. Not everything that looked like food was edible for man. Some fish, roots, and fruits were poisonous. It could be both disgusting and harmful to eat shark flesh, but it would become perfectly good if sliced and left overnight in sea or river water. Fish and other sea food did not need to be cooked: it was enough to cut them into small cubes and leave them to soak overnight in lime juice. The red mountain banana could not be eaten raw, nor could breadfruit unless buried in the ground until entirely fermented.

Manioc was a dangerous root if not grated and its poison filtered out. The best wood for making fire by rubbing was the bone-dry branches of *borao*, the hibiscus tree, split along the pith.

In Teriieroo's opinion, we could safely abandon all the tools of modern civilization, but there were two utensils even he could not do without: a cooking pot and a long machete knife. Without the pot, too much of the jungle food available would be indigestible for modern man, and without a knife we could not even sharpen the pry bar needed to get the crashproof outer husk from the shell of the coconut.

On the boulders in the river, there were small snails with spines on their shells, looking almost like tiny sea urchins. We had learned that they were bad to step on, especially with bare European feet that did not have natural leather soles like those developed on our barefoot friends. I watched my steps carefully one morning as I waded in the river looking for prawns. Perhaps there were more if I got across to the other bank. In midstream it was deep, and it was impossible to see the bottom through the swirling water. It was then that I stepped heavily on one of the damned snails, and lost my balance. Too much current to get another foothold, and I was swept headlong with the whirling water toward the estuary. This would have been nothing to the average swimmer; it just happened that I was not one of them. My greatest shame was that I could not swim at all. As a child, I had once tumbled off a bridge into a surging sea, and once capsized in winter when riding a block of ice on a lake where my father's workmen cut large cubes for the brewery icehouse. The result was an acute fear of deep water. No one could convince me that by moving my limbs I could float. Now I was head under water again, rotating, gasping, and waving, carried in the rushing rapids like a sack of potatoes toward the fierce ocean surf, which collapsed in tumbling walls as if pushed against the boulder beach by a thousand tanks. A deafening cannonade, thundering seas, a roaring choir of rattling boulders. In seconds, I would be smashed to bits. Quickly. Panic must yield to sober resolution. Self-conquest. Steady. With long, calm strokes, I began to move. I knew how to, but had never tried. With the greatest ease, I was free from the rapids and swam to shore, the boulders resounding like gnashing teeth in the foam from the deafening breakers a stone's throw beyond me. I stood for a long time watching the ocean fury from which I had just been spared. The tropical sun was hot. I went higher up, heading for a calm deep in the river. I plunged in and began to swim like a frog. Teriieroo joined me, crawling. Great! I did not tell him I had never swum before.

Teriieroo was too heavy to show me how to walk up a coconut palm. His grandson Biarne, named after his former friend, shot his body out in an arch and wriggled up monkeylike on all fours, as easily as I would have crawled along the floor. But I too knew how to climb a branchless pine, and I embraced the palm trunk with arms and legs, climbing up in good northern fashion, chest against the trunk. Triumphantly I found that the coconut palm was easier to climb than any pine, for the surface was indented by shallow rings around the trunk all the way up to the huge, fernlike crown. Up there I proudly waved down to my friends and tried to tear loose a coconut, but I could not. My breath was gone. Time to get down. I tried, but could not. The rings that had helped me on the way up now trapped me and prevented me from descending. The almost imperceptible sharp edges were all directed skyward. There I hung like a clown, high up in the top of a palm, unable to get down. Clinging to the branchless trunk, I began to get exhausted. I tried to arch my body out in Polynesian style, but almost fell down. I clung to the palm. Nothing doing. Exhausted, I let gravity work. The pain of an extremely sudden return to the soil was overshadowed by the feeling of parting from a tree that retained a considerable part of my skin. I felt as if worked over by a hammer on my behind and by a file and sandpaper on my front. These sensations were not improved by Teriieroo's discovering that half my big toenail was loose and required his putting his 275 pounds behind the job of pulling it all off with his pincers. Two weeks passed before I learned to climb a low palm the proper way, and to hang on while twisting off the tough stalk to the husk of the coconut, carefully keeping my hand off giant centipedes and wasps' nests.

Papenoo's pride was Teriieroo's car. He owned one of the extremely rare specimens on the island, and we sometimes spent more time cranking, pushing, and poking our noses into the metallic intestines, which none of us understood, than what might have been needed to walk the ten miles to Papeete. But Teriieroo, who would climb for miles in the hills, insisted on driving his Model T to Papeete. The reason was obvious and we drove with him. To walk in the woods and hills of Papenoo was sheer pleasure, for there we wore only an airy *pareu*, and the temperature felt like a pleasant dream. But going to town, we had to dress like civilized people. Teriieroo looked like an old-time banker when he put on a white

suit and twisted his pendent mustache. He swore at the huge tennis
shoes that hurt his big, sprawling toes, and tightened his tie with
the mien of a convict personally adjusting the noose around his
neck. I could not satisfy his curiosity as to what the original purpose
of this invention might have been. Transformed from lusty Polynesian peasants into serious citizens of a French annex to my own
world, we cranked, pushed, and wobbled our way to the low rows
of bungalow streets in Papeete.

Teriieroo had business to do in some colonial offices, and Liv and
I strolled in the streets among the busy Chinese, heading for Papeete's extremely colorful fish market. There we met Larsen. Larsen
from Norway. The thin man in a straw hat and striped shorts approached us and said he had recognized our accent. We had struggled through our school French to get some sensible information
about the zoological species for sale to those who had not come
only to gaze at the colorful spectacle. Larsen introduced himself as
a retired schoolteacher and local old-timer. Would we join him
with two of his friends in his Fautaua home near town tonight? We
went, and we met Calle Svenson from Sweden and Charley Halligan
from England. We were offered benches around a table on Larsen's
balcony. Beer was served while a kerosene lamp lit up part of the
tropical garden around us.

"Do you like Tahiti?" was the first question.

"The scenery, yes. We had never dreamed that anything could be
this beautiful."

"One cannot live on beauty alone. Besides, it is beautiful in
Sweden, too," replied Svenson as he fished a big moth out of his
beer mug.

"Not like here," I rejoined, and directed attention to the huge,
leathery banana leaves that groped for the black, star-spangled sky.
The moon shone on some heavy clusters of green bananas. The
soft air was filled with an exciting tropical aroma. Fertility. Luxuriance. Beauty.

"Things at home have turned wonderful in your mind because
you have been here too long," I continued. "Your senses are being
dulled to the fantastic surroundings here in Polynesia. We are just
out of the winter fog in Europe and are able to make comparisons."

Liv and I brought up all the trivialities and problems at home,
and how wonderful everything was on Tahiti. We wanted them to
realize how lucky they were, living in the island paradise of everybody's dream.

But big Svenson stuck calmly to his views. He was longing for home. He wanted to return to Sweden with his Tahitian wife and children. He did not want to see them spoiled by local immorality. I must not destroy his illusions.

"You are new here," he added. "Wait another month and you will share my view. You are a bit blinded, like all newcomers. Paradise lost, that's here."

Halligan emptied his mug. The timid little Englishman who never said a word had something on his mind.

"Those who return to their own native soil," he said calmly, "they rediscover paradise."

He had lived on Tahiti for twenty years.

"Where do you come from, then?" I asked, surprised.

He was from London. Yes, from London!

"Sure," Larsen agreed. "Just think of back home in Norway. There you can pick gooseberries."

Gooseberries? I was flabbergasted. Was he serious? Speaking of gooseberries here, where the trees were full of tropical fruits. I pointed to his untended garden. Trees and bushes full of exotic fruits and flowers. I saw a lemon tree in the distance and some branches with red coffee berries next to my arm.

"There's nothing like gooseberries. Just imagine standing in one spot in your garden, filling yourself with gooseberries." The thin retired teacher from Moss, Norway, tilted his straw hat back so that the lamp could reflect the happy dream in his face.

"You told us you had been here before," I said. "Why did you come back if you didn't like it?"

"Young man," said Larsen, "Tahiti was different then. It was something to be a white man here, but not today. The natives laugh at us behind our backs. I know their language and understand their jokes at our expense. They are getting conceited and spoiled, thanks to admiring tourists and boastful publicity. Every visitor to Tahiti writes a book. To make it sell, he must speak of a paradise. Who would otherwise care to read the book? People want some romantic place to escape to in their dreams. Tahiti must be represented as such a place. Polynesia must be served to Americans and Europeans as it was at the time of Captain Cook. To deceive ourselves, we introduce the ukulele to a people who had never seen a stringed instrument, and we import loincloths from France and straw skirts from the U.S.A. We even compose the romantic tunes we want them to sing, and then we make them perform for paradise-hunters in Papeete's bamboo cinema. Tahiti has to act primitively to bring in the tourists. To make books sell. To please the moviegoers.

And to let us foreign intruders off with a clean conscience about what our own kin have done to these islands."

Silence. We knew that what these three old-timers were telling us was not nonsense.

When Teriieroo came to fetch us, we drove home to Papenoo with mixed feelings. The splendid view of Tahiti at night, with palms and foliage silhouetted against the lagoon, was as intact as ever, but we had a feeling that we were on the spectacular stage of an opera house, where the painted scenery of the previous act had been left over to serve a coming cabaret.

It was good to get back to Teriieroo's bungalow. Papenoo was so different from Papeete. Certainly not as when Captain Cook arrived, but surely very little had changed since the days of Kroepelien or Paul Gauguin. The house was European, but the atmosphere was Polynesian. Whether for better or for worse, the mixture was honest. Nowhere in Tahiti had we seen a genuine Polynesian hut of poles and thatch. Every dwelling, however poor, was built from costly imported planks and roofed with corrugated iron. Teriieroo lamented this and stressed that the old-time houses of poles or cane, thatched with interwoven palm leaves, had every advantage in the local climate. They cost no money, were perfectly waterproof, and delightfully fresh and restful. Teriieroo's wooden bungalow was as stuffy and unpicturesque as all the rest. The heat of the tropical sun on the iron roof made us as drowsy as drunkards in daytime, and the clatter of the tropical rain woke us at night like frontline soldiers. Why on earth had he built in this way when the traditional Tahitian houses had all the advantages? Teriieroo smiled. Could we expect him to build in a way that would make everybody say he lived like a savage at a time when Tahiti had been civilized?

I did not know it then, but ten years later I was to come back to Tahiti, with my companions from the Kon-Tiki expedition. A wealthy paradise-hunter from America had now settled on the island and had built himself a huge, palm-thatched bamboo residence in Hollywood style, admired by all passing tourists. A number of foreign settlers with a flair for romance, a couple of restaurant keepers and recent founders of countryside motels had followed his style, and yellow thatch-and-bamboo plaiting were no longer an unusual sight among the palm trunks. Ten more years would pass before I came back again, this time with a team I had brought for excavations in eastern Polynesia. Even the Polynesians had now begun to build pretty and healthy homes of bamboo and coconut leaves, different in style from the buildings that Captain Cook had found, but a great improvement on the iron-roofed shacks, which were beginning to be considered old-fashioned and vulgar. Modern envoys from Hollywood had done their part in bringing Tahitian architecture, in a roundabout way, back to nature.

Four weeks passed in Teriieroo's home before a message came with the bus that Captain Brander of the copra schooner *Tereora* was planning to set sail for the distant Marquesas. Teriieroo grabbed a pen and wrote a message to Monsieur Pakeekee, a native from the Marquesas group who had been trained by the Protestant mission on Tahiti and had met the Papenoo chief there. Religion has always played a most important part in the islanders' lives. Religious buildings, priests, rites, and taboos have always held a central place in Polynesian community life, and it was an easy task for arriving European missionaries to convert the worship of old gods into that of a new one, so long as the basic concept of priests, ceremonies, and sacred assembly places remained. It has been both the delight and the dilemma of many a missionary to find how successfully he was able to convert a Polynesian community to his own sect, with the ever-present fear that a competitor in faith might achieve a similar success if he arrived in the same spot later.

Teriieroo's family would never miss a Sunday in the nearby Protestant church. Chieftainess Faufau would make sure that Liv wore the right hat, and placed a huge plaited specimen on her head which Liv, with little success, struggled to keep above her nose, as a heavy wreath of large shells around the crown helped to weigh it down. With Teriieroo's family of three generations, we made up a little procession down the road, with the chief and me in tennis shoes and white suits, followed by our two *vahines* in giant hats and long, loose Tahitian gowns, Victorian style. The singing in church was invariably a truly magnificent performance, as always in Polynesia, and was by itself a reward for our presence. The church was the one social gathering place in the community; only Papeete had its bamboo cinema. We had a feeling that our island friends stuck up for their own Christian sect with the pride and enthusiasm that football fans at home show for their clubs. On the very day of our arrival, Teriieroo had asked about our religious rating, and he beamed with satisfaction when we could confirm his belief that in northern Europe nearly everyone was a Protestant by birth. He accepted us as members of his own league and told us that the same sect was in the great majority in Tahiti also. In this well-intended spirit, Teriieroo now sat down and wrote his letter of introduction to his remote acquaintance, Pakeekee, on Fatu-Hiva, a letter that was destined to lead us into more adventures than we had anticipated.

About a week before our departure, a very special party was prepared on the floor of Teriieroo's big balcony. A long carpet of fresh, green banana leaves took on the appearance of a tablecloth when studded with aromatic flowers. Leis and garlands of fern leaves and sweet white *tiare* flowers produced an atmosphere of gaiety and happiness. The juicy vapor of baked bush pig and chicken rose from stone-lined underground earth ovens when I came back with Teriieroo, bringing a basket full of squirming prawns. Women had been fishing and pulling up roots, and children and children's children were shaking branches or climbing mighty mango and breadfruit trees to make sure that nothing pleasant to the palate should be missing that special evening.

No banquet, however professional and extravagant, can better regale guests than such a juicy, fresh, genuine Polynesian *umu* served without cost to rejoicing rows of Polynesian gluttons in the open air of a tropical night. Culinary art has always played a key role in Polynesian culture. Imitations in modern South-Sea-style continental restaurants are only dim reflections of what cannot be duplicated without tropical soil in the kitchen.

This evening, Teriieroo broke his own rule. He gave a speech while we all had our fingers in the gorgeous food. Big, flower-ornamented, and comfortably wrapped only in his favorite *pareu*, he got onto his feet at one end of the green carpet and pointed to Liv and me, who were squatting in Polynesian style at the other end. First in Tahitian and then in French, he told his many guests that, as they all knew, he had twenty-nine children by his late wives. But now he was going to adopt two more. In doing so, he also had to give them new names, since the old ones were Norwegian and too much of a tongue-twist for a Tahitian. Could anyone pronounce Liv or Thor? They all tried, one by one. "Rivi" and "Turi." Wild amusement. Nobody could.

That is why Teriieroo and Faufau adopted us under new names everybody could immediately repeat, except us. The chief had named us Teraimateatatane and Teraimateatavahine. It took us all evening, and contributed vastly to the enjoyment, before we learned to separate the components of our new names and pronounce them properly: Terai Mateata Tane and Terai Mateata Vahine.

Mr. and Mrs. Blue Sky. Only now, were we ready for our real introduction to Polynesia.

2. BACK TO NATURE

The islands we had dreamed of rose from the sea like the morning sun. The rising sun glowed red to the east, and the first Marquesas island was pale blue, like the shadows of fingers on the northern horizon. Steep, rugged, and menacing, the mountain masses hurled themselves ever higher as we sailed on, until they were soaring like rock fortresses high above the ocean. Tumbling, frothing, and rumbling like a distant thunderstorm, the endless sea beat wildly against these fixed obstacles in a world of living water. From a distance, the islands seemed far from hospitable. The first one we sighted, coming in from the southwest, was Uapou. Its incredible pinnacles stood out of the water like a cluster of reversed icicles, but as we came nearer, their color changed to a warm jungle green. As the schooner stood in still closer, we seemed to be approaching ruins of a seagirt castle, with wisps of cloud sailing around the towers like smoke. Then the palm beaches also rose, and we coasted alongside a lofty island, smaller but wilder and more spectacularly beautiful even than Tahiti.

As one island rose from the sea, another sank and disappeared, for there was a great distance between the islands in the Marquesas group. The Pacific stretched between them in many tints of blue, but around each island the water was as green as grass, due to masses of microscopic plant plankton that throve upon an incessant rain of minerals gnawed from the brittle rocks by the perpetual surf. Shoals of fish were attracted to this evergreen marine pasture, with dolphins and birds in visible pursuit. Swarms of sea birds followed the little schooner and plunged after the fish that continually struggled on the line we were towing astern.

We were much nearer the equator now, and as we came inshore, we could verify that here the Pacific reached its highest degree of fertility. One valley after the other opened in front of us and closed behind as we sailed past, all formed as deep, wild gorges cutting into the central mass of ridges and peaks. Only truly vertical precipices had managed to shake off the jungle and rise as naked, red rock above the chaos of luxuriant greenery that flowed down the steep ridges and bluffs to the palm-studded valley bottom.

The tropical heat alone was not responsible for this extravagant fertility. In the interior of the islands, the towering peaks intercept the westward course of the sparse but ever-present little trade-wind clouds, and squeeze the rain out of them before they manage to proceed westward. Therefore, fresh rain water always pours down from the mountains in rushing torrents and rivers, through dark jungles and friendly valleys, into the green sea. The tooth of time had gnawed greedily everywhere into the fragile volcanic rock. Caves and subterranean streams, pinnacles and grotesque carvings in the mountains, turned the whole scenery into a fantastic fairyland. In this exotic environment, we were to be set ashore. Here, somewhere, we were to dive into the unfamiliar jungle while the *Tereora* returned to the twentieth-century world. Once left behind on Fatu-Hiva, we should be deprived of telegraphic contact, in fact of any contact whatsoever, with the outside world. No message from anywhere until some unscheduled schooner should happen to call again at least several months ahead. If a war broke out, nobody could inform us. We had learned in Tahiti that whereas Papeete was shelled in the Great War, nobody in the Marquesas even knew that a war was on, until a schooner finally came up with the message that the war had ended.

It was less than a thousand miles up to Fatu-Hiva as the crow flies, but by schooner we had taken three weeks to get there. We had called at the low coral atolls of Takaroa and Takapoto, in the Tuamotu group, and we had seen how the civilization we were trying to avoid was slowly radiating from Papeete into surrounding Oceania. The trading schooner was the bringer of culture and was a profitable business enterprise. It carried a well-stocked store below deck, and by selling at high prices, doubled its business by getting back with a profit the same money paid to the islanders in return for working copra and bringing the heavy loads on board.

"It's all crazy," said Captain Brander of the *Tereora*, a jovial Englishman with white hair and a red nose, who loved the islands and his whiskey, although he never set foot ashore. A sort of retiring island Santa Claus. We had learned in Tahiti that this Pacific old-timer was a college graduate who had wanted to escape from it all. He admitted it:

"Crazy. But they want it, like everybody else. I detest our own civilization; that's why I am here. Yet I spread it from island to island. They want it, once they have had a little taste of it. Nobody can save them from the avalanche. I certainly can't. Why do they want sewing machines and tricycles, or underclothing and canned salmon? They don't need any of it. But they want to tell their neighbors: Look here, I've got a chair while you are squatting on the floor. And then the neighbor also has to buy a chair, and something else not possessed by the first one. The needs increase. The expenditure. Then they have to work, although they hate it. To earn money they don't need."

As usual, old Brander had remained on board as the *Tereora* anchored in the lagoons of two of the Tuamotu atolls a good three hundred miles north of Tahiti. Invariably it was his trading master, the brilliant Tahitian supercargo Théodore, who went ashore to attend to the business. Brander only brought the schooner to the desired destination. With Théodore, we had climbed into the lifeboat and waded ashore on the low coral atolls, to see what was going on. The natives were unloading corrugated iron and window glass in the baking sun. Others were wading out again with heavy sacks of copra. As we were invited into the home of an islander to get some shade from the burning midday sun, salesman Théodore triumphantly pointed out an old, discarded iron stove standing on the floor. There was no stovepipe attached, nor any chimney on the roof, for the tropical climate did not require that the oven should ever be lighted. The rusty thing was set up as a piece of costly European furniture.

On the second atoll, we had hardly set foot ashore when a group of excited Polynesians pulled us along between the palm trunks. There, in an open place of hard coral sand, stood a tall old automobile, motionless among the palms, like a long-legged foal straddling to keep upright. Flat tires. No road. For a modest fee, we were pushed onto this rolling royal throne, the pride of the whole island, and its envied owner actually managed to wind it up for a painful shake, dancing us around half a dozen trees back to its original site, accompanied by a host of pedestrians.

Nothing similar seemed to have reached the Marquesas group. We were first landed on the main island, Nuku-Hiva, in the northernmost part of this widely spread archipelago. Here was the residence of the French administrator, who at the same time was the only doctor in the entire group. He had no local means of interisland communication, since the lack of any sheltered harbor made it impossible to have larger boats than could be carried up on land. The Marquesas Islands have many open beaches of boulders or black, volcanic sand, but no deep bays, and the entire shoreline rises so abruptly from the bottom of the deep Pacific that no coral polyps have managed to build a protective reef around the shore as at Tahiti.

Before we left Europe, we had needed a special permit from the French colonial office to go to the closed islands of this group. French law forbade any visitor to remain ashore for more than twenty-four hours. Was it to protect the islands? Or was it to protect the visitor? Nobody had been able to tell us the reason.

From Nuku-Hiva, the *Tereora* turned south to visit the other islands in the group before the home voyage to Papeete. The schooner went under sail, but had an auxiliary engine in case the wind failed. We slept in double rows, with Polynesian passengers and their domestic animals on the cabin roof above deck. It was too stuffy and crowded below, and the deck itself was awash in rough seas. We slept in a row with a common rope over our chests and under our arms in case of excessive rolling. Islanders with trumpets and guitars, chuckling beauties, cackling hens, screaming babies, and a panic-stricken Polynesian pig aided wind and waves to drown the contagious groans from sick people who slept on the crowded floor below.

In daytime, we lay on our stomachs trying to penetrate the deep jungle with binoculars as the island coasts slid by. We were curious about the least detail, for one of these islands was to be our home. Beautiful, spectacular, but heavy, sometimes almost gloomy and deserted.

Brander watched us as we lay literally bewitched, gazing toward the new land. We felt small in this tremendous landscape, yet we were drawn to it as if by a spell.

"Austere and oppressive," said Captain Brander. "The heavy jungle and mountains seem to squeeze you small." He wanted us to come back with him to gay Tahiti, but we refused.

Our next call was Hivaoa, the second of the two major islands in the group, and our last stop before Fatu-Hiva. Brander strongly recommended to us that we get off there. This was the last spot from where we could contact the outside world. There was a little one-man wireless station, a French gendarme, an English shopkeeper, and a Tahitian nurse. One more European, a Norwegian copra planter, lived in a valley on the other side of the island. Paul Gauguin had spent his last years there, and we were shown his lonely tomb. Nothing doing. We wanted the island we had encircled on the map.

Next morning, we awoke in sheltered water as we slid in under the lee side of Fatu-Hiva's high mountain ridge. Shaped like a bean, this island is divided lengthwise from north to south by a knife-sharp comb, its two main valleys opening toward the sheltered, west coast.

"Where do you want to be let off?" Brander muttered as we came close to the rocks of the northern cape. He admitted he did not know this island, and his map could not help us. The old sailing chart showed no details but the rugged coastal contours and the available anchorages off the two main bays. It was decided that we should follow the coast as close as would be safe, and pick the place we wanted.

Sails went down, and with the engine at slow speed, we went closer inshore. Sheer, naked cliffs seemed to be hanging above our heads, plunging straight into the splashing surf. But as we moved along, the mountain curtains seemed to be drawn aside, and one by one truly paradisiac valleys opened to view, curving on to be lost in the island's interior. Out at sea, the jungle air met us again, stronger than ever. Fatu-Hiva. A rock-walled greenhouse.

Brander and Théodore for once were hanging on the rail like us, speaking in Polynesian to one of the crew, an islander who seemed to know Fatu-Hiva well. The question was for us to locate a place where we could be set ashore with the best chance of subsistence. The first requirement was drinking water. As we spoke, a mighty valley opened before us. It looked completely artificial, like the stage of a theater, with red flats or side screens jutting into the green palm forest from both sides. These fantastic side curtains were outlined with bizarre profiles against the greenery, as if cut from plywood by an artist with a sense for shape and effect, rather than being crumbling red tuff molded by rain and storms. A row of thatched bamboo sheds was discernible between the palm trunks above the boulder beach. Shelters for canoes.

"Hanavave," Brander explained, and nodded toward land. "Here there is plenty of water in the river and an abundance of fruit all the way up the valley. About fifty natives live here, according to this fellow. All in one village."

Liv was fascinated and immediately wanted to get ashore, but Brander shook his head.

"An unhealthy climate," he said. "The valley is very moist and the air filled with vapor. The natives here suffer from all kinds of diseases that may infect you too. Elephantiasis is terrible here in Hanavave."

With silent awe, we saw the mighty, theatrical rock curtains of Hanavave being drawn as we passed by. We were never to see a more beautiful composition of natural scenery. At short intervals, narrow gorges and ravines opened in passing review, sprinkled to the brim with jungle vegetation. But they were too small to ensure enough wild fruit for our survival. A friendly beach came into sight, with a palm-studded fruit forest crowding right down to the dark sand.

"*Aoe te vai,*" explained our Polynesian cicerone. No drinking water.

One little valley after the other passed by, each severed from the next by powerful walls and precipices. Either they lacked water, or they were deep and dark like canyons, too austere for us to live in.

Still another pretty little valley, with a waterfall. Still another hope. But here in Hanaui lived an old native couple with legs like hippopotamuses. We lacked the courage to go ashore, even though we knew that the filaria of elephantiasis were spread by the mosquitoes and not by human contact.

The last valley before the southern cape was Omoa. Wider and more open than any other we had seen on Fatu-Hiva, it disappeared in a big arc into the heart of the island. Exhilarating, picturesque, although not quite competing with Hanavave, the Omoa Valley abounded in wild fruits and drinking water. We could see with our binoculars how a river poured its frothing wealth of water over a boulder barrier into the bay, where the *Tereora* was now slowing down to anchor. Our informant estimated that a hundred natives lived packed together in a village close to this bay. Farther in, the large valley was entirely uninhabited.

"Here or nowhere," said Brander as the anchor rattled to the bottom. "You have seen your choice. Want to return with me?"

"We have only seen the leeward of the island," I insisted, and pointed to the long inland ridge which rose like the jagged crest of a dragon all along the axis of the island. "What about the east coast?"

Brander and Théodore, supported by the well-informed islander, were quick to explain that no schooner ever passed along the other coast. There was no anchorage and not even a safe place to land a lifeboat. The last to try was smashed, for the large ocean swells break with unimpeded force all along that coast, coming westward with nothing to stop them all the way from South America, four thousand miles away. The east coast was in fact barren and deserted. The tribes once living there were all extinct, and nobody even tried to harvest the copra on the other side of the mountain ridge.

I took a last look at the inviting green valley and the sky-scraping crest behind it. If we wanted to reach the east coast, we could possibly climb across.

We agreed to be set ashore in Omoa. The lifeboat was lowered and we said farewell to them all. Brander tried to persuade us for the last time; then he said he would be sure to pick us up on his next call, perhaps in a couple of months, perhaps in a year. The swells were rolling gently under us in the boat; they came into the open bay as backwash from the wild surf we could see and hear as it tumbled in cascades over the black lava rocks of the south cape. Strong, native oarsmen laid their combined strength behind the oars, and soon we rode in on the surf to a slippery boulder beach. Four Polynesians jumped overboard to hold the boat in the frothing back-surf, while four others helped us wade ashore with our belongings. Surf and undertow threatened to capsize the boat and, before we quite realized what had happened, all the eight men were back on their four thwarts, rowing with calm strokes back to the *Tereora*.

When we really woke up to what was going on, when years of dreams became reality in a matter of seconds, we found ourselves standing alone on an unknown boulder beach, watching the sails of the *Tereora* being hoisted, whereupon the two-masted schooner slowly moved away. We followed it until the white vessel dwindled and was lost among thousands of whitecaps that filled the ocean.

There we were on the beach, with our luggage beside us on the boulders. Two big suitcases containing Liv's wedding gown, my dinner-jacket suit, and all the usual apparel we had needed on the long journey as first-class honeymoon passengers from Norway. Nothing was useful now. A couple of cases containing bottles, tubes, and chemicals for collecting zoological specimens. Nothing could be eaten. I looked up into the palms fringing the beach. Coconuts. They gave me back some tottering courage. We should not starve. I drew a deep breath and looked at Liv. We both laughed humbly and reached for the suitcases. We had to go somewhere.

The sun and the singing tropical birds warmed us up. The sandy turf above the beach abounded in aromatic flowers, and the feeling of high adventure and happiness overtook us anew. Then we sud-

denly noticed people standing among the trees. There were many
of them. Watching us. Nobody moved and nobody greeted us. Some
were in loincloths and some in tattered rags of European make.
Copper-colored to brown, all were varieties of the Polynesian stock.
Most faces looked more cruel than those of their friendly relatives
in Tahiti and the Tuamotu atolls. But a couple of the younger
women and most of the children were beautiful.

Seeing that we hesitated, an old crone was the first to get into action. She shouted a few words that sounded like a flow of vowels,
softer than the Tahitian dialect. I did not get a word. Just shrugged
my shoulders and laughed. That made the old wrinkled crone bend
over and shake with laughter. Others laughed with her. She ventured forward, followed by the rest, and, to my surprise and fear,
she headed for Liv rather than for me. She licked her thin finger
and rubbed it against the cheek of Liv, who in her surprise was
incapable of speech. The old woman scrutinized her own finger
and nodded with an approving smile. Only later were we to learn
that the spectators had trusted me for what I seemed to be, but they
were sure that Liv was a Tahitian girl dressed up and whitewashed.
The old crone did not believe there were women in Europe. The
vessels anchoring on twenty-four-hour visits to the islands had
brought ashore many white men, but not one white *vahine*. White
men always came ashore for the brown girls, but no white woman
ever came for a brown man.

In the moment of general excitement, we found that all our luggage was gone. We could not ask for it, nor did we depend on it,
so we just followed the crowd between the palm trunks to an open
place with an enormous banyan tree surrounded by a boulder
bench. Scattered native huts were seen around, the most noticeable
being a wooden shack with the dreadful corrugated iron roof we
now profoundly hated. Here we were met by a young and timid
European-looking man who knew French. We spotted our luggage
on the wooden floor of his little bungalow as he invited us in, with
the silent reception committee crowding up to the open door. Our
very gentle host was far from talkative in either French or Polynesian, but to satisfy our curiosity he told us that his name was Willy
Grelet, the only one on the island who had grown up with a European father. His late father was a Swiss who had married a local
island girl and whose only friend had been Paul Gauguin, whom he
hardly ever saw, since they lived on different islands. Willy seemed
introverted and lonely, clearly keeping aloof from the rest of the
village people, all of whom obviously both respected and admired

him. We were to learn that he was a very honest person, even though he loved money, which he gathered wherever he could get it, and he was rich, but saved his earnings as there was nowhere to spend them. Between the poles supporting the floor of his bungalow, he had a primitive kind of shop, where the other islanders came to obtain merchandise in exchange for all their own copra, which Willy Grelet, as far as we could see, had under his control. The modest store contained matches, shirts, flour, rice, and sugar, as long as the stocks lasted. Little else could be detected in his bungalow, and the shop was open only at sunset, when Willy returned from his own copra work. Apart from work, his only passion proved to be hunting the formerly domestic animals that now roamed wild in the jungle; he therefore knew the island better than anyone else.

Before the sun set, it had so heated the iron roof that we could not sleep. The brown spectators kept pressing around the open door and sealed glass windows, and Willy seemed to be in no hurry to go to bed. The three of us remained seated around his kerosene lamp till the small hours, discussing our plans. Our island host clearly looked upon us as the strangest creatures that had ever come ashore, but he understood our plan. Far up the valley, we should find what we wanted, in the interior of the island, where the natives rarely went and where abandoned gardens were engulfed by jungle growth.

Most of the night, we spent compiling a small dictionary. Laughter had helped us ashore, but we also needed to know a few words to get farther than up from the beach. I had prepared in advance a long list of key words in Norwegian, and now Willy helped us to translate them by way of French into Polynesian. The difference from the Tahitian dialect was noticeable in the first phrase we had to learn. In Tahiti, "good day" was *ia ora na;* here it was *kaoha.* Consonants were not in great demand on Fatu-Hiva, and we struggled hard to distinguish between certain words:

no	= *aoe*
I	= *oao*
you	= *oe*
he	= *oia*
they	= *aua*
two	= *eua*
who	= *oai*
rain	= *eúa*

In addition, Oau and Ouia were local place names. The word for "nice" was *panhakanahau,* while "bad" was *aoehakanahau.* Nevertheless, the term they used for the "Polynesian" language was literally "human" language, a survival from the days when their ancestors thought that the white visitors were gods.

Polynesian words buzzed around my head with the mosquitoes as we crept to bed under Willy's large insect net. From the beach, we heard rhythmic thunder: the surf reminding us that we were on a lonely South Sea island, thousands of miles from anywhere.

Adam and Eve, when God drove them out of the Garden of Eden, must have felt the very opposite of us as we started our walk into the lush valley of Omoa at sunrise next morning. They left; we were arriving. The song of the colorful tropical birds resounded from all parts of the valley as they joined the Marquesas cuckoo in the early-morning concert. The mild, morning air seemed green with jungle aroma. Whatever unknown we were heading for, we felt we were returning to a luxurious lost garden that was ours for the mere asking. No fences and no guards. It felt like a dream.

It was the old, overgrown royal path we followed inland. Away from the village. The red, dented ridge which soared skyward at the bottom of the valley disappeared from sight as the jungle began to close above our heads. First, young coconut palms, resembling giant ferns; next, mighty jungle trees with moss-studded branches bearded by parasitic growths and pendent ropes of lianas. At intervals, we could hardly see the rays of the sun playing on the upper foliage, which was filled with hooting, fluting, fiddling, and piping creatures. There was life everywhere, although all we saw were little, fluttering birds and butterflies, and lizards and bugs pattering away from the exposed trail. We hurried to get ever deeper into this all-absorbing wilderness. We were keen on getting away as fast and as far as possible from the little cluster of village houses, where a complete lack of sanitation seemed to have brought all kinds of diseases upon the natives. We had waved to the last ones in the outskirts of the village. They waved back, shouted *kaoha,* and chattered unintelligibly. "Good day," we answered in their own language, "nice, nice; good day." Then we all laughed together. They seemed very happy despite their diseases, though some of them could hardly walk, their legs being as thick as their bodies. The elephantiasis from which they suffered had come to the island when the white man unintentionally brought the mosquito ashore. The last we saw was a little group of women sitting waist-deep in a pool of the river, washing themselves in milk-colored water with all their clothes on, while others were filling their gourd containers with drinking water a few yards farther downstream. They knew nothing about hygiene or contagion.

Just above the village, the river water, filthy lower down, became clean and fresh. The trail followed the stream, occasionally winding across the transparent water on smooth stones and sometimes cutting into the rusty-red soil of the riverbank. At the beginning, the trail was kept wide and clear of intruding bush, but as we advanced ever deeper inland, it became narrower and we often had to use our long machete knife. Willy had picked our guide, Ioane, his own Marquesan brother-in-law. He had a very definite idea of the place he would show us for our future homestead: the site of the last island king.

The grandmother of Ioane's grandfather had been the last island queen before the French annexation. Through her, Ioane had inherited the part of the island we were now heading for. We had learned from Willy that, even though the people might have died out, there was not a spot on the island without an owner. Everything was divided into family property that passed on to some heir, and even if a plot of jungle was abandoned and all but inaccessible, woe to the man who pilfered a banana from another man's land. If seen, he would be reported to the village chief.

Far up the valley, where the river was reduced to a rushing stream, the trail was gradually lost. Here we left the water and the valley bottom and began climbing in a complete wilderness of boulders, bush, and giant trees. Everywhere, hidden in the undergrowth, were ruins of moss-covered boulder walls. Artificial terraces. Everywhere, there was evidence of a persistent fight between stubborn garden trees and the returning, omnipotent jungle. Heavy walls with boulders weighing tons had been pushed apart by the muscle-shaped roots of trees so big that the three of us together could not encircle them.

Finally Ioane stopped. A spring of cold, clear water gushed forth at our feet. Next to it was an artificial plateau so overgrown that it was impossible to get a view of the valley or an impression of the place itself. This was the royal terrace. Here the last queen had lived. It did not look too inviting, but trunks of coconut palms and of breadfruit trees could be distinguished in the impenetrable chaos of foliage, and we spotted the huge leaves of bananas and of taro, besides the largest lemon tree we had ever seen, loaded like a Christmas tree with golden fruits.

If the site had been picked by the royal family, we could hardly do better elsewhere. We made it clear to Ioane that we had decided to stay, and he saluted happily and disappeared into the greenery. We had agreed, through Willy, that for a price per year equivalent to the value of an empty suitcase we were to rent the entire surrounding part of the valley, with the right to clear and build, and to eat all the fruit and nuts we could manage. In addition to this modest rent to Ioane, we were to pay a trifle in tax to the village chief.

For the first night, we had brought along a tiny tent, and before the sun set, I had managed to clear enough space to put it up. An inflated bag with a zipper opening. As night fell upon the jungle, we used matches for the last time. From now on, we were to save our evening embers under ashes, and if the fire died out, we had to rub another into life with the aid of split hibiscus sticks. That evening, Liv baked some *fei* and her first breadfruit, as large as a baby's head, and, as happy as children, we crawled to bed in our tiny tent below the huge, sprawling leaves. The mosquito was the only devil in our Paradise.

Sleeping in a tent is the next best thing to sleeping in the open. With nothing but a cloth wall to separate you from your surroundings, you participate in the faintest sound around, particularly so in an unfamiliar kind of forest. That night, we were to learn a lot about the natural environment that was to become our home, and yet there was much we did not understand. What made that ghastly cry as it seemed to leap across the canvas? It could croak like a toad and creak like a rusty door. There, something was rummaging in a pile of stones nearby. Was it a wild pig? Higher up the valley, something hooted like an owl. And we clearly heard the mewing of a cat somewhere just below our terrace.

Then we both heard someone approaching. We heard steps in the dry, fallen foliage, and the casual sound of cracking twigs. The sound came closer, then stopped. A long silence. Then someone tiptoed right up to the tent. A sudden silence again, while we listened, in complete darkness, with racing hearts.

Who in the world could it be, slinking up here at night and now standing motionless outside our tent? In our mind's eye, we both saw a revengeful native with elephant legs leaning over the little tent with a fishing spear, or perhaps a heavy stone, in his raised arms. They had no reason to love the white man here, where our worst diseases played havoc, where no one could read or write, and the cannibalism mentioned in the old encyclopedia persisted until very recent generations. If we disappeared, nobody would ever know when or how.

Lacking any weapon, I hurled myself through the zipper opening with an earsplitting yell. It is hard to judge who was most afraid, for outside was a wild white mongrel dog staring at the tent with a stupid expression. It suddenly became so madly frightened that it shot off like a white arrow into the bush and down the slopes, never again to venture into our domain.

Even so, we were not left in peace. In the calm night breeze, we heard scattered gunshots from far parts of the valley, a few of them even fairly close. This was crazy, for hardly anybody on the island but Willy Grelet could possibly possess a gun; besides, nobody could see an arm's length in the forest at this time of night. We had to crawl outside to hear better. We could see a few stars above. Then something hit the ground beside us with a tremendous impact. It resounded like a real gunshot, just like the ones we had heard in the distance. Something rolled toward me. A large coconut, almost as big as a rugby ball, since it still had the thick, leathery husk outside the shell, a shockproof cover to protect the nut from cracking when it falls from the crown of the palm. The jungle palms of the Marquesas group sometimes reach enormous heights to penetrate the jungle roof with their sun-craving crowns. As the breeze increased at night and shook the lofty palm leaves, ripe nuts loosened, and, heavy with milk, they made the silent night jungle resound with a sharp report each time one plummeted to the ground. One of the tallest palms was waving against the stars right above our heads; one tent stay had been lashed to its trunk. In a hurry, we untied the stay and pulled the little tent away into safety. A nut from that palm would rip the tent and be as fatal as a bomb if it hit us. In the dark, I cleared some more of the bush as best I could, and we covered ourselves with the deflated tent to escape the mosquitoes as far as possible.

As the sun rose above the Tauaouoho Mountains, hardly a ray fell upon our plateau. We were well walled in by the dense jungle, and not even the faintest breeze could enter and brush away the mosquitoes. We decided to clear the entire terrace and build some kind of dwelling strong enough to keep out the jungle beasts.

For breakfast, I brought back an insect-eaten cluster of ripe bananas I had found by roaming the terraces within hearing distance of Liv, and as I returned, she had already toasted some nut-like fruits that had fallen from a large local jungle tree. The water in the queen's spring was cool and crystal clear, with a most pleasing taste never found in tap water, and we were as happy as the singing birds around us, and aching to get to work.

Breakfast over, I grabbed the long machete and began to swing it like a sword against the jungle. With a single blow, the sharp knife severed the juicy banana stems like onions, and even the hardwood trunk of the breadfruit tree gradually had to yield, chip by chip. Familiar fruit trees fell one by one in company with unknown jungle growth. It was a bizarre job, like playing havoc in someone's garden. Liv pulled up creeping vanilla, ferns, coffee plants, and dragged down what looked like ropes with aerial potatoes attached. As the jungle roof opened above us and the undergrowth was thinned, ever more sunlight reached the ground and played on the mighty old boulder walls built up by generations of industrious hands. A soft breeze entered. When mud and rotten branches were dug away from the nearby pool with bare hands, and a short piece of arm-thick bamboo was hammered into the bank with a stone, the water of the royal spring squirted into a boulder-lined pool that made a perfect bathtub.

The trees of the lower terrace fell next, and a most pleasant view opened of the valley below, with its wealth of palms and tropical trees all fenced in by the red mountain wall on the other side, which increased in height, as it ran inland from the mouth of the

Opposite:

TAHITI was the closest we could get to Fatu-Hiva with a passenger ticket. In those days Tahiti had only one regular call a month, when a French steamer arrived after six weeks of ocean travel. On this island, we had to wait until some copra schooner could take us northward to the isolated Marquesas Islands, near the equator.

Overleaf left:

CHIEF TERIIEROO AND HIS WIFE, FAUFAU, gave us a warm welcome on our arrival, and invited us to live with them in the Papenoo Valley. A pure-blooded Polynesian, Teriieroo was chief over Tahiti's seventeen chiefs, and took pride in the old island customs.

Overleaf right:

TERAI MATEATA TANE AND TERAI MATEATA VAHINE were the names given to us by the chief when he adopted us, since no one on the island could pronounce our difficult Norwegian names, Liv and Thor.

Above:

THE POLYNESIAN WAY OF LIFE was introduced to us by the chief and his many children.

TROPICAL FRUITS were to become the major part of our diet, so we had to learn to recognize them.

CLIMBING A COCONUT PALM Polynesian fashion was a skill I had to master before we were equipped for survival on Fatu-Hiva.

Opposite:

AS PASSENGERS ON A COPRA SCHOONER, we started our three weeks' journey to the lonely Marquesas group.

CORAL ATOLLS in the Tuamotu group were visited en route to collect copra, or dried coconut kernels. The coconut palms provided the only economy of these islands. Few of the old-style Polynesian thatched huts were still in use, since civilization, spread by the schooner, had started to introduce wooden planks and corrugated iron.

Opposite:

THE MARQUESAS ISLANDS finally rose from the Pacific. As the rugged mountains of one island in this group sank into the sea, others rose in front of us, and we were able to visit most of them before the little schooner made a special call at Fatu-Hiva, where we had asked to be let off.

FISH ABOUNDED in these waters. During the long journey with a Polynesian crew, I had the opportunity to get acquainted with the two most dangerous marine creatures in the area, the shark and the moray eel.

Above:

BEAUTIFUL PALM VALLEYS slid by as the schooner went from one Marquesas island to the next. They ran from black lava beaches into wild mountains, but our questions always were: Did they have drinking water? Was there enough wild fruit to keep us alive? Were they uninhabited? These were our only requirements in choosing the place for our experiment of going back to nature.

valley, with peaks and perpendicular cliffs. On the very edge of the red precipice, we could see half a dozen white specks moving. Wild goats. Secondarily wild, like all other mammals on these islands. Giant cane and closely packed tufts of bamboo covered some promontories at the foot of the cliffs above the palm forest. To the right, we could see a couple of miles down the valley, but the little village and the ocean were hidden by a chaos of giant leaves.

Clearing roots and stones, we encountered old artifacts. A variety of stone adzes and gouges, ground and polished to perfection and made from heavy, solid stone, a bell-shaped stone pounder with a narrow grip-neck and a flaring base as perfectly curved and polished as if turned on a lathe, cowrie shells with the vaulted back sawed off to serve as vegetable scrapers, dented plaques of mother-of-pearl fashioned to grate coconut kernels, round hammer stones, and even a cracked but once beautiful wooden bowl. Some of them, we could use. A large, comfortable stone chair had once been set presumably for the king to overlook his own terrace, whereas a long bench paved with flat, smooth boulders was broken by growing palms. We repaired what was possible, and also saved a few useful or ornamental trees and shrubs, including a big bush entirely covered with strawberry-red flowers.

After three days of hard work, most of the clearing was done, and we began cutting branches and giant leaves to build our home. We had hardly started before Ioane came up the forest trail lugging our two suitcases, which we had intentionally left behind with Willy. We did not need them. We had nothing in them that we could use. We tried to make Ioane understand that they were to remain in Willy's house. But he made it clear, with signs and chosen words, that Willy was afraid of theft. What was more, Ioane was not satisfied before he had been permitted to admire what was inside the suitcases he had lugged up through the jungle. His eyes almost popped out of his head when he saw that we who walked

Opposite:
LANDING ON FATU-HIVA. We were set ashore with no provisions and without weapons, determined to live on what we could collect with our bare hands. There were no other white foreigners on the island, and we did not know the local language. The lifeboat returned to the schooner, which sailed away after the captain had promised to come back in a year. We were left on the beach of an island that had neither radio nor any other means of contact with the outside world.

barefoot and wrapped up in *pareu* were the owners of dark suits
and long gowns, shoes of various colors, white shirts, pajamas, and
underwear. Ties and shaving gear. Silk and a powder kit. He was
so eager to carry the suitcases away again that we had to hang on
to the undesired luggage and temporarily store it in the tent.

But now Ioane did not want to leave us. He made it clear that
the leaf hut we were about to put up would wither away and collapse, rain would pour in, wild horses would trample on us, and
all kinds of creeping things would enter. Bursting with a sudden
desire to be helpful, Ioane dragged me along, higher up the hillside, into a forest of giant, green bamboo. Most of the canes were
as thick as a man's leg and ran up like jointed water pipes to end in
clusters of long, thin leaves like fluffy ostrich feathers high above
our heads. Green as they were, the thick, hollow canes could be cut
with a single hard stroke of the machete knife. Unlike a tree, the
large bamboo when cut would not topple over on one side. Sharp
as a gouge, the obliquely cut end of the long and heavy tube would
drop perpendicularly to the ground like a spear and cut any hand
or naked foot that was not quickly pulled out of the way. With a
bleeding arm wrapped in leaves, I returned to our boulder terrace
with Ioane, each of us dragging a bundle of long, green bamboo.

Liv had picked a large pile of ripe oranges, and in a few moments Ioane, although he was middle-aged, was seen atop a giant
breadfruit tree, whereafter he wriggled monkeylike to the crown
of one of our sky-piercing palms, a feat I could never have managed even if I had not cut my arm. He left his harvest with us and
made signs that he had to leave. The sun was getting low. We liked
this amusing old rascal. He seemed so trustworthy, the way he
trotted barefoot about in the jungle with an elegant straw hat and
white shorts, apparently boasting all the time of his relationship
to the last queen. Whether we understood him or not, he grinned
and laughed, his brown face crumpling into foxy wrinkles.

It was barely daylight next morning when Ioane reappeared,
and, on the trail behind him, his wife and four other natives followed. They brought us pineapples and had come to show us how
to build a bamboo cabin. But, before work started, everybody, including Ioane once more, had to look at the unbelievable treasures
in our possession. First our tent, this amazing little roll of cloth
that could be transformed in a minute into a waterproof hut. I
could have kept on for hours pulling the zipper opening up and
down, a performance invoking the utmost respect. But Ioane wanted

the suitcases reopened, and the excitement had no end for the spectators. To them, the outside world was synonymous with the cargo of the trading schooner. Planks and corrugated iron. Corned beef and canned salmon. Enamel pots, matches, and underwear. Everyone shouted with joy as they struggled to peep through our tourist binoculars, which "moved the mountains." My little microscope transformed a blood-filled mosquito into a monster which startled Ioane's wife so much that she shrieked. And the shaving mirror, which magnified their already broad noses, made them laugh so much that they bent double as they took turns at poking their faces into it, making the most peculiar grimaces. Yet my wrist watch attracted Ioane more than anything else. He held it upside down and could not tell the time, but he made signs by measuring with his arms that he wanted a really huge one of the same kind, and he dug into our suitcases in the vain hope of locating one. We later realized that a large clock on the wall of Willy's bungalow was the envy of the entire island. If we had brought along one of these, we could have purchased a kingdom on Fatu-Hiva.

Recovering from the exhausting entertainment, our island friends set to work. Two men climbed the tallest palms with machete knives in home-made sheaths of hide, and coconut leaves ten to twelve feet long began sailing to the ground. The long stem of the fringed palm leaf was split lengthwise, and the women squatted on the ground to plait the fringes of two half leaves together, crosswise, as in basketry work. A framework for the house was raised from slender poles lashed together with hibiscus-bark rope, and the plaited coconut leaves were placed in overlapping rows like tiles to thatch the roof. A floor of slender rods was next lashed on a foot above the ground and covered with bamboo. The deep-green bamboo was first beaten flat between stones and plaited together in an artistic manner. Roof and floor ready, the walls were plaited by prefabricating in the same way two big rectangular and two smaller square sheets. When lifted on end and tied to the upright poles, these four plaited bamboo sheets formed the walls of a cozy one-room cabin about six feet wide and twelve feet long. Squares were cut from the walls and fastened back into place with bark hinges to form a door and three shuttered windows.

One day, during work, we had a visit that greatly increased our prestige among the islanders. I had just caught a rare kind of grasshopper in a glass tube and was dripping ether on cotton to preserve this zoological treasure, when a tall and skinny islander with his head cocked on one side came up the trail, his face distorted by the largest gumboil I had ever seen. His appearance, unfortunately, was grotesquely comic, and his compatriots just stopped work and roared with laughter, while the poor chap humbly begged me for assistance. Great expectations.

Ether, I thought. I had never had toothache, but the bottle in my hand reminded me of an old remedy. I soaked a large piece of cotton and jammed it in between his sparse teeth. He grinned and chewed but did not stagger. For a while. But after a couple of minutes he really began to sway and cross his eyes.

"Breathe with your nose," I shouted in Norwegian, and helped him close his mouth. He seemed just about to lose his balance. Our admiring audience was breathless with expectation. Had I used too much ether? Liv realized how worried I was when I groped for my collar, although I was dressed in a loincloth only. The ugly grin of the sufferer began to turn into a blissful smile that really scared me.

"Spit it out," I shouted, and he did. He puffed for a while like a dragon, stinking of ether. When he regained his balance I ventured another dose with the tall fellow safely seated. When the treatment was finished, he was cured, and time would show that tall Tioti would become our most indispensable friend on the island.

For a while, we were treated almost as old-time witch doctors. Poultry and meat from the village were left in piles at our feet when our visitors withdrew in the evening. Meat would not keep in the warm jungle, and so much arrived that it became a problem. We could not refuse a gift, and had no one to share it with. To avoid the smell, we simply had to carry all the surplus far away into the forest and bury it. Damn the wild dog I had scared so successfully that it never again ventured near our domain!

We learned a bit of Polynesian the hard way on the days the islanders worked with us. Willy had solemnly informed us that the Marquesas group was part of French Oceania, and if we needed any help the daily wage should not differ from what he had heard was valid in Tahiti, 17.5 francs per day. The word for 17.5 francs in the Marquesan dialect was *etoutemonieuatevasodiso*. This was the splendid word our friends, with a happy smile, reminded us of each evening when they set off down the mountain trail. But as with the trading schooner, so with us. When payday arrived, they did not care for useless money and wanted tangible goods in exchange. A suit would not be refused. Or our interesting binoculars.

Interrupted by long feasts of wild beef, chicken, and fish from the village, by long siestas in the jungle, and by frequent performances around our entertaining luggage, Ioane's helpful group returned for days on end before they finally disappeared forever. With them, the contents of our suitcases were gone, wedding gown and all. All that was left was the little tent, two traveling blankets, the camera equipment, and what we most desperately needed if we should ever find it necessary to think of the long journey back to civilization.

What I could never quite get over was that Ioane had managed to beg from me my wrist watch. For years, I had been looking forward to the day when I was installed in my own jungle home and could lay my watch on a rock and smash it with a stone. I had dreamed of the sound and sight of this crash of glass and burst of cogwheels as the symbolic fanfare for the return to nature.

I had the idea that man was a slave of his own little timekeeper. Continuously, it told him to move, to rush, to get ready. Time was supposed to be money. These islanders had plenty of time. Thus they were rich. They had no watches. We had watches, always depriving us of time. I never could forgive Ioane and myself that he had saved my watch from its cruel destiny and left me with an ardent dream never fulfilled. I told myself, and others—and I started by telling you—that I smashed it. I did not. Ioane got it. But he opened its back and poked around in it so thoroughly that it was never to deprive him of his time.

A new life started the day the village visitors had finished helping us to build our home and left with their rewards. Peace reigned in the valley. The tent was packed away and we moved into our new green home. Since the natives no longer brought us a share of their abundance, we had to think of our own kitchen. With my machete, I cut four straight poles of hibiscus wood and rammed them into the ground beside our cabin. Thatched with coconut leaves in the same manner as the bamboo hut, this open-walled shelter became our cooking place, with a stone-lined oven in Polynesian style. Ioane had already built a sleeping-bench along one short wall inside the cabin, and when I had knocked the foot end down to level, he had knocked it up, because his eye measure was better than my yardstick. Yet he ran away with the yardstick too, because it was of the amusing kind that jumped back into its cover by pressing a button. Sleeping on the nobbly bench of round branches would be like sleeping on billiard balls, so a thick mattress of banana leaves had to be piled on top. From split branches lashed together, I made two stools, a bamboo-covered table, and a little shelf. The rest of the inventory was also in true Robinson Crusoe style: our plates were large, shallow mother-of-pearl shells, which shone like rainbows in the sun. Our cups were coconut shells set in bamboo rings. When the shockproof husk of the coconut was pried off and the nut beaten all around its midline with a sharp stone, it suddenly burst into two halves as nicely cut as if severed by a saw. Our glasses were joints of ripe golden bamboo, and spoons and dippers were cut from the same hard material. Water was fetched in a jar-shaped container made from the rind of bottle gourds scraped empty and smoke-dried over a low fire. A piece of raw oxhide left by the natives was made into a long sheath for my indispensable machete, and remaining pieces became tough leather hinges for the door and window shutters, because the bark hinges cracked as they dried out. We had not disposed of our two travel rugs, for, after the tropical day, the night felt really cold.

Certainly no king could have a more pleasing residence than the one now erected on the royal terrace. If any person under stress had moved into such a home, he could not but rest and relax. Its simplicity and modesty would lead his thoughts away from all complex problems, and the matted bamboo walls seemed to absorb tension. The attractive pattern of the green plaiting became ever more engaging as the fresh bamboo matured and an increasing number of bars and panels turned golden yellow and intermingled with the green ones, like a live tapestry. At the same time and in the same way, the basketwork of the green palm roof began to flame into reddish brown. When we opened the bamboo shutters, the whole upper part of the Omoa Valley lay before us as our own royal garden.

Time took on different dimensions when it was measured by the sun, birds, and the appetite, rather than hacked into seconds and hours. Perhaps it was the lack of watches, or perhaps it was the fact that every moment was lived, felt, and registered in an environment totally new to us, where we had to keep alert to avoid being struck by a falling coconut, cutting our toes, or making a wrong step. Whatever the cause, although we were never bored for a fraction of a moment, every day felt so rich and long that a week became like several months. As I think back now on one year on Fatu-Hiva, it seems to have been more like twenty, it was so full.

The day began when the spectacular, parrot-colored Marquesan cuckoo awoke the slumbering jungle with its resounding trumpet calls. Not losing a moment, all the other birds of the forest began their chorus of joy, one by one joining in from different parts of the valley, each with a different tune and a different love story to tell. We could not help but wake up happy, absorbing every note of this melodious morning program, which began like an overture at the opera as the dimmed lights go up for the performance. So close to the equator, dawn came suddenly and yet gently, as if timed so as not to wake us up too briskly. The growing light stole in through the bamboo-framed window-opening with the last gusts of the chilly night breeze. The temperature would turn from chilly to pleasant the very instant that daylight was fully turned on. The dark dragon crest across the valley was itself a spectacle as it reddened in the dawn twilight to flame out like a cock's comb in the morning sun. For a moment, the jungle chorus rose to a real festival crescendo, and many of the birds seemed to be attracted to the little clearing around our cabin, where insects and worms could be readily spotted on the open ground. The parrotlike cuckoo, blue like the sky with yellow and green decorations, favored the thick foliage of the mighty breadfruit tree outside our window, while the palms seemed to teem with little fluttering singers, many resembling yellow canaries.

No part of the day could quite match the first morning hour, when the early sun began to play along the golden bamboo plaiting, for nature was never more serene and alert, and we were part of it. Somehow, all living creatures became more drowsy as the sun rose to pass the very zenith of the sky, blessing the crowns of the tropical forest with its magic rays. It never felt unbearably hot, for the constant trade wind from the east carried away the mounting heat and aired the landscape. It was not so much the heat that made one less dynamic nearer midday, as something to do with the air pressure, something that removed all unnecessary energy. The heat never bothered us in the Omoa Valley.

As the early-morning concert tailed off, we were already out of bed and down by the cool spring. We often surprised a beautiful wild cat with distant domestic ancestry that had the habit of sharing the spring with us. Sitting in the pool, it sometimes happened that shades we were unaware of seemed to fall from our eyes, whereby everything around us took on a breath-taking beauty. Our sense of perception seemed to be tuned in to a different and clearer reception, and we smelt, saw, and listened to everything

around us as if we were tiny children witnessing nothing but
miracles. All these little things were everyday matters, such as a
little drop of water shaping up to fall from the tip of a green leaf.
We let drops spill from our hands to see them sparkle like jewels
against the morning sun. No precious stone polished by human
hands could shine with more loveliness than this liquid jewel in
the flame of the sun. We were rich; we could bail them up by
handfuls and let them trickle by the thousands through our fingers
and run away, because an infinity of these jewels kept pouring out
of the rock. The melodious dance of the little stream below us,
formed of this treasure, tempted us to shake pink hibiscus flowers
from the branches and let them sail away, rotating and leaping
down the tiny rapids between the smooth boulders. They were
messengers to the sea, the magician's kettle that gave birth to
all life, the perpetual purifier that cleaned the ugly village water
from the river's mouth and sent it skyward and back to the hidden
birthplace of our little spring.

To rise from the spring and put our feet on the silky clay, in
the soft mud, or on a hard, warm slab, felt marvelous. From the
day the natives left us, our contact with nature was complete.
We felt it on our bare skin. The fine climate made it a relief to
strip off the clothes which the white man from cool countries was
now imposing on the tropical islanders and which cling to a sun-
baked body like wet paper. It felt just as good to throw off the
shoes, which would be in constant need of repair from stepping
from mud to sharp lava rather than from pedals to pavements.
The effect was one of added freedom and added intensity. Our
ever-wrapped skin was at first tender, like that of a reptile casting
off its slough and hiding until the new covering toughened. But
gradually the jungle withdrew its long claws and instead it felt
as if its leaves and soft branches stroked us in friendship as we
passed. Hostile to intruders, even the jungle is friendly to its own,
and protective to its offspring. It was good to feel the breeze, the
sun, the touch of the forest on our skins, rather than to feel
merely the same cloth clinging to the body wherever we moved.
To step from cool grass to hot sand, and to feel the soft mud
squeeze up between the toes, to be licked away in the next pool,
felt better than stepping continually on the inside of the same
pair of socks. Altogether, rather than feeling poor and naked, we
felt rich and as if wrapped in the whole universe. We and
everything were part of one entirety.

We were living in the most luxuriant part of the valley. The abundance around us reflected man's successful attempt to domesticate the wilderness. No attempt had been made to liquidate the environment in favor of extensive uniform plantations. Less useful trees had been replaced by more beneficial species of various kinds scattered about where place and soil permitted. The planters were lost while their domesticated jungle survived, not as victor over an extinct enemy but as a monument to human efforts. The people had died, not in a battle with nature but as a result of white man's desire to have them share in our own civilization.

Brought up in a city, the two of us would scarcely have survived in the jungle but for the blessings left by our island predecessors. The soil patiently continued to produce food even though no one came for the harvest, other than insects and beasts. Part of the forest behind us consisted of large plants of banana and *fei*. It was hard to distinguish between the two unless they bore fruit. Both have green, sappy trunks like giant flower stems, with a cross section as big as a plate, and both are crowned by tall bundles of leathery leaves groping for the sky like palms. But a reddish tinge is apparent near the root of the *fei*, and whereas the banana has its cluster of green or yellow fruits hanging down from the top of the stem like a chandelier, the *fei* has its cluster of red fruits standing erect and pointing skyward like the star on a Christmas tree.

As predicted by Teriieroo, the precious *fei*, or mountain plantain, which on Tahiti grew only in almost inaccessible cliffs, grew all around our cabin on Fatu-Hiva. It became our favorite, staple diet. Inedible when raw, it was roasted on embers and eaten dipped in the creamy white sauce of grated and squeezed coconut kernel. This coconut sauce was our only oil and served a multitude of purposes, culinary as well as cosmetic. Production was simple: We grated the nut with a serrated piece of shell and squeezed the crumbs by twisting them inside a wisp of coconut fiber. Dipped in coconut sauce, the yellow-green meat of the *fei*, sweeter than fried banana, had a special flavor of excellent quality, of which we never tired. Besides the *fei*, the forest offered us seven different kinds of real bananas, from a tiny, round variety, resembling a yellow egg with strawberry flavor, to the large horse-banana, almost as long as an arm, which had to be cooked and then tasted like baked apple.

It was unusual to come across ripe bananas hanging on the

plant. When we reached for one, it was like grabbing a finger on
an empty glove: it was already hollowed out by small fruit rats
and consumed with the help of lizards and tiny, yellow banana
flies. But there was plenty for all of us. We simply collected the
clusters when they were just about ready to turn yellow, and
hung them unsheltered in the breadfruit tree next to our window,
where the sun would ripen them in a day or two and under our
control. Their taste was unmatched by commercial bananas, which
have to be picked weeks too early so as to survive the long trans-
portation.

We had learned not to climb the slippery stem of the banana
plant to reach its cluster of fruit. With a hard stroke of the
machete, the entire stem cut like an onion and we rushed to grab
the cluster of bananas before it was smashed against the ground
as the whole plant fell. This seemingly vandalistic procedure was
due to the fact that neither a *fei* nor a banana plant yields fruit
twice. On Fatu-Hiva, the green stump remaining above the root
began pushing up a new plant immediately, and so fast that the
growth could be seen daily. The juicy inner ring of the onionlike
cut began to rise above the others and slowly pulled up the next
ring and the next. In a fortnight, the old stump resembled a flower-
pot holding a green pole as tall as a man, which now opened up
to unfold a green banner, the first, huge leaf. The new plant
crept up just slowly enough to seem to have its speed cautiously
adjusted not to scare us, not to wake us up to the fact that in the
forest there is no borderline between what we consider natural
and what we would have considered magic if it happened with a
speed that would catch our eye. Within a year, a big, new plant
had silently replaced the old one and stood there motionless and
mute, ready to offer a new cluster of tasty bananas to hungry
passers-by.

The coconut was almost equally important to our daily fare.
Most of the coconut palms near our hut were so incredibly tall
and they swayed so much that I could not manage to get to the
top, but there were always plenty of ripe nuts, covered with husk,
to be found on the ground. Some of them had fallen down weeks
before, and a baby palm was already putting its neck out like an
ostrich from an egg while a root was fumbling in the opposite direction, trying to get a foothold and pierce the ground. In these
overmature nuts, most of the hard kernel had dissolved in the
milk and begun to form a spongy, white ball looking like a brain,

edible, but with a sugary taste unlike the nut itself. Even the "marrow" of the stem on a young palm was edible, like a giant piece of crisp celery.

Most of the food plants kept up a nonstop production and yielded fruits and nuts all the year round. The spiny orange trees carried sweet-smelling white flowers and green and ripe, golden fruit side by side on the same branches, and so did lemon trees and lime. But not the breadfruit. This stout tree marked the seasons. Most of the old breadfruit trees were so big that I could not encircle the smooth trunk in order to climb it if the lower branches did not happen to be within reach. The impressive foliage resembled oversize oak leaves, and, scattered throughout the crooked branches, hung green, globular fruits as large as a baby's head. The tough, gnarled rind cracked when toasted black on embers, and loosened, when cooked, from the delicious white meat within. It was a starchy and filling dish, tasting like a cross between fresh toast and new potatoes. This fibrous meat could be torn apart with the fingers like bread, it could be sliced and fried crisp in coconut oil on a flat slab, and it could be buried in the ground for months or years and eaten as a pounded porridge when completely fermented.

The most important wild tuber we came across in the forest was the taro, the closest we came to potatoes. It had once been cultivated in irrigated swamps, but as the planters disappeared, it now grew wild in the swampy soil below the spring. A huge, heart-shaped leaf stood like a parasol above each individual taro root, and in between grew some other wild leaves of the same shape, but so big that we used them as umbrellas in the rain, and as body-sized "fig leaves" if native visitors should ever surprise us in the pool.

There was still more to harvest in the surrounding forest. Large, pear-shaped papayas. Small but extra-flavorsome mangoes. Wild pineapples. Tiny, red husk tomatoes. Pandanus, with its compound of nutlike kernels. The nobbly, blue-green *tapo-tapo*. And a single large tree with a gorgeous fruit looking and tasting like a red strawberry but as large as a cauliflower.

For drinks, we had mineral water from the cool spring, orange juice, lemon squash sweetened with squeezed sugar cane, and the milk of green coconuts harvested with a struggle from the lower palms higher up the hill. In Tahiti, Liv had learned from Faufau to prepare as a hot beverage a very tasty tea from the

withered leaves of orange trees. We often planned to gather and
roast the red berries of a few coffee plants that grew in the thickets
right behind our cabin, but got too fond of our orange tea.

It was not only the plants that had outlived their domesticators.
Stealing between the trees or trampling about in the open highland were the dogs, the cats, the horses, the cattle, the sheep, and
the goats that descended from former European stock, and the
bushy, long-snouted Polynesian pig, originally brought in by the
islanders themselves. The tiny fruit rat, a clean and happy little
creature, also brought by the Polynesians in their canoes as a
favorite dish, ran about in the thin branches outside our window,
stealing oranges. Or, rather, preventing us from stealing them from
him. No other warm-blooded species had reached these islands,
except birds and whales. Not even bats. And snakes were unknown.
Chickens had been kept on most Polynesian islands even before
the arrival of Europeans. When their owners died, many had
escaped into the jungles of Fatu-Hiva and survived wild. In the
morning, we heard the familiar crowing of the cocks far up the
valley. Ioane had presented us with some of his own domestic
chickens, but we had no fence and did not dare to clip their
wings for fear of the wild cat; so they flew merrily about like wild
geese, slept in the highest trees, and came down only to peck
what we left for food. Their eggs were laid all about the jungle,
so, in spite of careful searching, we were lucky when we found one.

With baskets plaited from palm leaves hanging from a carrying
stick across my shoulder, I spent most of the day exploring the
forest for food. At the same time, I was on constant lookout for
animals to save in bottles and tubes for the study of transoceanic
migration and microevolution, inspired by my former professors.
The idea of ever returning to the stale life of a modern community
seemed very remote indeed, yet my zoological collection could
be sent back on some future schooner to be studied by someone
else.

Compared with that of the continents and continental islands,
the Polynesian land fauna was poor, and Fatu-Hiva was no exception. But whatever there was, clearly had an important story
to tell. Creeping things abounded under every stone, among the
fallen leaves, and in the chaos of jungle growth. Colorful tropical
beetles and butterflies, spiders of all shapes, and an endless variety
of land snails in beautiful polychrome shells. The latter, especially,
would vary completely in type from one side of the valley to the

other, or on either side of a tall mountain crest. Differences in animals from one locality to another were intimately associated with a corresponding variation in the plant life. Never had I seen a region where the vegetation varied so profoundly from place to place. As the months passed by and we came to know more of the island beyond the Omoa Valley, we could see how the Tauaouoho Mountain Range was decisive for the whole pattern of plant and animal life. The distribution of peaks and passes along this ridge decided where rain was going to fall and where it was to drift by. Like all of Polynesia, Fatu-Hiva lay in the trade-wind belt, and the clouds always came in the same general direction, from America toward Asia. Where low plateaus and mountain passes let the clouds blow over unaffected, there was drought, the landscape was one of dry savanna, almost desert in places, with nothing growing except yellow grass and small ferns. But in directly adjacent areas, dense jungle, sometimes really impenetrable rain forest, covered the soil, because the rain poured down every afternoon and evening. This was where lofty ridges and peaks arrested the trade-wind clouds and condensed the rising mist from the sun-warmed islands as it was forced up into cooler altitudes. Every afternoon, the central mountains were wrapped in a thick cloak of clouds, from where tropical showers splashed only over the already verdant areas. Except when a rare tropical storm swept the entire surrounding ocean, the island rain was a strictly local phenomenon, as if the peaks were raised to milk invisible water from the blue sky, pouring it always over the same parts of the island, day after day. The flora and fauna were entirely dictated by this regular direction of wind and clouds. Never did we see a cloud drifting back from Asia toward America. Asia was downhill. This was an observation I recorded on my naked skin; it was literally to blow me on the course I was to pursue into the Pacific years later.

Experience taught us that the inner corner of the Omoa Valley and adjacent mountainsides were literally impenetrable. For thousands upon thousands of years, jungle trees had tumbled down into a network of trunks and branches, lying on top of each other and overgrown with thick green moss, parasitic ferns, and flowers, and interwoven with live trees and lianas. If we tried to force our way in, we constantly fell through and sometimes disappeared completely before reaching the real floor. Climbing along on the slippery and often rotten framework, we sometimes needed a full day to traverse a jungle ravine a few hundred yards wide, fighting our way with the machete and watching our footholds in an effort not to crash through as into a pitfall.

In these areas, even aboriginal man, with his desire to domesticate the wilderness, had achieved no success, as shown by the total absence of human traces. Nearer our home, the forest was far more pleasant and congenial, and as we began to know our way around, we moved with little difficulty. Here we stumbled upon human vestiges wherever we put our feet: mostly overgrown terrace walls and stone platforms, *paepae*, where native huts had once stood dry above the mud. But occasionally we met the former people too; their bleached or sometimes green-stained skulls and long bones could be stumbled upon in caves and crevices, and in a few areas carved slabs were set on end to mark a taboo enclosure filled with old human craniums. Sometimes, on the nicely cut slabs surrounding such burial places, were reliefs of squatting figures with their arms raised at right angles, as if meant to chase away evil spirits or undesired intruders. In a few instances, even a stone statue was erected, resembling a stout demon with giant, round eyes, an enormously wide mouth, stunted legs, and hands placed on the fat belly. Petroglyphs of men and marine creatures, staring eyes, concentric circles, and patterns of cup-shaped depressions were found down by the river, while, high up the hill above our cabin, overlooking the valley, was a large slab sculptured into a turtle. This was probably an altar for sacrifice. No archaeologist had ever set foot on Fatu-Hiva. Willy's late father had received a brief call from the German explorer Karl von den Steinen when he visited the Marquesas group in 1897 to collect ethnographica for the museum in Berlin. Three American ethnologists, Mr. and Mrs. Handy and Ralph Linton from the Bishop Museum in Hawaii, had studied the culture of the main islands, but nowhere in the whole group had anyone yet attempted archaeological excavation. New discoveries were made wherever we put our feet. Under the bed, we already had a big pile of finely polished stone tools and a growing collection of small images and ornaments carved in stone, shell, turtle shell, and human bone.

Never was any human voice but our own heard in the valley. We felt like the survivors of a forgotten catastrophe. We tried to visualize the daily life of our predecessors, their work and play, their loves and their problems. They ceased to be the exotic curiosities I had visualized while I studied rows of books in Oslo or the equally tidy rows of fine Marquesan artifacts I had made notes on in the Völkerkunde Museum of Berlin. Found one by one, just where they had been used and with a shape and function that concurred with our own local needs, these utensils showed us that their former owners had solved their daily problems in a way natural to us too. Their makers were not strangers at all; they were like Teriieroo and Faufau, like our friends down in the village, like us, or, rather, we were still like them, although we like to think differently because we have progressed in invention and changed our way of dressing. As for myself, I began to acquire a less strictly academic approach to anthropology than I had used to have at my own desk at home when trying to digest the many conflicting theories of scholars, few of whom had seen a trade-wind cloud and still fewer had set foot on the shores of a Polynesian island. The problem of how Polynesian tribes had found their way to these islands long before the days of Captain Cook, Columbus, or Marco Polo, began to interest me more than the itinerary of irrational coleopters and gastropods.

Weeks passed. What gradually burned itself into our memories more than any artifact or animal was the feeling of being an integral part of the environment, rather than something combating it. Civilized man had declared war against his own environment, and the battle was raging on all continents, gradually spreading to these distant islands. In fighting nature, man can win every battle except the last. If he should win that too, he will perish, like an embryo cutting its own umbilical cord. All other living creatures could exist without man; they did exist before man. But man could not exist before they were present, nor would he survive after they were gone. Living with nature was far more convincing than any biological textbook in illustrating the fact that the life cycles of all living creatures are interdependent. As city people, we had been secondhand customers of the environment; now we were directly part of it and had the strong impression of nature being an enormous co-operative where every associate unwittingly has the function of serving the entity. Every associate except man, the secluded rebel. Everything creeping or sprouting, everything man would spray with poison or bury in asphalt to make his city clean, is in one way or another his humble servant and benefactor. Everything is there to make the human heart tick, to help man breathe and eat.

The braided bamboo walls of our cabin let the jungle air pass through and fill our lungs to capacity. At home, when we had wanted a breath of fresh air, we would open a window, turn on a ventilator—today some would switch on their air conditioning—but who would give a moment's thought to the modest providers of the oxygen we gasp for? The baker supplies our bread and the farmer milk, but air is just there and free for everybody. Yet the largest city would stop pulsating and industry would collapse if it were not for weeds and wildernesses, for the inconspicuous roots that transform black soil into green leaves which emit oxygen throughout the day. Smaller plants, almost invisible to the eye, float about rootless, like green dust in the surface water of all the oceans. The water around the coastal cliffs of Fatu-Hiva was green with this marine pasture, but the illiterate village people down by the river's mouth did not know the functions of plankton. Nobody had taught them that to this green dust all moving creatures owe their life. Before plant plankton began composing the first molecules of oxygen, no fish could live in the sea. And before the same inconspicuous plankton had sent enough surplus oxygen above the surface to form a breathable atmosphere around our planet, no flying, creeping, jumping, climbing, or walking creature could come into existence anywhere. Thanks to modern science, civilized people know this. We knew it whenever we came to think of it. But our knowledge has not changed our conduct. The way in which our clean valley river was polluted by the ignorant village people before it reached the sea is followed on a larger scale by modern industry and all the cities of the world. Nothing has been found too venomous or poisonous to be piped into the sea. Although Columbus has shown us differently, the ocean still seems as endless to us as to any savage, and breathing comes naturally to everybody, so who cares for marine plankton or forest weeds?

In the airy jungle cabin, before we fell asleep, we would lie and inhale the exhalation of the surrounding forest. We were mouth to mouth with the breathing greenery, the one inhaling what the other expired. We and everything were united in a common pulsation, an endless machinery, a nonstop production line. The breath from flowers and plants that gives life to birds and beasts was paid back by them, and us, in daily doses of carbon dioxide and manure. Fertilizers of different quality were delivered by every moving creature in proportion to its capacity, most generously by vegetarian gluttons like cows and horses, while the wild dogs would generously lift a leg against a trunk to be sure not to waste a drop of their contribution. Worms and beetles dug the ground like real farmers, preparing the soil for the blindly fumbling roots, and with the aid of dogs and cats and other scavengers down to the size of invisible bacteria, they kept the jungle clean. They all cleared away rotting carcasses, and left it to flowers to fill the air instead with a variety of delightful, pleasure-giving perfumes.

The jungle is well groomed, and, in the wilderness, beauty has the same function as the pleasant scents: to stimulate and to attract. Beauty in never-ending variety peeped forth everywhere, high and low. Pleasing even to the eye of sophisticated man, elegant orchids hung as decoration from moss-covered branches, and slender hibiscus trees stretched their pink, red, and blue flowers out over the stream. Tiny travelers with waving antennae and eyes popping out of their heads also apparently took in the beauty, as a simple flower would offer a tiny insect attractive colors and a sweet meal for its help in carrying away a few pollen grains and thus aid an immobile plant in its fecundation. Each flower had its own ingenious design for preventing the insect from reaching nectar without stepping on the stamens.

With our own food literally falling into our hands, ready-made by twigs and tree trunks that had produced these tasty dishes from mere jungle mud, we felt ourselves as pot companions of butterflies and beasts. We served ourselves with anything that pleased us and took the meals, like the air, for granted. Only when we had sudden spells of intensive attention, as the jungle atmosphere seemed to wake us up from a sort of habitual slumber, did we differ from our four- or six-legged companions in the forest by asking ourselves naïve questions. It could happen when we ate a tasty fruit, that we took a second look at the mute tree that produced it and asked ourselves how one wood could come up with a delicacy so different in shape and taste from that yielded by another. A chunk or splint from an orange tree did not look all that different from a chip from a mango or a breadfruit tree, and yet, when the same mud was filtered through them, from the roots to the branches, it came out so completely different at the upper end. These simple tree trunks that fed us were in fact master cooks. The raw material they had used was nothing but what a child has at its disposal when making mud pies. The best cook in the world, with access to the finest choice of condiments and spices, could not convert mud into the wide variety of supreme dishes we got for nothing from these quiet trees. If a cook could do this, he would be a magician. In the jungle, we were surrounded by magicians.

One day I took a rest with my burden of *fei* under the foliage of some flowery bushes, enjoying the play of the midday sun among the glittering leaves. I detected a little, speckled spider on its way down the thin silk thread that it skillfully emitted for its own descent. Before reaching the ground, it seemed to change its mind and climbed quickly up to the leaf from which the cord was suspended, leaving the shiny thread to flutter in the faint breath of air. The spider seemed to be patiently waiting for something, although a single, waving thread could catch nothing. I had never liked spiders; they had always left me with the impression of being the assassins and gangsters among animals, lying in hiding with deadly weapons and striking at innocent little nymphs dancing by. But now I was beginning to change my mind. The nymphs in this forest were dancing swarms of mosquitoes, and they bit us day and night to the extent that we had started to leave undisturbed the cobwebs spun under our ceiling; they served as flypaper. We began to bless the spiders and the friendly little lizards that hid in the thatch and helped us in our battle against invading mosquitoes. After all, the spiders were no worse assassins than the beautiful cuckoos and innocent little finches fluttering about, catching the very same prey. And moreover, where would we be if there were not some control over the population increase in the forest? Every species would multiply beyond measure, and the clockwork of nature would stop from congestion. Even the abominable spider had its purpose. It did not kill for hate or revenge, but for its own survival as a desirable cogwheel in the global machinery.

The wind was almost unnoticeable, but the fluttering thread of silk was so weightless that it drifted out horizontally and was soon entangled in a twig on another bush. The lightweight spider ran across like a ropedancer and at first seemed to try to disentangle the end. But no, this was just what the little engineer had been waiting for. With its hind legs, it wound up the slack and fixed the end properly to the twig. The little creature clearly had something planned. It climbed the tightrope back to the first little tree, and higher up to another branch vertically above the first. On this trip back, it had spun another long cord, which was now tightened and made fast higher up. In a little while, it was back on the opposite tree again, and by a deliberate and correctly calculated choice of attachment points, an open framework was gradually constructed, like a vertical loom, on which the busy little artist could begin the intended precision weaving, all with the idea in mind that, once the job was intelligently done, it would be possible to catch a flying steak.

From different points along the upper thread of the frame, the spider let itself sink to the lower thread, spinning new threads with each descent. On landing on the lower cord, it carried each new rope end left or right to be fixed at precisely calculated points, figured out in such a manner that all the threads crossed each other at the same center—like the hub of a wheel, and as exactly as if worked out with precision instruments. I knew from my zoology studies that the silk threads so far produced and suspended were not adhesive, and the spider ran along them with the greatest freedom. But as it next took up its position at the center of the star, it was ready to put into operation another kind of gland. As it began revolving, it left behind a thread coagulating from a viscid fluid which the spider seemed to try not to step on. Beginning in the center, the little weaver started to walk in growing circles, letting out its glittering sticky thread to form a growing spiral attached to the spokes of the supporting wheel. When the spider was satisfied with the size of the net, it began spinning a tubular hideout under the leaf where the work had first started. The final touch was a cord tightening the net and stretched like a fishing line to the hideout, enabling the owner of the ingenious trap to hold the end and feel a "bite" as soon as something was caught in the net.

Who knows what went on in the mind of the little creature as it crawled into its waterproof den, grabbing the line like a fisherman to lie in wait for some result from its labor, a contraption as fiendishly concocted as any nets or lime twigs produced by Italian bird-catchers?

Hungry, I returned to the cabin, where I too had started building a trap. For some days, both Liv and I had felt as if our stomachs were craving for something other than fruits and nuts. Certainly the reason was the total change from a European diet. We were spoiled. Yet it began to bother us slightly. We could eat until our stomachs held no more, and breadfruit, taro, and coconuts were left on the bamboo table. We were never tired of this diet, we were just filled to capacity, and yet hungry. One night I dreamed I was eating a juicy steak, and I was angry with Liv because she woke me up in the middle of the meal.

Something had to be done. I girded my long knife and climbed up the hill, looking for fine bamboo. It must be possible to make a trap and catch some of the prawns we had discovered in the river. They were incredibly shy, perhaps because of the wild cats, and with a stroke of the tail they jumped back and were gone like a flash each time I lured them to my left hand with their favorite food, a bit

of coconut kernel. Even if they came close enough to stretch out
their claws like fossil mittens pinching the bait, their eyes on pivots
warned them of my other hand trying to catch them from behind.
But, that day, I had plaited the first crude trap of bamboo splinters,
with a one-way entrance and coconut bait. Now I, too, could go
to my den and wait for the result.

I danced in triumph the morning when I first found my trap
squirming full of dark river prawns, some with bodies longer than
my fingers and with thick claws. In a bag of large leaves, I brought
my booty home to the pole kitchen, where Liv was roasting *fei*. The
lavish jungle feast that followed was forever to remain a milestone
in our culinary experiences. We first devoured all the peeled tails
and bodies. Then we cracked the juicy claws with our teeth and
flushed the contents down with lemon juice. Now the *fei* in coconut
sauce tasted better than ever, and we really felt happily satisfied. A
new source of food was available. There was an endless quantity of
prawns in the river, and even some very tiny blue fish wriggled
into the traps together with the delicious crustaceans.

The sun shone as merrily as before on the golden walls of the
bamboo cabin. We missed nothing. We certainly did not miss civilization.

3. WHITE MEN, DARK SHADOWS

A landscape of peace. White doves seemed to add to the happy feeling of relaxation. They fluttered around the crown of the lofty palm that shaded my back as I lay in the clear river, fumbling to fix a bamboo trap between the slippery stones.

Suddenly I became aware that I was not alone in the forest, so I stole ashore and wrapped my *pareu* around my loins. I had heard stones rattling, and soon I detected the head of a dark person carrying a thin spear, lurking behind some large ferns. I had never seen him before, and he looked malicious. He seemed more Melanesian than Polynesian. His nose was flat, his hair short and frizzy, and his skin looked almost black in the sun.

He was so busy with his own activities that he had not seen me. Coming downstream, he carried a large bowl of calabash rind in one hand and a six-foot spear in the other. He waded slowly, all the time chewing mouthfuls of coconut and spitting the mash into the stream.

Then he lifted his spear and ran it into the water. A fine prawn hung on the thin point. Attracted to the freely floating bait of coconut crumbs, it now joined the rest of the catch in the gourd container.

"*Kaoha nui*," I shouted to the stranger in my best Polynesian.

He looked up and came toward me.

"*Bonjour, monsieur*," he said calmly, and offered me the tips of his fingers with a courteous bow.

"You speak French?"

"A little. I am Pakeekee, the Protestant parson."

Pakeekee, Teriieroo's friend from the missionary school in Tahiti. I still had Teriieroo's letter to him. When I had asked Ioane where to find Pakeekee, he had just shrugged his shoulders and shaken his head. I had taken this to mean that Pakeekee was not on the island. But here he was. I dragged him along to the bamboo cabin and gave him the letter from Teriieroo. With a mixture of delight and worry, Pakeekee struggled through Teriieroo's graceful handwriting, which proved to be a recommendation that Pakeekee should take special care of us since we were not only adopted by the chief, but, like Teriieroo and Pakeekee himself, we were Protestants.

Pakeekee did indeed take Teriieroo's request seriously, and he thought out the best way of taking care of us. He asked for two days to prepare himself, and then we were taken to the greatest eating party I have ever experienced. It took place in Pakeekee's plank-walled cabin down in the village. The gorgeous but solemn, almost ceremonial eating festivities went on for three full days. Morning. Midday. Night. We barely managed to get up on our feet and stagger around a bit before we were asked to sit down to eat again. The parson and his family had been in action in their chicken coop, in their pigpen, in their trees, and in the salt sea, and women and children struggled with sticks and leaves in the kitchen shed, where smoke and savory aromas filtered through the bamboo walls.

Besides a seat for the parson himself and us, the table was prepared for only one more person, the sexton. Women and children ate on the floor. When the sexton appeared, he proved to be no other than Tioti, the tall, comical fellow with the straw hat and the bad gumboil. The joy of meeting the funny and friendly Tioti again was mutual. Tioti twisted his face into open laughter, proudly exhibiting the spacious gaps between his teeth.

The parson made no secret of this being a purely Protestant celebration. Outside, we could see some of the village Catholics with their noses in a row along the top of the fence, watching baked pork and poultry disappear. We caught a glimpse of our friend Ioane, who seemed to have a long face.

"Are there many Protestants here on Fatu-Hiva?" I ventured as polite conversation as soon as the first meal was over and our host had signaled the end of the silence with a hearty belch.

The parson wiped his mouth and thought for a while, counting on his fingers.

"No," he said apologetically. "There are more Catholics. When Father Victorin visits the island, he gives people so much sugar and rice."

"But how many are Protestants?" I insisted.

The parson counted once more.

"One is dead," he said, "and then there is myself and the sexton."
He laughed humbly and hurried to add: "There used to be one
more, but he moved to Tahiti."

On the third day, we simply had no room for more, and the
kitchen was empty. As we slowly rose to our feet, Tioti went to fetch
a trumpet made from a huge conch shell perforated near the
pointed end. He strolled out onto the village horse path and blew
three long trumpet calls with such force that they echoed from the
hills. Then he came back and we all sat down to wait.

This strange performance was repeated at long intervals. After
the third trumpet call, the parson also got up and told us that he
and the sexton must now go to church: it was Sunday. Next door to
Pakeekee's wooden cabin lay a tiny hut of bamboo with a thatched
roof and not a single window. This was the Protestant church. Into
this, the parson and the sexton disappeared alone, and we began our
long hike inland, laden with farewell gifts in green leaf baskets. For
unknown reasons, we were never to be asked inside the tiny, bamboo church. Farther down, nearer the boulder beach, lay the white-
painted, wooden Catholic church, with an iron roof and a proper
spire. It was clearly more dignified to be a Catholic on Fatu-Hiva.

Together with whatever was left on the table, Pakeekee had sent
with us baskets filled with local curiosities. In one bag, I was surprised to find a large lump of white coral. According to the textbooks, there should be no coral here, no reefs of any kind around
these islands of the Marquesas. In fact, this group was renowned
for its black beaches of fine volcanic sand, in contrast to the white
beaches of coral sand famous on other islands in Polynesia. Still,
Tioti insisted that he had found this chunk of coral on Fatu-Hiva,
at a place where there was plenty more. Here was a zoological
mystery.

At sunrise, some days later, we joined our tall friend Tioti and
his charming little dumpy wife on a walk to locate the home of the
white coral. It was said to be a desolate beach known as Tahaoa.

Access to the place was both tortuous and cumbersome. Leaving
the Omoa bay, we had to climb up and down across huge rocks
which had fallen into the sea from the mountain above and formed
a narrow belt along the vertical coastal cliffs. On our right, the ocean
tumbled against the blocks we walked on and frothed beneath our
feet, and on our left, the rusty-red rock rose precipitously into the
blue sky. Large and small stones fell every day, especially after rain.
There was not much space left for a passage. The surf thundered
against the loose rocks and the compact cliffs, and sometimes we

had to hurry to jump on top of a big block to escape a chasing breaker and reduce its attack to a pleasant, salty shower. The fallen rocks gradually petered out, and we climbed on along a narrow shelf of hardened lava. Here the volcanic activity and the action of water had created caves and strange formations. We crawled across natural bridges and peeped into tubes and holes beneath our feet, where water gushed as the ocean roared in and gurgled out. In one place, it sounded as if an invisible train were passing inside the mountain, and, at intervals, a regular geyser of water gushed from a hole in the cliff above our heads.

Like Liv, I stepped with every care not to cut my bare feet to pieces on the sharp lava, while our two companions jumped about as if they were walking on a mattress. They could step barefoot on broken glass.

Toward midday, we rounded a corner in the cliff face and jumped down upon a beautiful beach. This was Tahaoa. I could hardly believe my eyes. Dazzling-white sand and scattered coral

Opposite:

THE FIRST NIGHT IN THE JUNGLE, we slept in a small tent. The forest around us was an abandoned fruit garden recaptured by the wilderness. The red mountain banana, *fei,* abounded in the valley, although in Tahiti we had known it as a rare delicacy that grew only on almost inaccessible mountain shelves. Falling coconuts and strange animal noises created an eerie atmosphere as night fell on the island.

Overleaf left:

TOP: CLEARING THE OVERGROWN SITE of the last queen's residence was like going berserk in a fruit garden.

BOTTOM: BANANA PLANTS and fruit trees of various kinds had to be cleared away before the sun shone once again on the royal site and a faint breeze blew away the insects.

Overleaf right:

TOP: OUR FIRST HOME was built of plaited bamboo and thatched with the woven leaves of coconut palms. The kitchen was a hearth sheltered by an unwalled roof.

LEFT: A WALL OF VEGETATION surrounded the clearing we had made.

RIGHT: OUR FINISHED HOUSE stood on the ancient stone platform that had once supported the house of the island's last royal family.

Opposite:

BACK TO NATURE. Below our cabin ran a fresh mountain stream with natural swimming pools shaded by palms and tropical vegetation. Delicious prawns could be caught in this clear water and provided a welcome addition to our vegetarian diet.

Above:

SUGAR CANE was sweet and juicy, and healthy for the teeth, as opposed to refined sugar.

PAPAYA grew on stems so slender that we could simply bend them down to pick the fruit.

BANANAS shone yellow where rays of sunlight penetrated the roof of the dark forest. The cluster of bananas was harvested by cutting down the whole plant, which grew and bore fruit again within a year.

Above:

OUR PANTRY was a large breadfruit tree next to our kitchen, where *fei* and bananas hung to ripen in the sun, since, in the jungle, ripe bananas were eaten at once by insects, lizards, and fruit rats.

THE ROYAL TRAIL led inland from the village near the beach, but became lost in the jungle far short of the Tauaouoho Mountain Range.

Opposite:

HOMEWARD BOUND WITH FOOD, I frequently passed overgrown ruins in the jungle. An estimated hundred thousand Polynesians were thought to have lived in the Marquesas group when the first Europeans arrived and introduced their diseases. During our stay, only some two thousand were left and the jungle was filled with the remains of former human activity.

PETROGLYPHS were discovered incised on large slabs in the forest, and included motifs otherwise unknown in Polynesia. The outlines of a fish enclose magic cup-shaped depressions and are surrounded by concentric circles. Behind the dorsal fin, such circles represent the eye of a one-eyed mask.

blocks as white as snow ran for nearly a mile along the open coast-
line. In front of the long beach was a wide stretch of very shallow
water, where the ocean floor emerged everywhere, forming a labyrinth of pools and exposed reefs. Immediately behind the beach, the
rock overhung, leaving space for only a very narrow strip of land
with a couple of tall palms and some low foliage.

The place was as beautiful as it was menacing, with a merciless,
compact inland parapet closing the gates to the island and forcing
a visitor to stay with the sea. There was a shallow cave in the rock
which would be the only shelter in case of falling stones. I saw it as
a possible refuge, but never thought we should come back months
later and resort to it because of threats other than those of falling
stones.

The light at Tahaoa was intense. We were almost blinded by the
sunlight reflected by hundreds of glassy pools on the reef, by the
glittering white sand and the water-polished coral blocks. The sand
was the product of crushed coral and myriads of shells. The high
surf, falling upon the outer edge of the reef, succeeded in sending
only some feeble rivulets of clear sea water landward through the
shallow labyrinth of the red, yellow, and green mottled ocean floor
surfacing in front of the beach.

Nowhere had we seen an aquarium like this. The shoreline was
studded with large and small conchs, leopard shells, turban shells,
cone shells, bubble shells, tooth shells, abalones, bivalves, and other
mollusks in a colorful variety that only the tropics can produce; and
live specimens, interspersed with sea urchins, starfish, and crawling

Opposite:

ANCIENT MARQUESAN ART, carved by stone-age people, was found
among the ruins. Hollow sections of human leg bone were carved
in the traditional image of the local god *Tiki,* and worn as ornaments in the hair. Flat sheets of turtle shell were similarly carved
as an intricate composition of figures and masks representing *Tiki.*
Placed alternately between pieces of white conch shell, all sewn
onto a fillet of woven coconut husk, they formed the *paekaha,*
or crown, of the ancient island kings (see also fifth illustration in
next picture section). Earplugs were also carved from human
bone and ornamented at one end with rows or complex groups of
tiny *Tiki* images. Stone idols representing *Tiki* were sometimes
carved as a double image composed of a male and a female back
to back, or as a single image nearly always male and invariably
with both hands placed on the belly.

crustaceans, were seen in the pools, where the water literally teemed with life. The bottom of the shallows were tapestried in all the colors of the rainbow by colonies of marine lichen, microalgae, and sea anemones: a painter's palette and a marine rock garden at the same time. Monochrome and polychrome fish wriggled, rested, and darted about everywhere, some speckled and others striped, some as stout as a pear, some as thin as a pencil, some as flat as a pancake. The artist who conjured up this fabulous imagery, the inventor who put it into motion, must have had limitless resources and tremendous fun. A genius with such capacity is independent of name and title, whether it be Allah, Holy Father, or the Laws of Evolution. It was here that our companion Tioti the sexton had picked up his big conch and brought it to Omoa in the hope of summoning Protestants to Pakeekee's little, bamboo church. If he had blown it here, he could have summoned Protestants and Catholics alike to a place of worship with walls that reached to heaven and a decor to the liking of their common god. It is hard to believe in different gods unless we enclose them within man-made walls.

Tahaoa's reef gave us a Sunday feeling, perhaps because the creatures in the pools seemed as relaxed as the sea birds above them, as they paraded back and forth in their colorful attire. All species were different in structure and decoration, each equipped with some ingenious organ or gear of its own. Some were so exuberantly ornamented that one felt inclined to look around for some fashionable and critical spectator for whom this gorgeous display of color and beauty was intended.

With a fresh background of biological studies, I could not help observing the perfect and perpetual balance between the species in this marine society which had never been touched by man. Not one species in a million years had managed to get control of the reef at the expense of the others. All seemed properly fed and equally healthy. If one kind of creature began to get too common, the surplus would be cut back with mathematical exactness. The excessive number would be reduced automatically by an incipient shortage of food of the kind required by that particular species, or by a temporary increase in the fertility and birth rate of some other species for which the first was the staple diet. This vital equilibrium between species was adjusted to perfection by features employed for both assault and defense. Safety shelters and shields of shell, and jointed armor with spikes and quills, were in service everywhere, and so were ingenious devices for escape and camouflage. Yet no species was so well defended that overpopulation could destroy the equilibrium. Daggers and spears, saws and hooks, tongs and pincers, snares and traps, suction discs, electrical fittings, and paralyzing chemicals were among the countless devices at the service of such species as were in charge of the birth control indispensable for the survival of an interdependent community.

We knew that giant sharks were patrolling the coast beyond the surf. But, in the shallow pools, we could wade about freely, without fear of man-eaters. Apart from taking care not to step on the ominous black sea urchin, all we had to be on guard against were the evil-eyed and ferocious moray eels, which could reach huge proportions in the Marquesas. But Tioti had assured us that there were not too many. Liv wanted to know why. Why were the pools not filled with this ferocious beast, which was fierce enough and strong enough to conquer all the friendly little creatures that flitted about?

The same natural law prevails in the tropical seas as in the Norwegian mountains, I said, reminding her of my favorite field research as a zoology student. The mechanism that brought about a constant balance between carnivorous animals and small rodents in the Scandinavian highlands had fascinated me and some of my contemporaries at the university. On biology excursions, and during our vacations, we had observed the fauna and made statistical curves of the variations in frequency of animals seen. There were years when the colorful little Norwegian lemming would multiply in such incredible quantities that great throngs would start on their famous migrations. Each female could produce a new litter of eight every twenty-one days, and the young would be ready to mate when they were only fifteen days old. The mass of these short-tailed, yellow-brown and black-mottled rodents would move fearlessly ahead in a straight line, and while swimming together across the rivers and lakes, many would drown and thereby infect the waters. Even ordinary field mice would have years when they multiplied so fast that they became a menace to the environment. Nature's unwritten and unexplained law of equilibrium was then immediately set moving, with visible consequences. By unknown mechanisms, this excess of food stimulated an abnormal fertility among carnivorous mammals and birds of prey. Foxes and ermine would breed larger litters; hawks and falcons would lay more eggs. Some of these beasts and birds of prey would mate and reproduce twice in a normal mating season. This sudden excess of carnivorous animals would quickly devour the excess of rodents, and in the following year our biological curves would show mice and lemmings back to normal, whereas birds of prey, foxes, and other carnivorous species could be observed in large quantities, searching restlessly for food. Failing to find the vast quantity of food that was the necessary basis for their own increase in number, the birds and beasts of prey, like the rodents, would soon drop back to their normal proportions. The environmental scale of living species automatically tipped back to a state of equilibrium.

"Only man, with all his supermodern arms and fishing gear, is able to tilt his own environment out of balance," I explained. "The moray eel, if left alone, will always spawn and multiply in proportion to its own allotted food supply, tomorrow as in the days of Adam."

We both felt happy that the world was big: between ourselves and our families in Norway the distance was endless. Man might exterminate game and fish in the forests and lakes of overcivilized countries, but the jungles of Africa and Brazil could never be threatened, and the ocean before us was so vast that it had neither beginning nor end. We felt as far from the civilized world as if we were exploring a different planet.

Liv was content with the brief seminar on animal birth control, although she wished I could have told her how it could be adjusted to the law of equilibrium so precisely that each animal pair always had exactly two of their offspring growing up. She had studied social economics, and pointed out that, if each pair had more than two youngsters that survived, then that species would multiply and begin to threaten the environmental balance. If fewer than two reached maturity, the species would die out. Now, she said, a fish might produce one hundred thousand eggs at once, so how could the moray eels know that they were supposed to eat exactly 99,998?

She left me puzzled, too, as she waded away. My textbooks had evaded that problem.

I put my face into the water to see better. Small red fish immediately sensed danger and wriggled away to pause above a spot of red marine "lichens," where they knew they could hardly be seen. I grabbed for some tiny, blue fish. They shot in between the bristling quills of the poisonous black sea urchin; somehow they knew that this was a safe stronghold against larger enemies, since the drawn bayonets around them had toxic tips with barbs like harpoon points that broke on touch and were next to impossible to extract from a wound. As my hand approached, gaping clams and pearl shells, with their doors ajar, hurried to close and bolt them so securely that no fingers could prise them open. A frightened little squid disappeared in a flash behind its own black smoke screen, as fast as a rocket, thanks to its own built-in jet propulsion.

I managed to grab the hard shell of a crab waving its antennae and staring at me with the eyes of a robot. It sprawled in my hand like a mechanical toy, fighting back continuously with its fossil mittens. Liv came wading back with an expression of having found a treasure chest, and unfolded her *pareu,* which was filled with resplendent mother-of-pearl, abalone, and cowrie shells. She was again disappointed when I, as a zoologist, could not tell her how each of these strangely shaped creatures could know how to make love. And how to eat the right things.

"Instinct," I said.

"Instinct," she repeated. "That's an empty word."

"Science has to coin a word even for things we do not understand," I explained. "Take, for instance, gravity. We do not know what permits us to walk on opposite poles of a round planet, so we call it gravity. We need a word even for the unknown."

"The word instinct is nothing but camouflage," Liv insisted. "Learned men use it as a scientific term to hide from ordinary people the fact that they don't know the answer."

She argued that neither crabs nor sea slugs would survive if all their activities were directed by their own meditations and reasoning. If Mr. Sea Slug does not think, she said, some other intelligence has to guide him. If we call it instinct, it becomes science; if we call it the Holy Ghost, it becomes religion.

"Yes," I agreed. "It is important to choose the right word for the unknown."

Tioti had caught a large, red and green mottled fish with an improvised wooden spear, and he was cutting it into small cubes. His wife soaked them in lime juice, which she squeezed into the hollow of a boulder. If left overnight in the lime juice, this would have been a delicacy, since all taste of raw fish would then have disappeared, but it was a bit too fresh for Liv. Secretly, she slid her first piece back into the ocean with a side glance as if she expected it to swim away.

With a stone, Madame Tioti began cracking the shells of live sea snails as large as walnuts. Dipped in the lime juice, they were truly comparable with fine oysters. But the third course was a real trial. As Madame Tioti served us, we found ourselves sitting each with a big, bushy sea urchin in our lap, slowly moving its long quills as if to warn us in case we attempted an attack. Eating with the fingers had become a habit, but not pincushions. I looked at Tioti in

his straw hat. Casually, he lifted his specimen by one of its longest
quills and smashed it against the white coral table. "It's not of the
poisonous kind," he said. He dipped his fingers inside the broken
shell; the contents looked like a rotten egg, spring green and rosy
red. I tasted mine and told Liv to be brave, to think of spinach and
fried eggs with oyster sauce. She ignored my advice and tried to
"shoo" her helping away from her lap as if it were a kitten, propos-
ing instead that I try to eat a sea slug while thinking of a sausage.

Few days had passed after our first excursion with Tioti before he
came back with more surprising information. He had seen our
enthusiasm for the creatures swimming in the pools of Tahaoa. Now
he wanted to show us a place where there was a large *i'a te kea,* a
"fish of stone." With the little home-made dictionary, we understood much more of what he said, but he knocked on the flat rock
to make sure we got the right idea. We thought he wanted to show
us a place with sea turtles, until he scratched the obvious outline of
a fish on a flat slab.

I refused to believe that there were fossils on an island of volcanic
lava, but it would be foolish to ignore Tioti, who had already shown
us corals where there should be none according to all learned
sources. I therefore girded on my long machete, and Liv and I once
more followed the sexton as a guide to biological curiosities. Two
other islanders led the way, as they were the ones who had found
the fish.

The quiet valley resounded as we hacked our way up the trail.
With machetes, we severed the branches and creepers that had
sewn up and closed an old path through the jungle. The itinerary
was inland and uphill, away from the sea and all living fishes. Black
clouds hung around the Tauaouoho Mountains ahead. The air was
unusually sultry, and our bodies glistened with sweat. We paused at
a fairly recent clearing where some incredibly tall and slender coconut palms rose high above the rest of the jungle. The sexton with
the straw hat clasped the nearest trunk, arched out his bottom, and
"walked" up into the blue sky with such ease that he might have
been climbing Jacob's ladder to heaven. The moss-grown palm was
about 150 feet tall and would have reached to the roof of a fifteen-
story building. We had hardly consumed the cool, sweet drink from
this heavenly harvest before all the leaves of the forest started rustling in a sudden wind of the kind that always springs up to an-
nounce a tropical downpour. It seemed as if the stagnant air was

forced aside by the enormous torrents of water on their way down. Birds fluttered into shelters as the downpour came drumming and gushing down the valley, and we hurried to prepare umbrellas from giant leaves. The tropical heat was gone in a second, and we stood shivering under our green umbrellas, uncertain of whether we were suffering or were having a grand time. What comes down over several days in temperate countries cascaded in a single violent shower, and then the sun peeped through the escaping mist to paint a peaceful rainbow over the palm-filled valley.

We disposed of our green umbrellas and pushed on through the wet jungle. Soon we reached a slope above a small stream. Here the forest seemed more open, where a truly giant tree had fallen and torn down everything it its way. It was a tree of a sacred kind, we learned, and it had almost certainly been planted in ancient times. Naked rock in the form of two huge slabs emerged near the upturned root of the tree, partly covered with invading coffee bushes.

Tioti pointed. Look, the fish!

There it was, over six feet long, head, tail, fins, and all, clearly outlined on the rock. Not a fossil, but the first petroglyph ever discovered on Fatu-Hiva. The only one of this kind known in any part of Polynesia. Petroglyphs, or line incisions, of small human figures had been reported from a couple of other islands in the Marquesas group, but here was a fish larger than a man and covered with cup-shaped depressions and symbolic signs. The dominant signs were sun symbols carved as a dot surrounded by concentric rings, some representing eyes in masks. I drew the machete from its sheath and started cutting down the surrounding bush. By joint efforts, big roots and thick coats of turf were torn away and the emerging rock was brushed with branches and fern leaves. Tioti became serious and big-eyed, like the petroglyphs themselves, as a large number of other figures emerged from beneath the black soil.

"*Tiki,*" he whispered solemnly. "*Menui tiki.*" Gods. Many gods.

Old magic masks with huge eyes stared once more into the daylight. One that was depicted behind the dorsal fin of the fish was a deity with a right eye only, and this was carved as large, concentric circles. Some masks had eyes and mouths only, and huge eyes were sometimes carved in isolation, always as concentric circles, scattered over the stone. Elsewhere on the rock were complete human figures with hooked legs and arms, a turtle, nondescript symbols, and something that puzzled me for years: a crescent-shaped ship, with a curved bottom, a very high bow and stern, a double mast,

and rows of oars. The vessels used in the Marquesas group since
the arrival of Europeans were dugout canoes and flat rafts, both
shaped from trunks or poles, so their bottoms were as straight as
logs. This crescent-shaped ship looked more like the reed boats of
ancient Egypt and Peru, not like the rectilinear Polynesian canoes,
even though at one time some had had separate ornamental pieces
sewn onto the bow and stern with coconut rope. Another parallel to
ancient America was the eye motifs scattered all over the stone. A
German scientist[1] had once made a special survey of what he
termed the independent "eye ornament," and pointed out that it
indicated pre-Columbian contact between the Polynesian islands
and America, since throughout the Pacific it occurred only in these
two areas, and in an exactly corresponding form.

Evening approached and, as the light changed, shadows filled the
slightest furrows on the rocks and revealed more staring eyes, which
suddenly stood out on a stone wall that surrounded a nearby, altar-
like platform. The forest was perfectly calm after the rain. Right
beside us, a pinnacle of red lava leaned over the jungle roof like a
drawn knife set to guard the ancient secret. Our three companions
wanted to get away.

The moon shone on the wet palm crowns below us, in the valley,
as we crawled to bed in the bamboo cabin on the queen's plateau,
discussing our discoveries. I felt we had touched the approach to a
riddle itching to be solved. Who had carved these eyes and the
peculiar vessel? Why did no two scientists share the same theory
about the whereabouts of the former Polynesian homeland, although
they were all looking in the general direction of Asia, from where
the canoes of the old Marquesans would have had to travel more
than one third of the way around the world against all prevailing
winds and currents?

My fascination for the unsolved riddle of Polynesian origins began to rise again. Perhaps it was Tioti's stone fish, which happened
to be a petroglyph rather than a fossil, that forced my interests a
further step up the biological ladder, from the transoceanic migrations of animals to those of man. From zoology to anthropology.
From now on, when roaming the forest for our daily bread, I was
more alert to petroglyphs and ruins than to mini-life between the
leaves or under the stones. Accordingly, my collection of small stone

[1] H. Schurtz, "Das Augenornament und verwandte Probleme," *Abh. Phil.-
Hist. Kl. Kgl. Sächs. Ges. Wiss.*, Vol. XV, No. 2 (Leipzig, 1895). For further
details, see Heyerdahl, *American Indians in the Pacific*, pp. 116–19 (London,
Chicago, 1952).

sculptures and other archaeological artifacts increased in proportion to the decline in the quantity of land snails and beetles preserved in my tubes and jars. I had to resort to Willy's shop to obtain packing cases for the loads of worked stone and bone piling up under the cabin floor.

Late one afternoon, Liv and I relaxed in the river after a long trip in the upper valley searching for wild fruit. We were comfortably seated in our separate pools with water gushing over our shoulders, while devouring oranges and juicy mountain mangoes. A cluster of giant leaves, leaning over us from the banks, shaded us from the strong sun, and life seemed almost too good to be real. Birds and flowers. We kept asking each other whether we missed anything, and could think of nothing we would like to buy. We cleaned our feet with coconut oil and rubbed jungle resins off with volcanic pebbles.

The pleasure of the fresh bath and the satisfaction of a healthy life in the forest still filled body and soul as we crawled ashore and began the short climb up toward the bamboo cabin. I carried a trap filled with prawns and Liv had pulled up a couple of large taro roots along the riverbank. These were to be our dinner.

Then, up the trail behind us, came a lonely rider, as slowly as a mourner. He was heading up the valley to look for breadfruit, and carried with him a large piece of pork from Pakeekee, neatly wrapped up in green banana leaves. It was more than a week since we had seen other people. The horseman looked sallow and fatigued, and spoke with the voice of a sick man. We felt a chill down our spines when he asked if the plague had not yet reached us. For the plague had come to the island with the schooner *Moana*, which had made a brief call in front of the Hanavave Valley, looking for copra. Now everyone on the island had been stricken. The plague had come with a canoe from Hanavave to Omoa. Many were already dead. The horseman himself was lucky to be recovering. Turning his horse to resume his journey up the valley, he assured us with a leer that the plague would take more time to reach us, so far away.

For a moment we were left speechless, looking at our hands and the green parcel containing the meat. The least feeling of being in an earthly Paradise was gone. The plague had hit the island. It would take a little more time to reach our lonely hideout.

We washed and scrubbed anew. We burned the leaves and baked

the piece of meat. But the food seemed to have no flavor. We did not even eat the prawns. We sat quietly watching the moon; then we crawled to bed.

Some days passed while we waited for the plague. We did not have to wait long, as we both began to feel its approach we expected the worst. But as the climax came I got nothing but a sore throat, while Liv had to disappear at very short intervals into the forest. That was all. Perhaps we ran a slight temperature, but we had no thermometer to tell. What a plague! We laughed. It was nothing but mild influenza.

Then, one day, the ever-merry sexton, Tioti, came struggling up the trail and knocked at our bamboo door, hat in hand. He neither laughed nor smiled. He, too, was sallow and coughed badly, the fever burning in his eyes. We could hardly recognize the tall, gay fellow.

Would I come down to the village and photograph his last son? All had now been taken by the plague. Bent and slow, he led our little procession down the narrow trail.

In the village we found truly tragic conditions. Piglets had been slaughtered and were being carried about. There were funeral parties in most of the huts. Everywhere, the atmosphere was grim. No gay *pareu* was visible anywhere. No human skin was exposed. Walking in the sun, people were as closed in as when shut up in their houses, where not a window was made to open. The men were tightly buttoned up and were wearing long sleeves and trousers, the women hidden to the ankles in shapeless gowns. Only feet were bare, stepping from mud to bed. There was no doctor, no nurse. There was no way of leaving the island. Nobody had heard of viruses or contagion, and hygiene was in keeping with that ignorance. It was ghastly to enter the huts, some of imported planks and some of bamboo, where young and old lay packed together on the floor, the dying coughing into the faces of their neighbors. I could visualize Teriieroo's and Kroepelien's reports of the early days, when the Spanish flu struck Tahiti and decimated the population. That was a real plague, when our two friends had driven away cartloads of corpses for mass burial. This was only common influenza.

In Tioti's hut, there seemed to be more air and space. Only one little boy lay neatly wrapped in white on a pandanus mat on the floor. His other children, we never learned how many, had been buried. This little boy, too, was dead, and they wanted me to produce a photograph of the kind they had all seen in Willy's house.

There was nothing we could do to help but to preach hygiene

and the value of boiling water. But nobody seemed quite convinced when we tried to describe a virus. An evil spirit invisible to the eye due to the lack of flesh made more sense to them than an evil germ invisible because of its tiny size. Devils and angels were familiar concepts to Protestants and Catholics alike, but nobody had come to the island to convert them to a belief in germs.

Our thoughts were filled with the tragedy as we left the mourning village, hurrying to our own jungle home. We were not only sad, but depressed. And we felt guilty as we headed for the airy bamboo cabin. We, as Europeans, should have spent the night locked up with our own germs in a stuffy shack of imported planks and corrugated iron, and they, as Polynesians, should have preserved the privilege of sleeping in our thatched bamboo hut. White man's barter with these islanders had not been fair. We were not proud of our own pedigree. It was hard to be proud of a white skin whose shadows fell so black on other people.

The influenza struck hard because it came to a people already riddled by other introduced maladies, such as tuberculosis, venereal diseases, leprosy, and elephantiasis. These, and smallpox, had played havoc among the formerly healthy islanders after their first contacts with culture bringers from the continents. White man can hardly be blamed for a healthy people's lack of resistance to his ailments. But today the battered islanders did not suffer so much from the lack of resistance as from the lack of knowledge of how to avoid contagion and combat disease. White man must be blamed for that.

If we in our hyperprotected cities and communities were to live the way we had caused the Fatu-Hiva islanders to pass their lives, we should have had far less chance of survival than they. They were exposed to contagion wherever they turned. Most of them suffered from some chronic disease. Tuberculosis and venereal infections were most common. Leprosy and elephantiasis were most visible. Child-bed fever and stillbirths accounted for the most deaths. More than once, we had shaken hands with an islander and found that he had only stumps for fingers, or that he lacked part of an ear. And one could not pass the village houses without seeing some man or woman sitting outside with legs as thick and heavy as tree trunks. Some had forearms as stout as their thighs. One man had a scrotum that would dwarf a pumpkin. From childhood onward, these people were used to such sights. To them, maladies were not abnormal; they were part of life.

These were busy days for our old friend Ioane, whom we had not seen for a very long time. He turned out to be the island carpenter and coffinmaker. When someone became too ill to rise from his floor mat, then Ioane came along, dragging his materials, and started nailing the coffin together right in front of the poor fellow's nose. There was one thing to be said for the Polynesians: they had no fear of death. To them, it was an opportunity to meet again the old folks whom they held in high esteem and their many dead friends and relatives.

As long as they lived, the Fatu-Hiva islanders never put on shoes. Their feet were too big. Even the parson, who at his three-day party wore a tuxedo jacket and shorts, was always barefoot, like the rest. But after death, when the shoes no longer hurt, they had new, white tennis shoes put on. The old custom of burying some favorite personal possessions with the dead still lingered on. In ancient burial chambers, bits of an eroded wooden bowl or elaborately ornamented earplugs of human bone might be found. During our stay, one man was interred with an old accordion and another with a deck of playing cards, clearly regarded as treasures. Indeed, the belief in life after death did not come with Christianity, and it was evidently thought a good idea to bring along something to entertain the ancestors.

We were filled with bizarre impressions as we crawled to bed on the rustling banana leaves in our moonlit cabin, once more alone with the jungle. Here, in the wilderness, we were safe, far away from anybody. But something bothered us both: something was not quite what we had expected. We had come to this island to rid ourselves of all links with a civilization whose true virtues we had begun to doubt. Yet we had just seen fellow beings down in the village who were in desperate need of some sort of cultural progress. Medicine. Knowledge of germs.

"Medicine is civilization," Liv commented laconically. "Without a microscope, Hansen would never have discovered the lepra bacillus."

I could not contradict her. Medicine was one of the blessings of civilization. There were, of course, several others. But I maintained that, except for music and the fine arts, the blessings of civilization all existed to make good the troubles caused by the abandonment of nature. Even music, I argued, even music has its merits because it compensates for the great variety of moods and sensations man lost when he abandoned his life in the forest. There is fine music everywhere between moss-covered stones and foliage, and I do not mean the singing of birds and the tinkling of a rivulet: I mean music without sound. Music beyond the eardrums. We have had to create flutes and violins to leave impressions deeper in than the eardrums, where nature used to play.

Liv admitted willingly that music was something she could not do without at home; she loved her records and she regularly went to concerts: but here she had not missed it for a moment. Wherever we walked, wherever we looked, we were filled with new impressions, new sentiments, changing emotions. The lights, the colors, the sounds, the perfumes, the touch, the shapes were never the same, and were always playing on our minds like a vast orchestra. We could hardly take in more music. At home, the four unchanging walls, the same dead furniture, the never-changing electric light, made us crave for music, for something to keep us alive in our hideouts deep inside our eardrums. Here, in the jungle, we felt as if music and real life were alternative approaches to the same inner reality.

Not so with medicine. It was nature that had given us disease, and man had developed medicine for his own defense. Viruses and lepra bacilli were pure products of nature, Liv pointed out; science had only detected them and was trying to dispose of them.

I had to agree, but insisted that Liv should bear in mind the reason why nature imposed more diseases on man than on any other living species.

"Because we live an unhealthy, unnatural life," Liv admitted.

"That too," I said. "But even more because we have defied perhaps the most fundamental law of the biological environment: the vital equilibrium between the species. Even guinea pigs or the parents of a mass of fish-spawn have to content themselves with an average of two youngsters reaching maturity. But not man. Dictators even encourage parents to help to overpopulate their countries."

With Liv and the moon as audience, I brought up my pet story of the lemming and the fox again. Man thought he was the fox, but he was really the lemming. Nature had sent its hawks after him. Five thousand years ago or more, we started to destroy vast areas of vegetation in order to cultivate a few selected types of plants in the largest possible quantity and to breed our selected types of beasts in the largest possible number. We crowded together in walled cities. We really began to change the world to our own liking. We did it at the cost of many parts in the complicated *perpetuum mobile* nature had built up, where the perfection of the mechanism depended on the presence of every single member. Before man started this undeclared war against the environment, he lived in more or less no-

madic family groups scattered about in nature, and there was no
chance for typhus or cholera bacilli to start epidemics. But when
man marched forth with his uniform herds in armies large enough
to tilt the environmental equilibrium, then he unknowingly triggered off some of nature's ferocious reserves: species latent in
nature until used against the harmful dominance of any one kind.
When multitudes of people crowded into towns and heaped up their
sewage and garbage outside the walls faster than nature could
clean it away, viruses, bacteria, parasites, and bugs, all previously
kept on the alert in harmless quantities, now got their chance to act.
They multiplied, and fell upon man, his crops, and his herds, as the
hawks and foxes upon the lemmings.

But, wise after his wounds and his losses, man soon began to de-
fend himself. First with herbs and boiling water. Next with true
science. He located his small and often invisible tormentors one by
one, and with pills and ointments, with vaccines and insecticides,
he took up nature's challenge. But nature has unlimited reserves
and resources. When one species failed, another was made to take
its place, and certain mini-members of the environmental police
force even adapted themselves gradually to man's remedies. Thus
the battle rages on, forced upon the increasing myriads of *homo
sapiens* by any other species in the environment that happens to be
fit for the assault, and with the simple purpose of restoring equilibrium to the disturbed *perpetuum mobile*. Should man, his herds,
and his crops ever decline to their allotted numbers, like mice and
lemmings, then germs and pests would drop off at the other end of
the scale, like the hawks and foxes. Nature's advance upon her own
youngest son, man, would peter out, and bugs and pests, germs and
plagues would do no more harm to man and his provisions than to
the balanced wilderness around our jungle dwelling.

There was nothing wrong at all with the fruit trees around our
cabin. Even the delicious *fei* grew here and there, scattered
among multitudes of other trees. Disease had caused this same plant
to vanish from the fields of civilized Tahiti, where man, in search
of wealth rather than permanence, had started arboriculture in uniform, commercial plantations.

Too much of anything automatically causes natural counterac-
tion.

"According to some social anthropologists, man's aggression
against his own kin is also grafted upon us by nature," Liv said,
turning the discussion from biology to her own field.

"If so," I said, "nature perhaps uses man the same way as it uses hawks and microbes."

It was otherwise difficult for me to believe that man was born more cruel than the monkey. But perhaps the presence of impressive numbers triggered off certain tendencies in man just as in other species. Hawks and foxes hurried to their nests and dens to mate twice in one mating season, triggered by the mere presence of large numbers of rodents. Emperors and presidents are incapable of running to their wives for the same purpose, so they run to their generals and get large armies of young men on the march to kill. They give prizes to parents who can help them breed like beasts of prey, for large numbers are needed to combat large numbers.

I suggested that perhaps even in man there was some unidentified impulse to kill, stimulated only by undesirable conditions, such as abnormal numbers. Maybe the drift toward mass murder was created by a combination of greed, fear, and jealousy. In the days when scattered human families lived from hand to mouth by what they plucked from the trees, there was nothing more to stimulate homicide than there would have been to tempt monkeys to kill each other. The difference came when man multiplied and found himself confronting other expanding crowds of men.

"I agree with you on the question of equilibrium in the animal world," said Liv, "but it remains a mystery to me why civilized man obeys any order to kill. That, to me, is the strongest indictment against civilization."

We were both about to fall asleep when Liv suddenly recalled Tioti's toothache. Was this, too, she asked, a question of guardian nature interfering?

She gave the answer before I had the chance to digest the question: toothache, liver trouble, and faulty blood pressure were not the servants of nature; they were defects brought upon man by unnatural ways of living. Wild geese had no liver trouble; elephants and giraffes had healthy teeth and normal blood pressure. Physical disturbances increase with distance from natural conditions.

A wild cock crowed as if in agreement. We had to get some sleep. Morning was not far away.

The sun was already baking the bamboo walls when we crawled from our bunk and headed for the cool spring. When we sat down by the open window with its great view, chewing crisp coconut, the sad conditions in the village still seemed to create a gray mist over the verdant valley. We could well be proud of civilized man as the inventor of medicine, but not as a culture bringer to other peoples. Disguised as global philanthropists, we had come with priests to these islands to bring from our own abundance precisely those products that might bring profit to ourselves. Nothing else.

We teach carefree islanders to abandon their ancestral huts in order to sell them imported materials. In order to sell them civilized clothing, we tell them not to expose their bodies even to the tropical sun and to stop making bark cloth, and we fool them into forcing shoes upon their healthy feet. We train them to eat bread and canned food instead of coconut and fresh fish, in order to make them dependent on imported grain and other expensive provender. We tell them to work—to work for us so as to be able to pay us for what we want to sell them. For though we seldom admit it, white man went to these people in order to harvest for white man's further progress.

We are sincere when we tell each new trading partner we meet that progress means to pack up and follow in our wake. We see no alternative road to a meaningful human existence. Other cultures, however old and classical, however sane and simple, are aboriginal and pre-European, so they have everything to learn from us. Wherever we go on voyages of discovery, we deliberately destroy existing cultures, and throw fragments of our own among the ruins. We are surprised if the hodgepodge result turns out to be decadence rather than prosperity. Other people, we assure ourselves, must be degenerate not to be able to benefit from the blessings of our civilization.

For we can take it. We have tablets to make us relax, and liquor to make us happy. Our doctors prescribe the calories and vitamins we need to be properly fed. We are therefore greatly advanced compared with the people we came upon in Polynesia, who, from sheer ignorance, ate and drank just what nature gave them and thus by no merit of their own happened to be as healthy as beasts. Formerly, when a Polynesian woman was pregnant, she merely stepped behind a bush and soon emerged with a new child. The reason why so many of them now struggle with child-bed fever is that they were so quick to pick up our diseases and so slow to catch on to the need of building their own hospitals.

We had seen the first automobiles reaching Tahiti, and a single one kept as a curio between the palms at Takapoto. They symbolized one of white man's pet philosophies: any device that saves us from using our muscles is a blessing. To save physical labor, we add motors to bicycles, to dinghies, to lawn mowers, to razors and toothbrushes. And we sit. We sit and do overtime to pay the bills for these gadgets, and run to our doctors because we are overworked, overfed, and stressed. The doctor presents another bill and tells us to do exercise, and then we buy a bicycle without wheels or a rowing boat without a bottom. There we sit cycling and rowing without getting anywhere, trying to regain the shape and the health of our progenitors before the motor was invented.

"Let's climb the hill today and look for ripe guavas above the bamboo forest," I said. We needed more breadfruit, too, and would begin to starve if we just sat moping, without thinking of replenishing our supply. Soon we were once more absorbed by the jungle and all its magic music.

As the days passed, the tragic toll of the ship-borne virus was forgotten by everyone on the island. The Polynesians are children of the sun, who live for one day at a time, with little thought for yesterday's problems and less for tomorrow's. We ourselves were once more swallowed up by the jungle in our search for food, with our eyes open for new discoveries.

One day, when we had ample provision of roots and fruit suspended in the large tree beside our pole kitchen, we decided to set out to collect some of the old human craniums we had seen tucked away among the overgrown ruins. Ancient Polynesian skulls were of great value to those who tried to solve the riddle of Polynesian origins, for the Polynesians were commonly very long-headed, in marked contrast to all the Southeast Asian islanders of Indonesia and Malaysia. This was one of the many reasons why nobody had found a tenable solution to the problem of Polynesian origins, as they could not, by reason of their head formation, be descendants of the Malays. Some even went as far away as Egypt and Mesopotamia in their search for the cradle of the Polynesian people. Some had suggested they were Jews and that they represented the lost tribes of Israel. In Germany, a strange political character named Adolf Hitler had started a party that despised the Jews and claimed that the only decent people were Aryans. After my visit to the Völkerkunde Museum, in Berlin, Hitler's chief anthropologist, Professor Günther, had even written and asked me to bring him a skull from the Marquesas Islands, since he was sure that the Polynesians must be Aryans. My own university, too, had asked me for Polynesian skulls. For this reason, rather than choose one skull here and another there, we decided to visit an old temple site on a lofty plateau near the sea, where we had heard there were hundreds of human skulls.

We had to pass through the village to get there, and we therefore wore shirts in addition to our loincloths, for the expected degree of decency. In the village, we picked up an old copra sack, and noted, to our annoyance, that one of the men started to follow us as we headed for the narrow trail winding up the promontory overlooking the bay.

From sharp curves, ever higher up a scorching mountain wall, we had a marvelous uninterrupted view of the palm-filled valley winding from the bay to the wild mountains far beyond our home, while, in the opposite direction, the blue and boundless Pacific Ocean stretched to meet the empty vault of the sky. Up there, with an impressive vista in all directions, was a large, open plateau, dry and scorched by the sun, with no vegetation except for some scattered coconut palms. We reached it with our uninvited follower mute at our heels. He was two steps away when we caught sight of some red blocks of volcanic tuff beautifully cut into rectangular slabs and set on end to fence in some terraces. Relief figures were carved on some of them, depicting straddling human figures with arms raised above their heads as if to scare away evil spirits or other undesired intruders.

When we looked over the low stone fence, we were amazed to see, closely packed together, a vast quantity of white human skulls grinning at us. There must have been more than a hundred, like a hatchery of ostrich eggs. Some were complete and bleached like coral by the strong sun; others were broken, fragmentary, and even stained green by age. I did not need calipers to see that most were typical long-heads, like Europeans, some more so than others. And I could not help noting the physiognomy of the local islander who was watching us. He, like so many others, certainly looked to me more Semitic than Aryan.

This unique display of skulls, with its wide variety of cranial indexes, was to me the first practical demonstration in support of a theory held by most scholars: More than one type of man had settled in Polynesia prior to the arrival of Europeans.

Our self-appointed attendant looked friendly, except when I lifted a skull to study its shape and its teeth. Although his own parents, and possibly even his grandparents, lay in the village churchyard started by the missionaries half a century ago, these were his own distant relatives, beheaded after death and deposited on this sun-scorched, heathen temple site. He knew none of them, for I could displace the skulls as much as I pleased, so long as I put them back again.

Although the ancient medicine men had selected this place because here the heads would rot more slowly than in the wet jungle, it was just a matter of time before all these grinning skulls weathered away and became like the green splinters scattered among them. Some would have to be saved for professional study rather than left to disintegrate for sentimental reasons. But our guardian had never heard of physical anthropology. Nor had he ever heard of equality between men and women, for to him a woman was only a *vahine*, useful for food and sex, while a man was a human being. I therefore left the empty copra sack with Liv, and strolled farther up the crest, with our mute spy close on my heels.

When we came back to the temple site, Liv was still sitting there. I alone noticed that the sack now seemed full of coconuts.

Before we left, we checked the teeth of all the skulls on this pre-European burial ground, even the teeth scattered over the ground from jaws that had already weathered away. Not one, single tooth showed signs of decay. In the skulls of some very old people, we could see that the teeth were worn down almost to the jawbone, possibly by sand in the food, but there were no caries at all.

Our friend Tioti, the sexton, would have been readily identified among this lot. And we could not help drawing comparisons with what we had seen on modern Tahiti. In Papeete, the civilized center of French Oceania, a liner from Europe called once a month on its way to Noumea, bringing a stock of flour and other groceries. The favorite breakfast in Tahiti had become white bread soaked in a bowl of coffee, literally made thick with refined sugar. Regrettably, the teeth of most Tahitians were now extremely defective. When we came to the remote atolls of the Tuamotu group, however, the simple diet was, today as yesterday, coconuts and fish. Sugar was consumed there, too, in considerable quantities, but it was not refined sugar. Young and old walked about chewing the unrefined juice directly from fibers of sugar cane. Their teeth were still as perfect as pearls, just as in the ancient skulls we carried in our sack as we started our climb down the steep mountain trail.

The shadows were long, and the low sun set as vertically and abruptly as it does only in the tropics, as we reached the village and lost our silent companion. With the bulky sack on my shoulder, we had safely passed the heart of the village and were just about to disappear into the dark jungle when someone shouted to us from the last hut.

"Hemai te kaikai!"

It was Tahia-pitiani, the beauty of the valley, who called us. We knew from our little home-made vocabulary that she had said: Come and eat.

"She does not mean it," I whispered, and tried to make the sack invisible. "It is probably only a polite phrase."

"Venez manger!" she repeated, to our surprise, in broken French. She apparently meant it, after all. We were in a dilemma, both because of our sack and because of the disease in her hut. We recognized a fellow with enormous legs among the men squatting in front of the door, and who knows what else we were to encounter? We agreed that we could not offend them by refusing the invitation, and so we stepped over to the group.

As soon as we got to the *paepae,* the elevated stone platform on which the bamboo dwelling was raised, we realized what we later amply confirmed: "Come and eat" was just an old, empty phrase, as we might say, "good evening." It was by no means an invitation, and I should have called back the appropriate phrase: "No, thanks, we are full!"

Too late. We were there, and they pushed a wooden bowl toward us. I put the copra sack down behind me with great care to avoid betraying the rattle of bones, and squatted down with the little group on the stones before the doorway. In the dark, our chock-full sack could, with luck, resemble a harvest of coconuts or mountain pineapple. The beautiful hostess, however, ran to light the wick of a tiny lamp. The scanty light did not penetrate the darkness below the dense crowns of the mighty breadfruit trees, but as it stood flickering on the stone pavement, it seemed to throw a suspicious glimmer into one of two large but shallow wooden bowls standing in the midst of the squatting party. In one were the sparse leftovers of raw and half-bad fish in coconut sauce. The other was totally in the shade, but we had smelled from a long distance that it contained *poipoi,* the staple diet in most of Polynesia.

Nowhere else was *poipoi* made as strong as in the Marquesas group. Breadfruit in large quantities was buried in deep pits in the ground and covered with large leaves. It was left to rot for a year, and sometimes much longer. When thoroughly rotten, the sticky dough was dug up and beaten with a polished stone pounder. Bits of fresh breadfruit also were sometimes pounded into this sour paste, which was eaten raw. Marquesan *poipoi* stinks so intensely that a normal nose can sniff a dinner party a mile away in the jungle. The islanders frequently told us that they were so accustomed to this sour dough from early childhood that they could not digest a sturdy meal without it.

There it was, in the communal bowl before our noses. Like the rest of the group around it, we just had to dig our three longest fingers into the sticky mess and comfort ourselves with the discovery that it was better fitted to the palate than to the nose. The darkness helped us. We ate less than our movements suggested as we dug in the dark bowl. Some enormous cockroaches pattered up and down the stone wall we sat on, and tickled and scratched our bare legs. They cleaned away whatever we carefully dropped behind us.

Some dogs came slinking along and sniffed cunningly at our sack of bones. Embarrassing. Fortunately, restrained belching from the dark announced that the dinner was over and the dogs rushed to their usual cleaning of the bowls. A big bucket of water was now passed from mouth to mouth. The dogs had already drunk their fill from it while we were eating.

The nightmare we had inflicted on ourselves was over. Children got up from the semidarkness around us, and we caught a last glimpse of a pair of legs, like those of a hippopotamus, that staggered away into the dark. The little ones crawled onto their pandanus mat inside the door, leaving us alone with our host and hostess. They were a most attractive-looking couple. She was slender and well shaped, with black hair falling in waves to her hips, and he was tall and strong, like a Tarzan. Their skin was like that of a fair Arab or tanned European. Both had thin lips and narrow, slightly aquiline noses. In build and physiognomy, they concurred with a common prototype in Polynesia, yet they contrasted in every respect with the characteristics of the Negroid Melanesians and the small, flat-faced Indonesians in the vast area of continental islands separating Polynesia from remote Asia.

After dinner, to our surprise, the woman spoke first.

"Veo is a hunter," she said, nodding toward her husband. "Veo knows the island well."

Both of them started whispering. Veo had found five large caves in the vertical cliffs of Hanahoua. This was an uninhabited valley on the other side of the high mountains, where the cliffs were so steep that nobody could get there on foot. He had managed to climb up to two of the caves, which were like big houses. Some large wooden images, *tiki*, barred the entrances, and behind them Veo had seen large quantities of old utensils, ornaments, and many more smaller gods in wood and stone. He had not risked going inside, since he knew that all such ancient burial caves were steeped in taboo.

Encouraged by his wife, Veo was fearless enough to offer to show us where the caves were to be found, in return for some reward. The problem was that Hanahoua was completely inaccessible except by sea, and the surf on the east coast was so fierce that a normal fishing canoe could not land. A government launch had once tried to do so but had had to withdraw to avoid being smashed against the cliffs. The only vessel fit to get in was one of the large, seagoing canoes, of which only three were left on the island. If I could get hold of one of them, with four strong men to help him paddle, then Veo would take us to Hanahoua.

The moon hung high above the breadfruit trees when we tore ourselves away from the secret talks and began stumbling up the valley with our bizarre load. I pushed the bulky sack in under our bunk, but had to take out three skulls and put them on a separate wooden tray, as the sack was too big.

A few nights later, I was awakened by someone shaking me gently.

"There is someone here," Liv whispered in my ear.

I lay on the outside of the bench, and opened one sleepy eye wide enough to see a big moon through the window and to assure both of us that the tiny cabin was empty.

"But I heard a noise," Liv insisted.

"Probably the cannibals beneath our bed," I said comfortingly and wanted to sleep on.

That was when both of us sat up, wide awake. There came a desperate rattling of dry bones from beneath our bunk. We both bent over and refused to believe what we saw. The three death's-heads on the tray were shaking and nodding as if arguing about how to get out of the cabin. All understanding left us.

A sudden scream from Liv made me start. A black shadow shot through the room. I saw the thin tail as it struggled down through the bamboo plaiting. An innocent fruit rat had crawled in through the neck opening of one of the three craniums, and, packed together as they were, all three had nodded and rattled as the nocturnal visitor ran around inside the unstable vault.

As we peeped out, the eerie, moonlit palms seemed to wave and mock at us beyond the open window.

4. EXODUS

Alone in the wilderness. Nothing but jungle. An underworld of shadow with rays of light falling like blond hair from the crowns of the giant trees. Jungle in the midday sun. Everything motionless. Not a sound from sky or earth. Complete silence. Only some coconuts falling, at long intervals, very far away. The world reduced to the soft touch of cool grass along my naked back and a sweet smell of rich soil and vegetation. Stretched out with closed eyes and sprawling limbs beside my heavy burden of *fei* and firewood, I enjoyed the feeling of fresh blood streaming through every part of my body and fresh jungle air filling every corner of my panting lungs.

Resting motionless, I could see the sun through my closed eyelids, alone in the sky, as lonely as I, and as motionless and silent as everything else. The earth had surely stopped rotating. Not a creak, not a rustle, and somewhere on this planet there was supposed to be roaring traffic in bustling streets. What a crazy, unbelievable thought.

Another coconut fell, to emphasize the absolute silence. The world had come to a complete standstill. I had to roll over onto my stomach to feel that at least I could move and make noises. Then I found company. A little brown ant was struggling to find its way with a bit of dry straw through the jungle of leaves and grass below my nose. Another of the same kind came zigzagging in the opposite direction, and in passing patted its colleague with its feelers as if to say, "That's fine, old boy, the queen is waiting for a piece just like that." I wondered if I could give the little fellow a lift with its burden, but it showed not the slightest sign of fatigue and struggled on with all six legs, head first or head last, waving its feelers as vigorously as if the trip had just started. Whoever saw a tired ant? Fatigue—that is, disagreeable fatigue—is restricted to hunted animals, slaves, and modern man. It is as great an effort for an office clerk to walk five blocks with a loaded brief case as it is for a jungle dweller to cross a valley with a goat on his back. It is as hard to get up and climb or run when you have been seated for years as it is to get up and walk when you have been in bed for months. The body is strange. Spare it, and you get really tired for almost nothing; use it, and almost nothing makes you really tired.

I leaped to my feet. I had heard a horse neighing down in the valley. Above me, on the open, highland plains, there were wild horses. But down in the valley there was never a horse unless there was a man on it. Somebody was on his way up the valley, and Liv was alone.

I hurried to lift the carrying stick onto one shoulder and hastened down the hillside as fast as the dense growth and my bare feet permitted.

Liv was sitting alone beside the poles of the kitchen shed, grinding coconut with a serrated shell once shaped for that purpose by one

Opposite:

PAKEEKEE was the Protestant parson on Fatu-Hiva, which had about two hundred inhabitants. His congregation was restricted to his own sexton.

FATHER VICTORIN, the Catholic missionary, lived on Hivaoa but made occasional calls at the other Marquesas islands with the schooner. Devoted to his cause, he had all the other island souls enlisted in his own faith, and constant animosity existed between him and the parson, in which we became involuntarily involved.

TIOTI was the Protestant sexton and Pakeekee's only friend. A good-natured person, he became our main guide and helper on the island.

PAHO, the parson's twelve-year-old adopted son, was a Polynesian Peter Pan, an attractive little devil, full of vitality and mischief.

Overleaf:

LEFT: FEELING LIKE A KING, I could actually put an ancient Marquesan royal crown on my head for the occasion (for detail, see last page of previous picture section, top right). Or was I the first hippie?

RIGHT: FEELING LIKE A QUEEN, Liv had luxurious bathing facilities in her own royal garden, while colorful birds fluttered among the palms.

Opposite:

SUFFERING FROM ELEPHANTIASIS and mentally deranged, Haii, who had collected scorpions to drop into our cabin, gave us a strange greeting as we passed through the village. He had been eating *poipoi*, or fermented breadfruit mash, from the large wooden bowl at his swollen feet.

Above:

ON THE MOUNTAIN TRAIL. Tioti and young Paho took us into the highlands of the interior, because it became too risky for us to remain in our jungle cabin when hostility developed in the village. We had to take food with us, because there was little or nothing to be found in the mountains except insects and lizards for our zoological collection. The interior of Fatu-Hiva had never been mapped, and the high altitude created a fresh climate, too cold for any Polynesian to endure at night.

Opposite:

PAHO WITH A WILD PIGLET he had caught with his bare hands, defying its fierce parents, which chased him with their sharp tusks.

LIV ON THE STALLION TUIVETA, which was born wild in the mountains.

OUR DRINKING COCONUTS were soon finished, but there were freshwater springs in the mountains. On the high plateau, the temperature would sink to 60° Fahrenheit (15° C) at night, which felt extremely cold after the tropical heat in the valley.

Above:

HOT MEALS were welcomed in the highlands. Liv is heating a can of corned beef donated by the parson, to be eaten with some of the provisions we had brought along from the forest: bananas, coconuts, and a pandanus fruit, which looks like a pineapple but consists of segments that are cracked and eaten like nuts.

of our Polynesian predecessors at the site. She was waiting for the *fei*, to try out a very special recipe she said she had concocted. Hungry, I dug into the heap of dead ashes until the old embers appeared, and with a couple of dry twigs the fire burned as fast as if we had turned on a switch. We always took great care about preserving glowing embers from one day to the next under a pile of ash. We never missed matches except when we had to light a new fire by rubbing a pointed twig along the dry marrow of a split hibiscus branch. That was quite a job.

We had hardly got the fire alight before we had to cover it up once more. A young boy appeared on horseback with a message from Captain Brander. The *Tereora* had anchored in the bay with Captain Brander and a French friend of ours on board. The captain insisted on seeing us on the schooner and would not weigh anchor until we had shown up.

We were received with both joy and amazement when we climbed up the *Tereora's* rope ladder from the dugout canoe that carried us through the surf of the Omoa boulder beach. The amazement was due to our being in perfect health and having no intention of leaving the island. Rumors of unknown origin had reached the islands far to the south, claiming that we were down with elephantiasis and merely lay waiting for a ship. Brander despaired and was irritated in an almost fatherly way when all his efforts to persuade us to go along to Tahiti failed. We sent with him a little stack of letters to our parents, and told him to assure chief Teriieroo that we had never felt better in all our lives and had no intention of returning to the modern world, ever.

A French artist named Allaux lay on the *Tereora's* deck creating paradisal paintings. We knew him, because we had reached Tahiti

Opposite:

RESTING UNDER A MANGO TREE. Large trees, which gave shade from the midday sun and juicy mango fruits for the thirsty throats of travelers, stood at long intervals along the mountain trails; they had been planted by the ancient islanders.

WILD HORSES, descended from domesticated ancestors brought to the island by early European voyagers, survived in the wilderness after their masters had died from imported diseases.

THE SECONDARILY TAMED TUIVETA was small but incredibly strong and sure-footed. We could ride along on the edge of precipices, even at night, and the horse would never falter or stumble.

on the same liner. When we returned in the canoe to the boulder beach, he came along with the object of seeing our jungle cabin. But the sand flies and mosquitoes ashore made him change his mind. He disinfected their bites and returned to his pencil and palette on board, where the breeze carried away all winged visitors and where he could continue in peace to paint a real paradise. We recalled the words of the little teacher on Tahiti: Nobody gives the modern world a true picture of Polynesia. Fair enough; our friend could not add sand flies to his landscapes.

The *Tereora* weighed anchor and left. She was like a busy breath from a distant world. A long time would pass before she came again. We let the wilderness swallow us up once more as we returned to our own peaceful hearth deep in the valley.

Veo was to take us to the treasure caves. The sexton, Tioti, would help him get the big canoe and the necessary paddlers. We waited in vain, since none of them showed up, but the speed of the clouds across the Tauaouoho peaks indicated that the wind was stronger than usual. The sea was probably agitated.

At last, one afternoon, the sexton appeared on our royal terrace carrying a bundle of fresh fish. That was a sign that the fury of the sea was abating. The village people had been out fishing from canoes.

While Liv prepared a superb meal of baked fish and taro, Tioti and I sat down on the old stone seats at the edge of the terrace to discuss our plans. But the sexton sat writhing and scratching his back, a sure sign that something had gone wrong. And we were soon to learn what. Père Victorin had been landed on the island when the *Tereora* had called. He was the little Catholic priest who had spent a lifetime traveling between the Marquesas Islands and from whom Pakeekee and Tioti tried to steal parishioners each time they blew the giant conch trumpet in front of their bamboo church. The trouble was that the priest had not left again with the *Tereora*, but had remained ashore, in his little plank-walled house beside the Catholic church.

"So what?" we thought. He would not eat us.

But Tioti was apparently of a different opinion. Ioane, the coffin-maker, and several others had hurried to tell the priest that two white foreigners were living in the jungle and only came out to associate with the Protestant parson and his sexton. Père Victorin had been shaken by this unpleasant piece of news. No strangers would settle ashore on these islands unless they were missionaries risking their health for their faith. We were clearly Protestant

missionaries sent to help Pakeekee in his clandestine efforts to en-
tice away from Père Victorin's register the names of souls already
saved for Christianity by the Catholic mission, the first to reach
the island. We could visualize the father's concern when we recalled what Captain Brander had told us as we visited the Takaroa
atoll on our way up. Two Mormon brethren had recently landed
there and converted all but two of the three hundred local islanders
to their own faith. The two who had refused to become Mormons
were the clergymen, Catholic and Protestant, who thus remained
all alone with a big plank church apiece.

We laughingly instructed Tioti that he could comfort the father
with the information that we were not missionaries. We had come
to collect animals and not souls.

But Tioti continued scratching his back. He was really worried.
He was not concerned about the father, but about his own enemies
on the island. They were always terrible to him and Pakeekee as
long as the father remained ashore. They were not even saluted.
But as soon as the father left, things went back to normal, for after
he had gone, people thought less about religion.

Surely Tioti was exaggerating; yet we began to feel uncomfortable when he gave us examples of what we had to be prepared for.
We learned that Haii, the old man suffering from elephantiasis of the
scrotum and both legs with whom we had eaten in Veo's hut, had
once mixed his own urine with orange beer and brought the mixture
as a gift in a gourd bottle to the parson's house, thinking that this
would be the best way to pass his own disease on to Pakeekee.
Surely there was something similar in store for us too. There were
even easier ways of harming us, who lived alone, far from everybody.
One thing was sure: it was useless now to plan a canoe trip.

When Tioti left us, we felt very uneasy. We did not know what
to believe. It would be irresponsible to ignore his warning, but
what could we do? Only one thing. We had to feel out the situation
ourselves.

As soon as we were left alone, we went down to see Veo and
Tahia-pitiani, in the first of the village houses. Tioti proved to be
right. Veo was visibly uncomfortable at our visit. He let us know
that nobody would lend us a big canoe for any sensible price,
and what was worse, nobody was willing to paddle. To show that
they maintained a sort of clandestine friendship with us, the couple
confided a secret: someone in the village had ready a big female
scorpion with all its poisonous young, and all of them were to be
smuggled into our cabin.

Never before had there been scorpions in the Marquesas group. But recently a pregnant specimen had apparently come ashore with cargo from some schooner, for I myself had collected a couple of big ones under the boulders on the beach.

I was deeply angered and wanted to hurry straight to the house of Père Victorin, but Liv calmed me down and insisted that we should take no hasty steps. After all, we could not get away from the island.

The whole night, we lay on guard, listening for unusual sounds and making plans, rejecting them all, one after the other. Long before sunrise, however, we got up and dug out the old tent and put it into a sack together with our two plaids and the iron pot. We had decided to take refuge in the lofty mountain plateau until things had calmed down in the settlement.

We walked with our pack down the long trail into the sleeping village and knocked at the shutters of Tioti's hut. The dogs had already awakened the entire village, and Tioti peeped out, his straw hat firmly on his head. He quickly saddled his own horse for Liv, and fetched Pakeekee's for carrying our sack, as well as a large store of coconuts, taro, and fruit. We even got a couple of cans of corned beef that had come with the *Tereora*, for there was no food but juicy mountain mango and guava in the highlands.

It was still twilight as we proceeded down through the village center to reach the narrow trail that led to the highlands of the interior. The clatter of hoofs brought several natives out of their huts from sheer curiosity. They did not salute us with their usual "*kaoha nui*," but merely stood motionless, whispering among themselves, with a mixture of surprise and contempt on their faces. We also passed the house of the father. He was sleeping.

At the northern corner of the bay, our little caravan entered the good trail which wound its way upward through dense shrubs of guava where wasps abounded everywhere. Liv rode in front, then Tioti and I followed on foot, and behind us, leading the pack horse, followed Paho, the parson's twelve-year-old adopted son. As we rose slowly above the dark valley, the sun rose with us, and so did our spirits. We laughed at those down in the deep valley who thought they could crush us. For a while we had forgotten how wonderful life was. Now it came upon us again, that exuberant awareness of complete freedom and happiness. We had everything. The sun and the whole universe were ours. Our property knew no demarcation; we had severed all links with private possessions and were as free as the cuckoo and the mountain goats. Like us, they owned the whole world. Our home had no walls, no fence. We saw and felt no boundary short of the horizon, which kept extending with each curve in the steep trail.

The red morning sun was now aloft and sailed above the rust-colored crest on the other side of the valley. The breeze was fresh, and the endless, truly endless, ocean seemed to curve uninterruptedly around our planet as around Mount Ararat in the days of Noah.

Finally, we rode up to the very roof of the island. The jungle was no more. It had dwindled into mere grass and low ferns with the hard-trodden track rolled out like a red carpet, as red as the volcanic spires that loomed at the trail's end. We were high up and inland. On our right, the mountainsides fell away, the rugged remains of former crater walls, into the verdant canyon of the Omoa Valley. We could tell from the opposite ridge that we were in line with our bamboo cabin. It lay hidden deep beneath us under the dense jungle roof, which, from this height, looked like thick moss with palm crowns standing out like fluffy, green flowers.

The air became thin and cool as we rode onto an open highland plateau. We had to breathe deeper and noted how we seemed to wake up to sharp reality after a long jungle dream. Had we been slumbering down there? Up here, we were certainly wide awake, and we entered a world that nobody had mapped. A world different from anything we had seen. A white area on the navigation charts. A desert, according to some remarks in the very scanty literature on the Marquesas group. No two among our native friends had concurred in their memories when trying to describe to us this highland region.

Riding into it, we understood why. We found the most varied, beautiful landscape we had ever seen: peaceful mounds and hummocks in rolling plains interrupted by wild glens and deep scars, always with cliffs and spires rising up in the background. This was no desert. The glens were filled with dark, impenetrable jungle. The hillocks rose bare and unshaded, covered with nothing taller than grass and ferns.

On the slopes and in the plains were sun-baked savanna with open woodland, and areas where only tall tree ferns threw their round shadows, like parasols raised at random in the rolling landscape. A multitude of flowers was gathered to worship the sun up here, for down in the valley the dense crowns of the jungle trees intercepted the rays from heaven, which gave all their blessings to the large forest timber, leaving nothing for the puny flowers to

thrive on in the shade below. Rare butterflies and beetles in gay
colors danced among the mountain flowers, and little birds fluttered
from tree to tree.

People had never lived up here. We were nearly three thousand
feet above sea level, and although the climate was invigorating to
us, it was far too cold for the thin-blooded natives. Tioti and Paho
shivered and their teeth chattered. In their opinion, we should never
survive up here. Nobody came up here to sleep. One would freeze
stiff when the sun set.

We told them of our country, where even the surface of water
sometimes froze so stiff that people could walk on it and break
it like window glass, and where rain on cold days fell to pile up like
heaps of salt or sugar on our hats and on the ground. All this was
terribly amusing to Tioti and Paho, who laughed wildly, their teeth
still chattering. Finally, we had to leave them to their belief that
these were terribly funny jokes; otherwise they would have regarded
us as barefaced liars.

Young Paho was a Polynesian Peter Pan, an attractive little devil,
full of vitality, caprice, and mischief. On horseback he would rush
along the jungle trails like a cowboy. He would leap out from behind a rock with the yell of a Tarzan, and run up the loftiest palm
faster than any adult. He would lie and steal and seduce the village
women, but we could not help admiring him for his sparkling energy
and keen sense of humor.

As we strolled along the red path between thick ferns and guava
bushes, Paho suddenly let go of the pack horse and disappeared
with long leaps down the hillside. Two paces and a wild leap, two
paces and a wild leap, until he was lost from sight below the bushy
slope. After a while, we heard a heart-rending, piercing shriek, and
soon afterward Paho reappeared with something fighting violently
in his arms. Only a piglet could yell as dreadfully as that. To stifle
the ugly shrieks of his angry booty, the triumphant Paho yodeled
louder than any jungle king as he came struggling up through the
tall bushes with one hand around the belly of the hog and the
other clasped around its snout.

Then I held my breath. We saw the hairy black back of a fully
grown boar bouncing through the bushes from the right, and another
from the left. They rushed with raised bristles straight for the boy
who carried their shrieking offspring.

We all yelled from fear to warn Paho, but as the first boar went
for him with head down and tusks turned up like ivory horns, he
made a bullfighters' leap to one side and let the heavy beast shoot by.

Another jump for the next one, and still another the other way, without dreaming of letting go the fat and furiously struggling piglet. He brought it to us as if nothing had happened, while two ferocious wild boars were kept at a distance by our yelling and throwing stones. But when the sexton tried to tie the fat piglet with a piece of bark rope, it bit his hand and ran happily away, bouncing like a football among the ferns. I had to grab Paho to stop him forcibly from a second pursuit.

Not far away, Paho showed us a cool spring. It was a mere pool in the red soil, with the impressive name of Te-umu-keukeu, or "The-hearth-of-the-goat." Here we decided to make our camp, and, as we loosened the packs from the horses, Tioti and Paho lost no time in saying good-by and hastening back along the trail up which we had come.

We were left alone to camp in the most picturesque landscape we could have dreamed of. We chose a spot below a lonely tree covered with blood-red flowers, and gathered feathery ferns for our bed. Some distance behind, was the edge of a mountain forest with types of trees and palms that were unknown to us, and behind rose the ridge that divided the island lengthwise. In front of us, the open grassland left a free view of lower hillocks dotted with tree-fern parasols, and beyond them were the dizzy cliffs of the Hanavave Valley and a glimpse of the open sea. As evening came, it was really getting cold, and we struggled desperately to light a fire below our iron pot. Finally a sweet aroma rose from the pot. Our coconut cups warmed hands and throat with tea from sun-dried orange leaves.

Happily, I rolled over a big stone as a table for the baked bread-fruit which Liv raked out of the cinders. Below the stone lay the only snake in this Paradise. A poisonous centipede, as long as a hand and golden like a bracelet, lay there writhing to protect its treasure: a large cluster of pearl-shaped eggs. I made sure to close the zipper of our little tent and shook the rugs well before we crept to bed, as the thin moon took over guard of Fatu-Hiva's fairyland. And we were to learn that we were not alone in the mountains.

We woke up at the drumming sound of approaching hoofs, far heavier than those of any boar. Were some natives coming for us? Our horses started tugging at their ropes, and whinnying either from fury or from fear. The heavy hoofbeats halted. Wild cattle? Wild horses? It could be a wild bull roaming to safeguard its own herd. We had been told that there were plenty of wild cattle in the highlands. Wild horses too, and even donkeys. The sudden silence made our hearts beat. We lay ready to spring. But nothing came close enough to stumble over the stays of the tent. At long last, we fell asleep and dozed till the early sun warmed the canvas. Then Liv crawled out and raked the embers out for a blazing morning campfire, while I grabbed the pot and headed for the spring. We looked in all directions, but were completely alone.

Shortly afterward, we caught sight of our nocturnal visitors. Three beautiful wild horses, with tails hanging almost to the ground, were standing motionless, watching us from the edge of the forest.

For generations, these animals had run wild in the uninhabited highlands. Like the dogs and cats of the jungle, they were all descendants of domesticated ancestors. Only the Melanesian pig, tusked and as densely bristled as a boar, was present in the Marquesas group when the European arrived. Traditions insist that even the pig was unknown to the first Polynesian settlers: it was recalled as a subsequent gift by a native voyager named Haii, who introduced both pigs and chickens to the Marquesas group less than three centuries before the Europeans entered the Pacific.

Knowing only the pig as a domesticated mammal, the natives of the Marquesas group were most astonished when the first European sailing ships set ashore new kinds of four-legged animals. They were all taken for strange varieties of pig. The goat was called "pig with teeth on the head," and the horse was called "pig running fast on the trail."

After our experience of the influenza epidemic, it was easy to visualize how these various four-legged breeds had run for the jungle and the hills, driven by desperate hunger to break all ropes and fences, when their human masters no longer showed up.

Our chief concern was not to get involved with a pack of wild dogs. Large and tiny mongrels of all shapes and colors hunted in packs. Howling and barking, they would pursue flocks of goats or sheep and even catch an occasional calf. If one of these dogs was killed in an assault on a boar, the others would ignore the pig and throw themselves with ferocious howls upon the companion that had fallen to the boar's tusks.

Wild cats climbed the trees, looking for fruit rats, catching birds and robbing nests. Even the fruit rat would rob birds' eggs, and no twig was thin enough to prevent this little thief from advancing. The cats and rats were obviously threatening the bird life of the Marquesas, and many species were becoming rare. Sea birds were best off: they hatched their eggs on barren reefs and on slippery cliffs which cats and rats could not reach.

The lack of archaeological material in the highlands was compensated for by the presence of an animal society that offered a rather unique study in ecological adaptation. There was not a moment left for boredom, in spite of the fact that we had our food in our packsacks, so we lost no time in providing for our survival. Our horses provided for themselves; they needed nothing but the ever-present pasture. For us, there was very little to add to the food we brought: an occasional coconut palm and banana plant amounted to no more than what could easily be counted and quickly consumed. Besides these, there were only a few giant mango trees with peachlike fruits smaller than those down in the valley and with a flavor less like that of pine needles; also, numerous guava shrubs with fruits resembling yellow apples each enclosing a giant, juicy raspberry. But everywhere were traces of wild beasts that had been harvesting the best before us.

Although we enjoyed every breath during our refuge in the lofty highlands, the open view made it as difficult for us to hide as it was easy for us to be on guard against approaching visitors. Tioti's and Veo's warnings had made us more alert for human beings than for any wild beast.

On our third day in the mountains, we spotted what we feared: a whole group of natives on horseback emerging slowly from behind a barren hill. On top of the hillock, they stopped for a while, outlined against the sky long enough to spot our camp. Then they came galloping toward us across the grassy plain.

Reaching us, they stopped and saluted without alighting from their horses. Their faces were far from friendly and yet expressed more curiosity than menace. They had clearly come to check if we really were living in the highlands or were up to some sort of secret stratagem. Perhaps they thought we had descended into the Hanavave Valley as agents of Pakeekee. They had grim, suspicious expressions as they came up to our tent, but left visibly relieved when we had shown them a jar filled with tubes of centipedes, snail shells, beetles, and butterflies. They lost no time in getting back on their horses, and left us alone.

We felt safer after this visit. Yet we never left our two horses except when exploring some jungle-covered glen. One of them, the larger, was born wild in these mountains. He was a fine stallion named Tuiveta. The people of Omoa sometimes rode into the hills to catch young foals with lassos. Proud and strong, these horses had an inborn balancing skill. The mountain trails often followed a narrow ledge with jagged rocks or frothing surf far down below. Our stomachs curled up when the horse insisted on drifting along always on the extreme outer edge, where it could nibble at a narrow strip of grass that generally hung over the side. The bridle was nothing but a bark rope tied around its muzzle, and if we tried to turn the horse's head farther in, against the wall, it began to rear and prance about at a hair's breadth from the precipice. We had to let the stubborn beast balance where it would, even though, when sitting on its broad back, one's outer leg often hung free over the abyss. We soon learned to trust these horses blindly, however, for they never made a wrong step. Even on a moonless night, they could move along a narrow mountain ledge when we could not even see our own feet. Only once had we heard of an islander disappearing forever into the abyss with his horse. But the trail was said to have been wet then and slippery after rain.

We were to feel the dizzy suction of cliffside vertigo once when we were advancing along a rock shelf above the Hanavave Valley. Liv walked in front and I followed on foot with the two horses at my heels. I led the vigorous, wild-born stallion Tuiveta on a rope. It carried all our pack, while the other, more subdued, mare followed peacefully behind with no burden. The shelf we followed on the cliffside was not much more than two feet wide in places, and as we had never passed this way before, we preferred to walk, since on horseback we might perhaps jam a leg between the horse's belly and the rock. The rock wall rose skyward beside the left arm, and less than a full step from our right foot it fell away in the opposite direction, straight down into the deep upper gorge of the Hanavave Valley. We proceeded slowly while leaning carefully inward, trying not to let any threat of dizziness spoil the terrific view. Suddenly three wild horses appeared in front of us, one behind the other on the narrow shelf, and the way was blocked in both directions. They were a strong stallion, a smaller mare, and a tiny, curly-haired foal. The mare and the foal threw themselves about and disappeared behind a corner in the rock, while the courageous stallion took up a pose like a bronze monument, determined to protect his kin.

Tuiveta threw his neck back, whinnying his challenge into the sky, and then wanted to get past the two of us, who blocked the narrow passage between him and the strange stallion. His wild opponent valiantly took up the challenge and began trotting slowly straight toward us. I first hung on with all my strength to the tough bark rope around Tuiveta's muzzle, but he ignored me completely, got viciously wild, and rose on his hind legs to prepare his forward thrust. I yelled to Liv that she should throw herself flat against the rock, and did the same myself as Tuiveta tore loose from my grip and dashed forward. We felt the bump of the passing horse, and the two stallions met beside us. For a moment, they posed with muscles quivering and necks crossed like the foils of two fencers, seemingly testing each other's courage. Then things began. They bit and kicked and reared and whinnied. We expected, any moment, to see one of them tumble off the edge and disappear into the abyss, just as we had seen a wild goat sail down through the air off a cliff while some dogs stood and watched their prey vanish. But the two stallions made no false step. Our packs, however, were flung high into the air and disappeared over the cliff's edge. Only the little tent and our two rugs got stuck in a crevice farther down; the rest disappeared forever into the depths. We were left with no food whatsoever.

Tuiveta won the battle. The wild stallion withdrew with admirable dignity when the mare and the foal had been given ample time to escape. And Tuiveta offered no resistance as I ventured forward to grab the rope around his muzzle. Proud as he clearly was of the victory, he seemed embarrassed as he turned his head to observe the noticeable lack of his own pack.

After a day with nothing to eat but juicy mountain mango and guava, hunger forced us down from the hills. It was like filling one's stomach with peaches and pears, delicious and refreshing, but our bodies craved for something more. We longed for fish, meat, coconuts, and breadfruit. We longed for prawns and *fei*. I thought of the fat little piglet, but we saw the hogs no more. We had to ignore the fact that captive scorpions and perhaps other abominations awaited us in the valley. Dreaming of food, any kind of starchy or filling food, we rode silently along the red carpet winding down from the lofty interior.

We felt like different people, with a new appetite for life, as we descended into the warm Omoa Valley. Although hungry, we were replenished with energy after our days in the cool highlands. We realized that we had been sluggish from jungle dampness when we had left the valley without confronting the person said to be the source of the change in the natives' attitude. Reaching the valley bottom, we now headed straight for the house of Père Victorin.

Behind the Catholic church lay two small bungalows with shaded verandas, glass windows, and roofs of corrugated iron. One was empty and long abandoned. This was a former *gendarmerie*, where a French administrator had lived at the beginning of the century, when the island was still densely populated and aspired to become part of the outside world. An old tambour lay tossed into a corner of the open balcony. In the bygone days of glory, Ioane had used it, marching along the village paths beating it whenever a schooner had anchored in the bay. Those days were long gone.

Some natives gazed at us with big eyes as we tied our horses and headed for the other veranda, where someone in a long black robe was sitting, surrounded by children. He was trying to teach them the alphabet. None of them could read. He rose as we came up the stairs, and, for the first time, we met Père Victorin. Short and slender, he seemed to disappear in a robe far too big for him. With the utmost courtesy, he received us and offered us a seat. And there we sat.

Awkward. I had never met a Catholic priest before. Hardly even a Protestant minister. Pakeekee was just about the first. With a mother who believed in nobody but Darwin and a father who believed in the Christian faith but never went to church, I was baptized but was the only one in class who had refused confirmation. My image of a priest was just as vague and unrealistic as my image of a girl had been when I was a young boy: They were human beings of course, but of another kind, and an ordinary fellow would not know how to behave in their company.

The little man in the black gown seemed to feel as awkward as I did. These were the days before the split branches of the Christian Church had started on the road toward conciliation. He fixed me with inquisitive eyes and a broad smile, to encourage me to speak. He helped me by asking if we came from Europe. We started talking about ourselves, and indirectly made it clear that we had not come to interfere in the struggle between Pakeekee and himself; we had come to study the premissionary life of the islanders and to investigate the origins of the local fauna.

The father gently sidetracked this topic, and began telling us about his own experiences in the Marquesas. Ever since he was sent from Lozère, in France, thirty-three years earlier, he had been traveling alone between the islands in this group. Alone he had walked for thirty-three years among the sick and dying; alone he had slept in murky huts and eaten *poipoi* and other obscure native dishes. Always alone. These people never showed him personal friendship. Nobody entertained him. He was not born with any sense for palms and flowers, and to him, as to Captain Brander, the natural things of the island were dreary and depressing. To him Fatu-Hiva was the church with his little cabin behind, where the floor and walls lacked any sign of female attention. His pride and passion was a book where all but two of the island's souls were listed as saved from the shades below.

As the little man spoke, he kept pulling his long black cassock down to his high black boots. Yet we saw what he tried to hide: his white legs were swollen like melons. The poor man had elephantiasis. He had given everything, including his own body, to the cause he was sent for. We then began to understand his fear of our having come to back up Pakeekee. He was like a philatelist, afraid of losing a single stamp once the album was complete.

It was almost with a sort of awe that we rose at last to salute the little man with the piercing, unhappy eyes and the enormous legs. We were hungry, filled with a pleasant appetite for food and life. We had each other, the jungle cabin, and an unwritten future before us. Père Victorin had none of these. He looked tiny, pale, and sad as he stood motionless, watching us lead the horses back to Pakeekee's and Tioti's huts. We wished he could have seen us heading straight up the valley instead. We were certainly not going to do him any harm. We would never again have any ill feelings because he had involuntarily caused us trouble.

5. TABOO

Our yellow bamboo cabin shone like a golden castle. It seemed so big after the crawl-in tent: we could actually walk about inside it. Yet the huge jungle leaves enclosed it and towered above it as if it were a dollhouse. This was our home. It felt almost as if we had been born here. Yet we had come back only for a short visit.

No sooner had we filled our stomachs with a fresh harvest from the gushing stream and the royal garden trees than we followed Tioti's advice to get away for a few more days. Tioti was waiting by the sea to take us in his own tiny dugout canoe. It could carry all three so long as we kept to the leeward side of the island.

Tioti had made the canoe himself in typical Polynesian fashion, by scooping out a tree trunk and giving it stability with an outrigger, a pointed log held far off one side by two slender cross poles. The vessel was twice as long as a bed and half as wide as a bathtub, barely permitting us to squeeze in with some provisions.

Liv lay in the rear of the canoe, half buried in heavy clusters of bananas, while Tioti and I swung our paddles and dipped them silently into the long, smooth ocean swells. The morning sun made the jagged mountain island look like a jungle in flames. A few small trade-wind clouds sailed like puffs of smoke high above our heads, while only feeble gusts of wind stole around the corners of the island to whip up peaceful ripples across the long, low rollers.

Tioti, the sexton, was talkative. But he seemed more intent on convincing us of the power of various local devils than of the potency of any god. There was only one god, and although Tioti never said so, he seemed to visualize him safely locked up in the windowless bamboo church of Pakeekee. Devils, however, according to Tioti, were roaming about everywhere on the island. The surest place to meet them was on some taboo ground. A couple of generations ago, all local people were experts in dealing with the devils, insisted Tioti, almost with envy in his voice.

But Liv and I were not good listeners. We were fascinated by the strangest fishes we had ever seen, and felt we were witnesses of the legendary day in the story of the creation, the distant period in the story of evolution, when the first living creatures tried to move up from the sea onto the land. We were close inshore, since there were no successive rows of breakers where the cliff walls fell vertically into the deep sea. Only the slow swells rose and sank, up and down the smooth rock face beside us, and we had for a while enjoyed watching the myriads of red, gray, green, and black crabs at water level which scuttled in all directions and in and out of cracks and cavities in the mountainside. The pale-green water was so clear that we could see the polychrome growths of algae and sea anemones deep down where gaily colored fish swam about. Huge tropical lobsters, some with bodies as long as a human leg, peeped out of cavities, covered with knobs and spikes, and competing in brilliant patterns and designs. But nothing was as strange as the fish that seemed to feel best out of water. No larger than a man's finger, pitch black and large-headed, this strange creature would ride up on the crest of a mounting swell to gain impetus before it leaped high up onto the dry rock. It seemed to take hold on the rock by suction and kept leaping about well above water level, like a legless frog. There were great numbers of them glittering in the sun. They would remain wriggling and moving about on the rock face, or they would jump from one stone to the next or even stretch out calmly on their bellies as if enjoying the sun. This whimsical little fish leaped around as if afraid of getting wet by the spray, until finding it timely to dive back into the sea, only to spring ashore with the next wave.

Tioti could see nothing worthy of our attention in a fish that did not serve one's belly, but rose in the canoe to run his slender, three-pronged spear into a couple of the rainbow-colored lobsters. He was clearly concerned about us, feeling that we did not pay adequate attention to his briefing on the whereabouts of the local devils. We had at first doubted his words when he told us about the coral reef, and again when he spoke of the huge stone fish, and now we did not believe that he could show us real devils. Some of the devils were still hanging about, more or less idle, since the days when they had helped Tioti's ancestors, just as God helped Tioti now. Had we not heard of Tukopana?

We had not heard of Tukopana, and agreed to pay careful attention to a real lesson in devilry that could even be testified to by the French administration on Hivaoa. For Tukopana was the last great medicine man, still active when the Europeans arrived, and although he lived on Fatu-Hiva, his dealings with the devil were famous all over the Marquesas group. Tioti entirely lost the rhythm of our co-ordinated paddle strokes as he came to the point.

Before Tukopana died, he had summoned the king and the people in the Omoa Valley and had shown them two demonic-looking statues he had carved out of white rock. One was big, and the other was small. After his death, he said, his own spirit would enter the larger statue and it should therefore have his name. The soul of his deceased, favorite daughter would enter the smaller image, and together they would continue to guide the people of Fatu-Hiva during generations to come.

And Tukopana died. The two white images were raised on the burial plateau above the Omoa Valley, where we had been to study the accumulation of human skulls. Twenty years before, a French governor had come to the Marquesas, where he had heard of the two beautiful statues on Fatu-Hiva. To him, they were valuable curios. He forced four Fatu-Hiva islanders to carry the statues down to the government schooner, and he took them to his residence in the Atuona Valley, on Hivaoa. Tukopana and his daughter were set up before the door of the governor's bungalow, to the despair of all visiting natives.

Shortly afterward, a terrible storm fell upon the islands. Torrents of rain poured down for days on end. At last, a huge flood broke loose high up in the mountains of Hivaoa and thundered down the valley of Atuona. Coconut palms and large breadfruit trees were torn up by their roots and tossed about, and the flood headed straight for the governor's house. The governor escaped, but his bungalow was smashed to matchwood, and when the flood subsided, Tukopana and his daughter were gone as if they had sunk into the earth. Until the present day, people have been searching everywhere for the two precious statues. But all in vain. And the governor built his new residence far from the old site.

Tioti was silent for a long while after he had finished his story. We paddled and paddled. We were lifted up by one swell and slid down the next. The coast seemed endless. Small valleys opened up between the rocks and closed as we passed. Valley upon valley. Deserted and forgotten. Some speckled goats, wild as antelopes, climbed about high up on the precipices, and once a bristly black boar stood on a beach sniffing and staring nearsightedly as the canoe slid by. Then it calmly went on gnawing at a fallen bread-fruit. It would be quite wrong to say that these valleys were un-inhabited; they teemed with formerly domesticated animals. Only their human masters were gone. They had gone west with the wind, according to Tioti. These pagan people had not gone to heaven. Their souls had followed the sun, which passed through a tunnel under the ocean to reach its own home, in the east.

That the home of the traveling sun was in the east was something Tioti had heard from all old people. It was in the east that the sun and the souls concluded their underworld journey, and that was the place where the eternal sun rose every morning. Ancient voy-agers were still remembered as having sailed on long return voyages to the legendary fatherland of the former god-kings. Although the spirits of the dead were believed to follow the sun to get there, these living voyagers had taken a short cut by sailing due east, toward the sunrise. The eastern horizon was referred to as the "upper" side of the ocean, for current and clouds came in a con-stant drift from that direction. Everything except the immobile is-lands themselves was in constant movement "down," toward the west. Everything: the sea, the clouds, the sun, and the starry night sky. Tioti warned us that if we kept on paddling until evening, we should get past the shelter of the north cape, and then we should ourselves be caught by the downhill drift, unable to force our way back to Fatu-Hiva.

The sun hung directly above our heads as the fantastic stage of the Hanavave Valley opened before us. The palm-studded show-place, with its giant side curtains carved from the red rock as if hanging in folds, seemed more bizarre and breath-taking than ever, as we arrived in Tioti's tiny canoe, primed with his stories of ghosts and ancestors. Watching the rows of towering side curtains sliding one behind the other like moving giants as the canoe headed into the bay, we felt like Lilliputians in an enchanted world, and could well understand how superstition and necromancy could spellbind the local families, whose whole world was bounded by these eerie walls.

Far in, at the very end of the long valley, was a blue mountain ridge where we could see a speck of bright sky shining like a lamp through a hole in the solid rock face. Wind and rain had dug a tunnel straight through the mountain peak. Tioti told us that cannibals from the Hanahoua Valley, on the east coast, used to come swarming through this opening in former times, whenever they launched their treacherous attacks on the people here in Hanavave. In days past, people could climb like goats and had even cut ledges for trails along the vertical rock faces. The tunnel, with the awkward name Tehavahinenao, was now inaccessible from this side and said to be filled with human bones. The trail up the rock wall was weathered away; otherwise, we could have reached Veo's treasure caves in Hanahoua by passing through the lofty tunnel.

Before we steered into the menacing succession of high breakers thundering in across the shallows leading to the beach, Tioti noted a glittering shoal of fish which he recognized as being particularly palatable. He rose and threw his spear into the air in a high arc. It fell in the middle of the shoal, and the quivering shaft remained upright in the water, evidence of a perfect hit.

In landing, we noticed nothing but smiling faces and the hospitable calls of "Come and eat" as we dragged our canoe ashore and walked inland through Hanavave village. But we shouted politely the appropriate return salute, that we were full, and showed them our catch from the sea. There was clearly no hostility here, and yet a face with the remains of a leprous ear reminded us of Captain Brander's warning about the many contagious diseases that flourished in this valley, so we were not tempted to settle. We had come ashore to satisfy Tioti's desire to have us meet a real devil.

Tioti had called on a skinny local friend named Fai, and made him join us to carry our sea food and the bananas. Tioti himself had speared a breadfruit, which he carried across his shoulder on the point of a stick. The two friends were whispering together in front of us, and as they spoke Fai slackened his pace and became visibly less enthusiastic about joining our party. I took the load of fish for fear that he would run away. But when Tioti laughed and scorned him for being afraid of devils, Fai decided to come along. If we insisted, he would show us the abode of devils, one of the very few places that were still taboo and where none of the still-living islanders had ever set foot. There had formerly been all sorts of taboos, but in our day nearly all were forgotten and disregarded. There were some few rules that were still respected, however. It was taboo and brought bad luck if anyone stepped across the place where another person was feeding chickens. And it was still worse to put a wooden bowl upside down on one's head. Devils or evil spirits were still watching a very few places in the forest, where an intruder could not venture without falling victim to some fatal accident within three days. Fai would point out to us such a place—from a distance.

As we reached a small, pebble-bottomed stream and Fai raised his hand and pointed, Tioti turned and wanted to hurry in the very opposite direction. He was suddenly hungry and could not wait to find a place to fry the fish. On the double, he led us back in the direction from which we had come, through a large, friendly forest where only orange trees grew, in incalculable quantity. There were oranges everywhere, on the trees and on the ground. The branches of some of the trees were bent toward the ground like those of weeping willows, so heavily laden were they with green and yellow fruit. We ate and we drank, and we picked all we could carry. Never had we eaten oranges so juicy or so extraordinarily tasty as in the orange forest of Hanavave.

Tioti headed back to where the jungle began and the orange grove ended. Tioti had matches. Fanning a flaming heap of orange twigs with his inevitable straw hat, he spread a sweet smell of roasted breadfruit through the forest. As the scorched rind cracked and exposed the floury white delicacy within, Fai raked baked lobsters and fish out from between the red-hot stones. To hell with the devils! They could wait. What an exhilarating, absorbing experience it was to tear apart with our fingers this day-fresh food and sacrifice it to our human selves!

Fai told us that only about fifty people lived in the cluster of huts down by the sea. One of them was a Chinese who had a tiny store where he bartered copra with the other villagers, like Willy in Omoa. This was all that remained of the once mighty tribes of the Hanavave Valley, where at one time three kings ruled simultaneously. One kingdom lay inland at the foot of the high mountains, one in the middle of the long valley, and one by the sea. All three had been jointly at war with the Hanahoua people, on the other side of the mountain tunnel. The stone chairs from which the tunnel had been under constant watch still stood in the jungle. Whenever their common enemy did not show up, the three kings waged war against each other. The medicine men, communing with the devils, could often foretell when the enemy was preparing to strike. For this reason, they were always consulted in times of war. They would fall into a state of ecstasy and dance frenziedly with death's-heads rattling from their belts, while they spoke with voices not their own, guided by some devil. Whatever came from their lips was interpreted as advice or warning.

With high spirits and heavy bellies, we rose to our feet and discovered that we were only three. Fai had disappeared. Tioti was on his toes in a flash, ready to run and look for him, but I heartlessly turned Tioti around and reminded him that he was the one who had insisted on showing us a devil. Now that we all knew the place, there was no need to look for Fai.

Tioti laughed: he was not afraid of any taboo. He was a sexton. He was a Protestant. No devil could get him.

So, side by side, we crossed the little stream and soon we were back to the place where Fai had silently pointed. On the other side, the bushes were so dense that we searched in vain for a place to penetrate. It was impossible even to crawl in. It could very well be true that no human foot had tried to enter for at least a generation. We had to resort to my machete.

The taboo place was dark and humid as we were swallowed up by the foliage. But we had entered much worse jungle areas; the ground here was solid, at least.

Our progress was stopped as my long knife struck a hard stone. A moss-covered wall as high as my head was hidden behind creepers and foliage. Huge blocks had been squared and set atop each other, and the soft green covering of moss made the fissures almost invisible. We must all have been equally excited. Slowly I hoisted myself up onto the wall. Liv and Tioti followed. We found ourselves upon a large, elevated platform, also nicely composed of heavy and well-fitted blocks. The jungle roof closed in above us, creating a dark and somber atmosphere.

Liv and I were silently wondering how the ancient architects had managed to handle these huge blocks, which had been quarried from hard basalt, since all rock in the neighborhood was fragile tuff. Then a suppressed exclamation from Tioti told us that he had found something. Pushing aside some branches, he showed us two huge slabs of beautiful red stone, tilted against each other like the gables of a house. They were partly covered with turf and roots.

We started to remove the vegetation from the slabs carefully, each of which appeared to have the size and shape of a normal thick mattress, but cut to perfection with rectangular outlines. They proved to be decorated with old sculptures in high relief. Nothing similar had been seen before anywhere in the Marquesas group or in all the rest of Polynesia.

On one slab there was a row of seven grotesque human figures. Some were carved as if meditating, with one hand under the chin; others had both hands on the belly; and still others had their hands raised as we had seen them on slabs surrounding burial grounds. Some had huge, outstanding ears and looked almost like animals. In the center, between these demonic creatures and also in relief, was a small but artistic double figure: Two tiny human images with their hands on their bellies had been carved side by side, with a common pedestal beneath their feet. The other slab had only three figures, their backs likewise attached to the red rock, but all three were carved in a dancing posture: One arm was at the hip and the other was arched above the head.

The smooth background surface of the slab had been less exposed to erosion than the high reliefs, and we could distinguish incision lines forming rectilinear, interlocking labyrinths.

Tioti kept his hands away from the *tiki*. All human images were called *tiki* in the Marquesas group. *Tiki* meant "god" to Tioti's ancestors, but not to him. To Tioti, *tiki* meant "devil."

A terrific cloudburst interrupted us and we ran for shelter beneath some giant leaves. Tioti was visibly relieved when the rain stopped, after a few minutes. When we returned to the gabled red stones, we saw a white, triangular slab fitted as a seal to one end. The other end was solidly walled up. I carefully tilted the door slab to one side and found an opening down into complete darkness. This began to be exciting. Liv held her breath. Slowly I wormed myself, feet foremost and on my belly, into the opening. That was too much for Tioti.

"With my big lamp you could chase away the devils," he suggested, and wanted to run to the beach, where he had left a kerosene lamp in his canoe. I asked, instead, for his matches, and got them, whereupon Tioti jumped down from the platform and disappeared.

The opening barely left me room to wriggle through with my arms above my head. Feeling with my feet, I touched something and let go. I slid down to a soft floor and, fumbling about, I knew by feel that I was in a small chamber with smooth stone walls. I moved a bit farther in, hoping that some light would enter through the opening behind me, but I could see nothing. Total darkness. I was standing on something. I struck a match; it flared up but died instantly in the raw air. I had seen nothing but a section of the masonry wall beside my hand, and then the darkness seemed worse than ever.

The next match just fizzed. Tioti's whole box was wet. I squatted down and struck one in the hollow of my hands. A grinning white face looked at me for a second, then pitch darkness returned. Another match. Damn it, the wrong end! I struck another match. The grinning face again: I was standing on a dead person.

A pale-yellow skeleton lay beneath my feet, partly covered with mold. It could not be very old, for a little colored bottle of European origin lay beside the skull. Probably this was the pagan tomb of Hanavave's last medicine man, who could well have lived half a century earlier, when the first missionaries visited the island. Like Tukopana, in the Omoa Valley, he had beseeched his rows of *tiki* with their taboos to keep evil spirits away from his tomb. The worst among the evil spirits so far witnessed in Polynesia was white man, so I crawled out of the taboo chamber and let the old medicine man rest in peace.

It was easy to find Tioti. He was waiting on the other side of the stream. And, to our surprise, Tioti proudly showed that Fai was with him. Fai made sure we realized he had not run away at all; he had just wanted to find for us the location of another taboo place. It was not very hard to find: he pointed to a little finger-shaped pinnacle that rose above the jungle roof right beside us. Its name was Motu-nui, or "The Great Rock."

When we reached it, we found that this pinnacle had vertical walls smoothly polished by the wind and the rain. Some bushy trees on a shelf high up above our heads sent some tough, lianalike roots down to the floor of the valley in search of humus, and they served us as ropes as the three men of our party began to climb the taboo rock. Liv was furious, because she had to wait in a tree down below, out of reach of wild beasts, as this was a men's enterprise.

Only the humiliating idea of remaining behind with a *vahine* tempted Tioti and Fai to join me in the climb. They did not fear the climb itself, but what the taboo might bring upon us. Fai seized the creeperlike roots and led the way with me at his heels and Tioti's head below my feet. I was soon bothered by vertigo and kept my nose close to the rock. A sheer drop. This was certainly not for women.

A loose piece of rock was detached near my knee and began falling. I yelled a warning as I glanced between my legs and saw Tioti's broad straw hat moving below me. Then I closed my eyes and waited. Surely, this was the end of the sexton. Of that, I had no doubt. I did not venture to look down again, but meekly asked what had happened. I did not expect a reply.

"Tioti's head was harder than the stone," said a calm voice jokingly from below. The sexton had twisted himself to one side.

We reached the shelf we had seen from below. Fai was the first to get his head over the edge and then wanted to get down in a hurry. I had to force my way past him. The mountain shelf was filled with skeletons. Behind the shelf was a shallow cave or rock shelter, filled with old wooden troughs containing craniums and human bones. Bandages of white *tapa*, bark cloth beaten from the rind of the breadfruit tree or from the now extinct *eute* tree, were wound around many of the skulls and bones. From the roof of the rock shelter, long braids of black human hair were suspended. Among the many cribs or troughs, each of which was carved from a single piece of wood, stood a box made of hand-cut boards nailed together. European clothing with buttons was wrapped around the bones inside. Was this evidence of early barter or the remains of a shipwrecked sailor who had ended his days among cannibals on Fatu-Hiva?

Fai had hurried back over the edge and we heard him shout in despair below. He had collided with Liv, who was struggling up the pinnacle all alone. The unexpected encounter could have been fatal, and Fai was beside himself with fear and excitement until he and Liv had changed places, she safely above and he with a clear passage below.

This was excitement enough, and I was relieved when we were all on the ground and headed for the village on the bay. Our two friends were so confused and agitated at the idea of having broken

Opposite:

ABOVE THE HANAVAVE VALLEY. Mountain trails, once cut into the rock by Polynesians when the island was densely populated, would have been overgrown and lost if not kept open by the wild descendants of once domesticated animals, notably cattle, horses, goats, sheep, boars, and dogs.

ON THE ISLAND HILLS. The flora and fauna of the island were dominated by the perpetual trade winds, which always blew from east to west, from South America toward Australia and Asia.

Above:

ABOVE THE OMOA VALLEY. The valleys of Fatu-Hiva were all surrounded by the steep walls of extinct craters. Erosion had opened all of them toward the sea. Dense jungle crept up from the valley bottom wherever it could get a foothold. The flora of the interior highlands varied from impenetrable rain forest to semidry savanna with grass and ferns.

Opposite:

BEFORE THE BATTLE. Farther along this narrow mountain shelf, three wild horses blocked all passage ahead. Tuiveta stood his ground in a battle that ended with his pack in the abyss.

BACK TO THE JUNGLE CABIN. Deprived of all our provisions, we were driven by hunger down to the luxuriant jungle, where food hung on the trees and prawns could be caught in the river.

Opposite:

WITH A SPY AT OUR HEELS, we visited an old burial ground to study and collect ancient Polynesian skulls. Our Polynesian shadower kept watch over us all the time, but when I went farther off, he followed at my heels, so Liv was left alone and able to fill a hemp sack with specimens for anthropological studies.

HUMAN CRANIUMS were found everywhere in caves and nooks. Although many teeth lay scattered about beside the skulls, all were perfect and without the slightest sign of caries, in contrast with the poor teeth of the modern Polynesians.

Above:

A GHOSTLY ATMOSPHERE prevailed in our lonely cabin one night, when three skulls started to rattle in their hiding place under our bed. The mystery was solved by the moon, which lit up the valley below and sent some sparse rays through our window, revealing the cause. (See page 84.)

Opposite:

EXPLORING TABOO GROUND. The forest was full of *paepae,* ancient masonry platforms for thatched bamboo houses that had long since disintegrated. Some *paepae* had been declared taboo by ancient medicine men and often contained burials and old artifacts. Most of the skulls were long-headed, unlike those of the Malays and Indonesians, but like many of those found in pre-Inca burial grounds in Peru.

Above:

SACRED JUNGLE TREES sometimes reached enormous dimensions and offered shelter to those who dared to break the taboo.

THE TAUAOUOHO MOUNTAIN RIDGE divided the island lengthwise in two, like the crest of a dragon. We were always curious about what was on the other side.

CLIMBING A TABOO PINNACLE, we found a burial ground on a shelf high above the valley.

the taboo that, in their state of mind, almost anything was likely to happen. They expected calamity from every direction. They had broken the taboo; punishment was certain.

None of us slept too well that night, on the floor of Fai's little, unfurnished cabin. The sinister sound of coughing from other huts mingled with the barking of nervous dogs, and the sickeningly sweet smell of copra seeped between the sticks that formed the walls of the airy cabin. Tioti rotated continuously, like a windmill.

Next morning, we were down early by the black boulder beach. We were leaving the valley. To launch a canoe was no joke even on this leeward side of the island. There was nothing to provide shelter. The westbound ocean swells sent their undulating offspring fanning around the north cape and entering the open bay. Here they rose up into long rows of frothing breakers that in turn collapsed like salty waterfalls, thundering against the black boulders on the beach. The Polynesians knew how to handle their boats in this surf just as a European knows the gears of his car. They would stand motionless for a time with the canoe lifted, ready to run, while waiting for the right wave. Which the right wave was, we never managed to learn. Perhaps it was slightly smaller than the rest, or not so closely followed by the next.

Tioti, Liv, and I now stood with one canoe, waiting for the right wave. Still a poor swimmer, I hated this moment. We stood in safety, high up on the steep slope of boulders reached only by the spray, holding the canoe by its cross poles, ready to rush forward. When Tioti signaled that the right wave was breaking, we rushed ahead into the whirling water, leaped into the canoe, and, in order to get over the next roller before it rose on end as a vertical wall, paddled as if a devil were really on our heels.

Opposite:

EXPLORING A TABOO CAVE. The whole valley outside, with all its inhabitants, had once been buried by an avalanche. Tioti and Fai are carrying an outrigger canoe into a cave supposed to contain a subterranean lake called Vai-Po, or "Water-of-the-Night," in native traditions.

STRANGE MUSIC resounded from all directions as Liv and I embarked to investigate the sacred lake.

TRADITION CLAIMED that a secret passage continued under water and up into an inner chamber, where the skeleton of a medicine man was supposed to be seated at a stone table.

I scarcely had the time to make more than two or three desperate strokes before I saw something that made me throw the paddle into the canoe as I flung myself on all fours at Tioti's feet. A spout of water rose like a fountain through a round hole in the bottom of the canoe. Damn that sexton! Yesterday, upon landing, he had removed a plug to empty the canoe, and today, in his confused state of mind, he had forgotten to put it back again. The plug had been left ashore. One rising breaker after another tipped us high up on end as Tioti alone tried to keep the bows of the canoe straight into the surf to prevent its capsizing. At the same time, he struggled with his little paddle to force us farther out to sea, out beyond the grip of the dangerous breakers, which were trying to push us into the churning chaos cascading against the rocks. Liv had grabbed the bailer, a coconut shell, and was desperately scooping while I reduced the waterspout with the palm of one hand, fumbling for something to replace the wooden plug. The shaft of the sexton's paddle went like the spokes of a wheel, first on one side of the dugout trunk and then on the other.

The tiny canoe was half filled with water by the time Tioti grabbed his hat and used it to help Liv to bail: we were safely outside the reach of the surf. With a twisted tuft of coconut husk, I managed to plug the scupper hole. We were safe, bobbing peacefully up and down on the long swells of the friendly, open ocean. The danger lay landward, where we still could hear the surf and the boulder beach itself roaring and rattling like a pride of lions. I had not quite realized before that the ocean is never as treacherous or as ferocious elsewhere as it is near a coast, the part that is generally seen and judged by most of us.

When I shook my head at his oversight, Tioti shook the water from his straw hat and put it back on again. "Taboo," was his only excuse.

We were not yet homeward bound. We wanted to explore the coast farther northward, as far as a deserted valley called Taiokai. There we were tempted to look for a legendary underground lake referred to by Fai as Vai-Po, or "Water-of-the-Night." No foreigners had hitherto been told of this lake, and only Kapiri and Keakea, two natives from the Hanavave Valley, had been inside the cave opening and seen the water disappear into darkness.

The eerie stage of Hanavave once more closed its curtains, and no more valleys opened in the mountain walls as we slid northward beneath what seemed to be overhanging skyscrapers of windowless rock. Behind us, bobbing up and down in the rolling swells like ourselves, was Fai, in an even smaller dugout. Our plan was to carry his little canoe into the cave if we found it.

The sun was getting very low as we reached our destination. The unimpressive valley of Taiokai lay before us, and here we were to land. We knew it was just as awkward to get in as to get out. In landing, too, it is essential to wait for the right wave and not get too far in before the decisive moment. Again we heard the rumbling and rattling of the surf and the boulders between us and dry land, reminding me of the nerve-racking drum rolls that precede an acrobat's dive from the dome of a circus tent. We trusted Tioti. He was a master of the craft.

But not today. Unbelievably, he lost his paddle grip at the most critical moment as we chased along, surfboard fashion, on a glassy wall of water. The outrigger, which was floating alongside us at the end of the cross bars to give stability, suddenly rose out of the water. The last I saw between the rising cross bars was Fai leaping ashore, dragging his tiny canoe; then the heavy log of the outrigger swung above our heads as our canoe turned bottom up and the three of us disappeared from each other's sight in the whirling masses of water. A good surfer might have swum to a more pleasant landing than we had, who were rotating out of control until thrown headlong against the barricade of water-smoothed boulders. I landed neck first and saw the Taiokai palms growing upside down in a sprinkle of stars until my head stopped rotating and I saw Liv and Tioti struggling to get to their feet. All three of us had come ashore with nothing but bumps and bruises. With Fai's help, we dragged Tioti's solid dugout hull bottom up, away from the suction of the surf, and placed the two canoes high up on land.

Night fell as we wrung the ocean out of our salty rugs after assuring ourselves that everything had been delivered by the waves, even Tioti's hat. "Taboo" was his laconic comment as he put it back on his head.

In the dark, the dense bushes prevented all progress inland from the beach, even though Fai tried to find an opening by the light of the kerosene lamp, which he had brought safely ashore for use in the cave. Failing to penetrate, we lit a campfire atop the barricade of pebbles and boulders thrown up by the surf. Here we attended to our cuts and bruises with leaves and strips of hibiscus bark while drying ourselves and our sodden rugs as close to the flames as we could get. Then we adjusted our stony bed as best we could, and fell asleep on the stony beach.

But for the fact that we were totally exhausted, we would not have had a wink of sleep. I was awakened in the dark by the complaints of the others, and my first impression was that a million ghosts and devils had come out from the black jungle wall beside us. I saw nothing but stars and a few red embers from the dying campfire, but everywhere in the dark I could hear the rattling of the dry bones of invisible visitors. I felt something cold with sharp nails nibbling at my neck, at my foot, and at my bare waist. I kicked, but struck nobody. Without reflection, I began to strike out right and left wherever I was touched. Without a whimper, whatever I struck seemed, in a disgusting way, to come apart: loose knuckle-bones and bony fingers with claws rolled rattling down my body onto the stone mattress as I sat up. Each loose bone continued to move by itself among the stones, scratching for a hold with sharp claws and rattling about unperturbedly with the ghastly sound of dry bones, trying to climb back onto me again.

All this must have happened in seconds, or one of us must have awakened all the rest, for I had not heard Liv's whimper and the wild exclamations of the two men until the moment when I had felt the bony fingers touching me all over.

Several times, Tioti shouted a name unknown to me while Fai fumbled for his lantern and lit it. Only then did we really wake up. We found ourselves surrounded by thousands upon thousands of what looked like white knuckle joints, as big as chicken eggs, crawling about on crooked, clawlike fingers like the legs of giant spiders. Those that were clearly visible within the ring of light from the dim kerosene lamp proved to be large snail shells, bleached by the sun and taken possession of, as portable fortresses, by one of the strangest of all crustaceans: the soft-bodied hermit crab.

Never in my life had I seen so many, and even our native friends were completely amazed at their quantity and sizes. The smallest were like a grain of rice, the largest—and they dominated the pebble and boulder beach entirely—were as big as large hens' eggs or even a child's fist.

Again we could only use the empty word "instinct" to explain the inaudible voice of nature that instructed this creature, as a tiny youngster, to search for an abandoned snail shell of suitable dimensions to put on as a suit of armor. Crawling alone into the big world, it was never in doubt about what to do. Inspecting old and vacant snail shells for one of suitable size, it seized the one of just the right dimensions and skillfully threaded it on behind as a protective covering to its soft and shrimplike body. The body curl had been made by nature to assume the shape of the spiral in the snail shell, and one claw was made much larger than the other and of precisely the right shape to serve as a close-fitting lid that shut the door of the stolen house. With time, the young hermit crab outgrew its childhood dwelling and began to look for a more spacious apartment. With all its vulnerable hind body curled up inside the snail shell, the long-legged hermit stalked about, with its borrowed house always on its back, inspecting the available supply of empty shells in the sea or on the beach. When it found a vacant shell, seemingly tailor-made for the period ahead, the dissatisfied tenant positioned himself with his old house beside the new one, and only if the size was correct did he cautiously extract his long body-curl from one house and thread it into the next. His brothers and sisters, uncles and aunts did likewise, and although no other vulnerable animal would think of this ingenious solution for body protection, hermit crabs in all oceans know that this is just the right thing for them to do.

There are other kinds of crabs that are no less ingenious and have thought out a different way of self-protection. Or, if crabs do not think, they have been tipped off by whatever has done the thinking. The dromia crab, for instance, knows that all members of its family are expected to go in search of a certain kind of live sponge, which they collect and transfer to their own dorsal shell. The potato-shaped sponge grows as big as or bigger than the crab itself, but is extremely light in weight, and, walking about on the bottom with this ever-present burden on its back, the smart little fellow hidden beneath is perfectly camouflaged. The obvious idea behind it is that sponges are not edible, but the cautious little crab is.

Another kind of crab, the spider crab, seems to have been tipped off about a rather similar and no less ingenious idea. All members of this strange family detach young seaweeds from the coastal rocks, and, with the skill of experienced gardeners, transplant them with their claws to their own hard backs for camouflage. The clear intention and successful result is that, wherever they move about, they can hardly be seen for the garlands of seaweed that wave above them.

The intention of the countless hermit crabs that ruined our night's rest would be hard to determine. Like people in a street, some were probably in search of provisions, or out to find a partner in love, or they were looking for an apartment that would better suit their growing needs. Seen with our eyes, they were a disorganized,

crazy lot, with no planned intentions but to rattle and crawl everywhere, nibbling us for no purpose and pressing themselves under
us in great numbers without finding anything. If we brushed
them away to get peace, they quickly withdrew into their bunkers,
closed the door, and rolled the whole house away. A moment later,
shading their facial masks with the huge, armored mitten, they
would peep out with black, pivoted eyes to discover that they could
safely stretch out their legs again and stalk along on the interrupted
mission.

In this crowded beach community, not even a dog could have enjoyed a sound sleep. Yet I must have been unconscious in the end,
for I did not notice anyone get up until I saw Fai fighting his way
out from the bush with a huge load of breadfruit and a few oranges.
He went back for further loads and dumped them into Tioti's canoe,
while the sexton speared some fish. Searching the beach, we too
picked up a number of large sea snails still living in their own
houses. Whereas the hermit crabs patiently awaited a vacancy, we
were more cruel: We used the snail shells as individual frying pans
and ate the contents for breakfast.

Stiff from sleeping on stones and shells, we set out to search for
the cave opening by following the mountain wall at the end of the
beach. Taiokai was not an attractive valley. It had once been
densely inhabited, but a catastrophe had struck the area. The
entire mountain ridge above had suddenly come down in an avalanche and covered the valley, with all its buildings and people. Everything disappeared under the falling masses of stone. The tidal
wave that rose from the beach went far across the ocean. But the
rock walls surrounding Taiokai still seemed to overhang and to be
ready to tumble down again. Most of the valley was filled in by
an inhospitable stone ramp, covered only by low brushwood and
no real forest. At the edges of the great ramp, a few man-made
walls could be seen, partly buried by the avalanche. During our
restless night, we had heard the sound of falling rocks time and
again.

Partly hidden by huge fallen blocks at the foot of the mountain
wall, we discovered the low but broad entrance to a natural cave.
We crawled in across the boulders, and, in the half light, saw a cave
of great dimensions. Crawling down a rocky slope inside the mountain, we came to a beautiful white beach, and here lay a pond or
lake. Since light did not enter from anywhere but the distant opening behind us, all the rest of the large grotto was swallowed up in

darkness. From various directions, we heard the melodious tinkle of drops falling into the water. Nothing more could be seen and nothing could be done without Fai's canoe and kerosene lamp. We went back to fetch both.

This was Vai-Po, the "Water-of-the-Night." We lighted the lamp and saw a low roof undulating like a petrified sea with agitated waves, turned upside down over a small lake as calm as if it had been covered by a sheet of ice. The lamp threw motionless reflections everywhere; only when we moved it, did we move hundreds of shadows in the irregular roof.

We put the canoe on the water and held our breath: Beautiful, crystal-clear tones, as if from gently beaten xylophones or silver bells, spread across the lake and filled the air. Click-clack-cluck-clock-click. The tiny waves from the canoe spread over the calm, dark water and struck the many invisible projections and cavities with a harmonious tinkling.

I jumped into the canoe, where Liv was sitting, and pushed off. Tioti and Fai were squatting partway up the slope as if petrified, Tioti without his hat. A spooky light from the opening fell on their backs and made them seem unreal. Silvery bands of the same light danced toward us on the sky-blue water and mixed with the warmer, red and yellow reflections from the lantern in Liv's hand.

I moved a few paddle strokes away from the beach, and immediately the tinkle-bell orchestra began again, coming from all directions. Unforgettable beauty of sound and color. I ventured a few more strokes across the blue into the dark. Soon the sexton and Fai were lost from sight, together with the play of color, as we slid behind a rock promontory. Darkness and silence pressed in around the dim lantern. We were out of sight, but we heard Tioti asking Fai if the place was taboo, and if there were currents or monsters in the water. Fai did not know.

Liv took a *tiare* flower from behind her ear and dropped it upon the surface within our circle of light. There was no current. I tasted the water. Very cold, and surprisingly good, although it had an almost unnoticeable salty flavor. A few more careful paddle strokes. Then something hard struck my head. The ceiling was coming low. We bent double in the slender canoe and passed on. Then the bow hit the ceiling. We could get no farther without swimming. But the "Water-of-the-Night" continued under the rock.

A legend known to Fai held that somewhere in this farthest end of the cave, an opening could be found by diving below the surface of the water. By swimming into this secret entrance, a narrow tunnel could be found that led up to another cave, at a higher level and perfectly dry. Before the people of the Taiokai Valley were buried under the great avalanche, the local medicine man was said to have had his hideout in this secret cave. His skeleton was still supposed to be sitting there in a stone chair beside an altar.

We were both tempted to get into the cold water and check if the legend was true, but Fai's old kerosene lantern gave no light below the surface and we were without a rope. Then we heard Fai's excited voice. He had been outside and found that the weather was changing. We beached the canoe and climbed the slope to find our two friends gazing at large clouds slowly emerging over the edge of the overhanging walls. Tioti scratched his back, a sure sign of trouble. This time it was the weather. The wind had changed its speed and direction. A period of fine weather, permitting safe ocean travel, was about to end. There was no time to lose if we did not want to get stuck in this menacing landscape for an indefinite period of time.

First we ran to bring both canoes into position on the steep boulder beach. Then we ran back and forth along the water's edge to look for the smoothest passage through the thundering surf. I checked to see that the plug was in. We rushed waist-deep into the foam and threw ourselves into the canoe. We shouted, we paddled, we stared left and right for the threatening cascades, we got drenched, we steered, we were riding obstacles on our wooden horse in mad leaps between sky and water. And then we were in the open, out on the calmly rolling ocean.

Fai was heading for the Hanavave Valley and stuck to the coast, while, with Tioti, we chose a straight course farther out to sea, aiming for Omoa non-stop. This was the third day after breaking the taboo, and our two friends were equally sure that something was bound to happen now. The only reason for venturing into the open ocean was the feeling that the overhanging rock face of Taiokai seemed even less trustworthy.

We soon discovered that the swells had become shorter and steeper than on the outward journey. Water splashed in so frequently that we had to throw our big hoard of breadfruit overboard in an effort to gain a maximum of freeboard. Tioti kept only the fish.

In passing the bay of Hanavave, we waved our paddles to Fai as he disappeared behind the closing mountain gates, and then

we were alone with the sea. The tropical sun sank vertically into
the water and left our part of the world in sudden darkness. A
brilliant array of color fanned out for a moment over the sky where
the donor of the day had withdrawn, and then we felt completely
enclosed by the tropical darkness. Occasionally we could see some
stars, as huge clouds slid past and for a moment left us with an
obscure impression of Fatu-Hiva's skyline against some southern
constellations. But, for most of the time, we continued without any
sign of land. Tioti seemed to steer by wind and waves.

The waves grew continuously higher, the arching backs of the
long swells were becoming sharper, and a few began to hiss, with
patches of foam showing up as light flashes in the night. For a while
the canoe would rush downhill, and the next moment start a steep
climb or slant along a madly sloping plane. It had ceased to be fun.
The canoe had too little freeboard to tolerate much more of this. We
did not see the contours of any wave, and thus we were quite un-
prepared for any treacherous crest before it suddenly poured into
our laps. Then all three of us had to bail for our lives. Time and
again, the little dugout was so full that Liv's coconut shell would
have seemed ridiculous if not supplemented by a big gourd shell
and Tioti's hat, for the hull had to be emptied before the next wave
broke in, since two drenchings would have filled us to the brim.

If the water level inside and outside the hull were ever permitted
to meet, it would be useless to bail any more, explained Tioti. Not
that the wooden canoe would sink, he added comfortingly. We
could keep on paddling, with our heads above water, if it were not
for the sharks. We had not been followed by any on the way north,
but the water we were bailing out now contained blood from the
fish, and for that reason we could be sure that sharks were already
following us in large numbers.

With special organs that enable it to smell with its whole body,
a shark can detect a drop of blood at incredible distances. Whenever a wounded goat fell into the sea, triangular shark fins would be
seen chasing in from all directions, and the same thing happened
whenever a fisherman cleaned his fish over the gunwales of his
canoe. We knew that the largest blue sharks in the world patrolled
the coastal cliffs of the Marquesas Islands, some of them doubling
or even tripling our canoe in size.

No night had ever felt to me as nearly endless as that one out of
sight of any landmark, struggling to keep afloat in a half-submerged
bathtub of a boat, surrounded by invisible hissing waves and silently

pursuing man-eaters. Up and down, sideways and around; it was good that nobody was seasick.

All three of us were afraid. Any second, we could lose the battle. We put away the paddles and we grabbed them again. Bail and paddle; paddle and bail. And there again we could see the skyline of our island outlined for a moment by stars. But we saw nothing that resembled the contours of Omoa.

Tioti slightly adjusted our course. He was silent. Scared like us, and surely more convinced than ever that this was the devils' final retribution. He had warned us. Now we should see.

A sexton who believed in taboo! I was as irritated as he was. It was his fault that everything had gone wrong the day before. He had lost his head not because of the taboo but through autosuggestion. Now he was sitting there thinking of the devils of his cannibal ancestors rather than of the god of Pakeekee and Père Victorin. Any moment, he might involuntarily play another trick on us. It would suffice for him to move carelessly or to lose the hat which we needed for bailing. Why did he not think of God instead, of something positive? In the dark, where I could neither see nor be seen, I began to think of some of my childhood lessons. Christians were supposed to believe that faith could move mountains. I was irritated by the sexton, because he put his faith in a revengeful devil and not in a helpful god. He believed in both. I did not believe in devils. Right now I was not so sure whether it would not be a safety precaution to believe in a god. Perhaps my father, who did believe, was right and my mother, who did not believe, was wrong. Or perhaps she too believed, the difference being that his god was borrowed from an ancient book written by early Jews, and hers was taken from the more recent publication of an Englishman named Darwin.

As we paddled and bailed, I told myself I was a blind fool. Even in pitch darkness on an empty ocean, or perhaps more easily there, I should see that the greatest power of all was not man and what he could see through his microscope, but the ever-present nothing that squeezes breadfruit out of a dry branch, directs the spider in its spinning, and tells every hermit crab to look for an empty snail shell. After living for months with nature, had I not seen evidence of superhuman ability everywhere? Evidence of something highly realistic, for which science had not yet coined a name: the power stimulating nature to creation, followed by intelligent evolution and maintenance.

We felt tiny in the boundless night: Something really big must exist to take care of everything hidden from man in this vast darkness. The universe seems bigger in the night: When it is light, it is easier to deceive oneself with the impression that what we see is all there is.

Truly this night was without end. I was tired, scared, and afraid that Liv was near to exhaustion. I sent a humble wish for survival and a successful landing out into the dark, to the benevolent power I scarcely could believe in and yet confronted no matter how I reasoned. Somehow this gave me comfort and courage. It seemed as if extra strength went into my paddling. Tioti noticed it and made heavier strokes too. We picked up speed, and less water seemed to splash in. Perhaps it was all autosuggestion, but if so, it was because a kind god had been substituted for an evil devil.

Now the waves were definitely less crested, and we saw black rocks nearby. Soon we could hear the surf. Finally, we even saw dim lights from some of the cabins in Omoa, and Pakeekee, who must have expected us, had lit a huge campfire in front of the palms.

We turned the bow straight toward the fire. Between us and what seemed Paradise was once more the deafening roar and thunder of an agitated surf. All was still and black but for the flickering flames above the boulder beach and some half-naked brown bodies running between the palm trunks throwing branches onto the fire.

We stopped and held the canoe dancing restlessly in one spot at the very birthplace of the surf. Then the sexton shouted, "Go!"

A chasing crest lifted us up and threw us forward at racing speed, with other frothing breakers tumbling both in front of us and behind. Water boiled and rose around, up and up, and as the heavy wall of water rumbled against the black boulders, we were grabbed by strong arms and dragged up to the campfire.

We were safe in our home valley.

"Taboo," was the dry comment of the wet sexton as he shook his hat.

"No," I said. "This is the third day and we are safe ashore."

"Because God was with you," explained Pakeekee.

"He was," said Tioti, "because I am a sexton and a Protestant."

6. OCEAN ESCAPE

The rain came. Not as a sudden deluge that carried away our cabin and the skulls below our bed, but as a sneaking thief who stole the sun and left us in wet misery. Not a drop came through the thatched roof, but dampness penetrated everywhere and everything. The crisp banana leaves of our mattress lost their springiness, our blankets grew heavier, and the smell of mold began to transcend the gay aroma of spice and flower. No thundering avalanche was heard crashing down the mountainside, but day and night our ears were filled with the sound of water: water that dripped, dropped, dribbled, splashed, sputtered, gushed, and streamed everywhere. Mud. Our cabin was a boat in a sea of mud.

It was not tempting to venture out in search of food except in the moments, between showers, when the sun emerged. The sun seemed hotter now, as if it were burning with renewed ardor to dry up the mess in the jungle. Yet, all too suddenly, it disappeared behind a curtain again as the next bursting cloud spurted its liquid load down upon the forest. One thing was comforting: In this weather, no one could sneak around our cabin, even in the dark, without leaving footprints on the ground.

During the early days of this rainy period, we continued our nomadic life, in the mountains, in the jungle, and by canoe along the sheltered, west coast. Once, when the weather seemed promising, we returned to the spectacular Hanavave Valley, which teemed with archaeological sites. In the thickets covering a rock promontory, we came across a temple terrace of beautifully cut red stone, where decayed remains of wooden images three feet tall stood leaning, gazing at us with huge round eyes, their bodies gaping with the wounds of old age. There were caves high up in the rock faces, sealed with stone masonry, but we were unable to reach them.

One evening, when we came back to the Omoa Valley, Pakeekee saw us as we passed through the village, and he had clearly antic- ipated our arrival. Tioti was with him, and their *vahines* had pre- pared a gorgeous meal of pork. After the party, we were invited to join a very special fishing enterprise.

The sky was clear as the night fell upon the island, but it was dark, for there was no moon. We found the sea as calm as a sleeping beauty when we reached the beach and launched two small dugout canoes. Pakeekee and Liv entered one, and Tioti and I the other, accompanied by Pakeekee's adoptive son, the little rascal Paho. In the bow of each canoe, they had tied a bundle of dry *teita*, a ten- foot-tall local grass resembling thin cane. Each bundle had been wound around with bark rope to form a great torch.

Well out in the bay, we set fire to these two torches. Snapping and crackling, they flamed up and lit the surrounding water while a rain of sparks danced into the night air. Back on the land, silhou- ettes of palm crowns waved above the beach while innumerable stars sparkled above our heads. The black water immediately began to teem with tiny fish, but we paddled out of the shoal and went farther along the cliffs in the direction of the Tahaoa reefs. The second canoe followed closely behind us, gaily lit by the flames. From high above, we could hear the hoarse cries of large sea birds nesting on the lofty mountain shelves.

Suddenly, flying fish began to sail about us. They shot out of the night water like big, glittering projectiles and passed through the torch light before they dived back into the black sea on the other side. It was flying fish we were out to catch, but not with a hook and line, and not with a fishing spear. We were to catch them in the air like birds.

After a little while, we found ourselves at the center of a very lively scene. The sparkling torches had an amazing effect. They brought the flying fish out in great numbers. The streamlined fish came gliding through the air, attracted by the flickering light. We had never seen such big and heavy specimens anywhere. They were the size of our forearms. They sailed through the air with the speed of an arrow from the bow, and some of them struck the side of the canoe with a heavy thud.

"Mind your eyes," warned the sexton. The glittering projectiles seemed to lack any steering control as they whizzed past our faces.

The sexton had risen to his feet and stood balancing in the narrow canoe, fencing in the air with a net on a bamboo pole. He caught one fish and quickly reversed his net to dump the catch into the canoe. I grabbed the fluttering projectile, which was incapable of taking off from the bottom of the canoe. It was as helplessly grounded as a glider. With its tail, this fish had to work up a terrific speed under water before it could leave the surface and glide through the air for a hundred yards or more by spreading out its overlarge pectoral fins. The fish was a compact bundle of muscle, and I needed both hands to secure it. The back was as black as the night sky, the belly white, and the sides embellished with silvery blue lines. What a perfect shape for speed! Man was still making square automobiles then, and scarcely more than fumbling at streamlining his clumsy airplanes. The fish stared at me with huge, black eyes which stuck out from its head like balls and were capable of gazing in all directions, while it spread out its flying apparatus: mottled wings as thin as cellophane, held by a fan-shaped group of thin spokes.

There was the next one in the net! It had become more than lively in the canoe when I saw another coming over the bow with its course set straight for me. Before I could turn aside, it hit me in the stomach with such unexpected force that I fell off the loose thwart, to Paho's wild amusement. It was a true hit, but my assailant fell with me into the bottom of the canoe; thus we had caught three. I heard screams and roars of laughter from the other canoe as well; they clearly had the marine projectiles shooting at them too.

As more and more of the big fish sailed through the air, we were reminded of the snowball fights of our childhood in wintry Norway. The glittering fish raced between our canoes, above and below and straight through the arena of light. The sexton got one that sent his hat dancing overboard. Paho got one in his neck. We sprawled and fumbled in the air and in the water for fish, and laughed so much that we rolled over in the canoe, soaking wet with sea water and spray. Flying fish skirted or hit us continually. Paho and I ducked and twisted to escape, and Tioti fought and fenced around himself with the net to catch them.

At last the torches burned down, but Tioti pierced the remains with a stick so as to burn the stump to the very end. As it fell hissing into the black sea and only the stars twinkled in the darkness, no more of the capricious fishes came out of the water. Only sea birds cried from invisible cliffs high above.

At the bottom of our own canoe, I counted thirty-five large flying fish, of which quite a number had entered without the aid of the sexton's net. This was enough to share with Veo's family and many others, but the sexton would not give up. We paddled back into the bay and dropped a line into the water, using bits of flying fish as bait. Tioti said this was the right time and place for *kao-kao* fish. And in a few moments we had four large fishes with heads that were drawn out into long beaks, plunging about among the flying fish. A long time passed and nothing touched the bait. I almost fell asleep.

The sexton rattled his paddle hard against the gunwales. But he had no fish. We waited a little longer. Then he drummed again with his oar, raising a great noise in the calm night.

"Why are you doing that?" I asked.

"The fish are asleep," replied the sexton.

A week passed, and two, and three. The rain poured down with ever shorter intervals, and the mud rose in the jungle. Gradually we had to suspend our nomadic activities. We were forced to restrict our movements to the area around our cabin, because ugly boils and open wounds had appeared on our feet. We had been bothered by them for some time but had managed to keep going. Now they were getting serious. Liv had three boils as large as teacups growing on her forelegs, while I had open wounds on my feet and ankles. Her painful boils expanded from inside, without visible reason, until they burst, whereas my wounds had begun as almost unnoticeable grazes I got leaping ashore among the boulders on the beach of Omoa the night we returned from the taboo adventure. Whenever we waded in sea water, our feet would swell like balloons, and the constant rain made it impossible to walk in the jungle without getting covered in mud up to our knees.

For days on end, only hunger forced us on expeditions in the immediate vicinity of the bamboo cabin, since we spent most of our time striving to keep our feet clean and dry, while washing our wounds with boiling water. We had no medicine of any kind. We remembered the teacher Larsen on Tahiti, who had told us to take ointment along to cure us of tropical boils. We had refused to bring anything of the sort. None of modern man's inventions. To learn the true virtue of civilization, we had left behind all its blessings and benefits together with what we considered its evils.

One day, the sexton came up the valley to look for us, worried that something evil had happened to us. To our delight, he brought a bundle of fresh fish. He looked at our troubled feet and identified the wounds as *fe-fe*, a disease he said we could cure in a week if we

used the right herbs. He disappeared into the forest and came back
with his hat full of yellow hibiscus flowers. They were immediately
boiled until they became a kind of porridge, which was padded
steaming hot straight onto our open wounds.

Tioti left, happy to have repaid me for having cured him of his
gumboil earlier on. He told us to continue for a week with poulticing
our ankles and legs with boiling-hot hibiscus flowers.

So we did. And Liv's boils flattened out, but only to become converted into raw areas precisely like mine. And there we sat and listened to the rain, day after day, with large, green banana leaves
wrapped around our legs to keep the hibiscus paste in place. Our
meals were not what they used to be. Coconuts. Coconuts and
breadfruit. And lemon juice. The rain seemed endless. The jungle
floor was streaming from one pool to the next. The air was saturated
with warm humidity. The *fe-fe* wounds did not heal. On the contrary, they grew in size as the skin slowly withdrew in all directions.
Sometimes the pain could be felt right up to our groins and we
had to keep to our bed. Our moldy bed. If we slept on our sides or
on our backs, we smelled mold from the bamboo walls, and if we
turned over onto our stomachs, we smelled mold from our mattress.

Insects of all kinds invaded the bamboo cabin to escape from the
water and the mud. Minute, yellow ants came marching in armies
through the plaited floor, and thin, two-way roads packed with
these tiny busybodies crossed the walls like living yellow wires. To
rescue our meager provisions, we suspended coconut cups from
the middle of thin bark strings stretched across the room like a
clothesline. But scouts among the intrepid little ants soon saw
through our trick, and as daylight broke on the following morning,
we found the suspended coconut cups yellow with ants, while the
strings looked like rusty wire, packed thick with crawling ants
which seemed to move in layers on top of each other.

There were ants in our bed too. We tidied the piles of large
banana leaves on which we slept, and thereby we disturbed three
separate communities of ants swarming in all directions to rescue
their hatcheries of tiny eggs.

We tried to keep the poles on which the cabin rested surrounded
by water, but insects flew in or dropped from the jungle trees. The
countless pools of water everywhere were ideal breeding places for
mosquito larvae. Mosquitoes, which had bothered us to a modest
extent before, were dancing in thick clouds wherever we moved.
Every inch of our bodies was bitten over and over again until we
were driven almost out of our minds with despair. The ants on the

cabin floor carried away the endless hundreds of dead mosquitoes
we swept off our bodies and limbs with blood-stained hands.

After one night when Liv had been rolling to and fro on the floor
in agony and despair, tormented by the hungry little winged devils,
we surrendered. We could not win. Nor could we survive if we were
to remain involuntary blood donors to these masses of greedy assassins.

With our bodies itching and burning as if we had bathed in acid,
we limped down to see Willy in the village. For cash, we bought
part of his own personal mosquito netting, and to keep the mud
from our *fe-fe*-infected feet we also bought a pair each of the funer-
ary tennis shoes. They were so large that we had to tie them on with
bark rope. We stretched a piece of the netting across the open window in the bamboo wall, and used the rest to form a little tent
above our bed. The result was marvelous. We slept until the next
afternoon.

When Liv lifted the net and jumped into her large, new shoes to
head for the spring, she had barely left the cabin steps when I
heard a scream.

I ran to the door expecting the worst, but found her alone, dancing on one foot. A black spider, as big and hairy as an eight-legged
mouse, ran out of her shoe and disappeared among the ferns. She
had been bitten on a toe. I knew the terrible effects of the tarantula
and other giant spiders when they bit. But I knew nothing about
this local species. We squeezed out blood and rubbed the marks
with lemon. Only experience was to tell us that the hairy giant that
had hidden in Liv's shoe was more awe-inspiring than dangerous.

Slowly, another tormentor got the upper hand in our cabin, a tor-
menter from which neither netting nor shoes gave the slightest protection. A very fine dust, as thin and white as flour, began to be
pushed out from tiny, round holes in the plaited walls. It was
wafted down to the floor, hung in moist cakes among the wicker-
work, or whirled about in the room. It penetrated everywhere. It
covered us like snow while we slept, and we inhaled it with every
breath and ate it with every mouthful.

Ioane and his assistants had known that this was bound to happen. They had built our house from green, unripe bamboo, real-
izing that this material would be devoured gradually by boring
wood bugs. The bamboo they picked for their own walls was bone-
hard and yellow from the very moment it was cut, and sometimes
even soaked for a week in sea water. But, by building a house that
would last us only a few months, they would have a good chance to

come back and earn more trade goods by working for us a second time.

And the white powder was wafted down upon us from thousands of holes in the walls; it whirled in and out of the netting, and left us with a constant taste of bamboo flour between our teeth. Liv dusted every day, but new dust appeared at once. Tiny black rumps and heads occasionally peeping out from the holes were all we saw of the army of dust makers.

The only roommate we could tolerate was Garibaldus. Garibaldus was the name we had given to a large lizard, or rather, gecko, lodging one floor up, in the thatch of our ceiling. Garibaldus was as large as a newborn kitten, and he paid his rent under our roof by helping us to clean up the confusion of ants and other insects. He was even bold enough to devour a large poisonous centipede if one climbed into the house. But Garibaldus was no noiseless acrobat. He ran around, drumming on the worm-eaten bamboo walls, shaking cascades of white dust down upon us. And while we were sleeping down below, Garibaldus sat in our thatch ceiling croaking, purring, and screeching. And he was indecent in the extreme. Garibaldus dropped his visiting cards and, as if by accident, they always fell on me. In fact, they must have been carefully aimed, for, if the two of us down below changed seats, Liv was never hit. I was the invariable target. And if I banged my fist on the table and threatened to bottle him up in one of my collectors' glasses, then Garibaldus gurgled with laughter and disappeared as quick as lightning into the thatch.

In our loneliness, we acquired another animal friend in Poto. *Poto* is the local word for cat, and that is precisely what Poto was: a beautiful, young, wild cat. Resilient as a small tiger, with striped fur and a bushy tail, this vigilant beast of prey never ventured into our cabin, but came stealing onto our terrace in search of jungle mice and lizards. Poto became a daily visitor once Liv set out a shell filled with the thick, creamy sauce she made by squeezing the white oil out of grated coconut. Poto first showed her taste for coconut sauce when she stole some that had been prepared for our own breadfruit dinner. We caught sight of the cat from the window as she jumped up onto our stone table in the kitchen shelter and put her head into the coconut shell. Obviously, a wild cat had never tasted anything half as delicious as this sauce. When the shell was licked clean, the happy feline washed the cream off her snout with her paws and rolled playfully about on the slab. Then she must have heard a sound from us in the cabin, for in a flash she was gone in a big leap from the terrace. But, next day, the curious head reappeared above the stone wall. The coconut shell on the kitchen stone was too tempting. It was found full again, and Poto became a daily visitor.

Poto became almost tame. At first she was amazed to see tall jungle dwellers walking on their hind legs, but as the days passed she ventured to drink coconut milk at Liv's feet. This was when our two domesticated chickens became jealous. Only two of the several hens we had received as gifts during the early days behaved differently from the wild birds of the forest. They came regularly to be fed with coconut crumbs. Although bred from their eggs as females, the two belligerent hens stalked about on the open terrace, their chests thrust out like two cocks, fighting at every opportunity. When Poto was detected stealing their coconut crumbs, she was assailed so ferociously that she disappeared like a tuft of hair over the edge of the terrace, with the two madly flapping hens at her heels.

In a futile attempt to pacify the two hens, we had once asked Tioti to bring them a young bridegroom. But when the brave knight with his red crown was let loose on the terrace, sparkling in colorful elegance, the two feathered *vahine* really had a fit. They stopped fighting between themselves and quite uncharmingly leaped upon the poor cock, who shrieked in despair and ran away into the forest. We later found a few gay feathers beneath a hollow tree. The cock had hidden until it was killed and eaten by some wild beast. The two masculine hens paraded more proudly than ever, chests out, on our terrace, and hardly stepped aside even for us. They seemed ashamed of laying eggs, flying deep into the jungle to do so in secret, ignoring any responsibility for hatching their abandoned products.

No sooner were the two hens out of sight than Poto reappeared, heading for her cream. While the noisy hens sounded like an approaching avalanche as they came fluttering down over the roof, Poto moved as silently as a cloud. One day, Poto introduced a boy friend, Panther. Panther was about the same age as Poto, but had reddish fur and was more timid. Poto encouraged Panther to come along to our cleared terrace and made straight for the kitchen shelter. She turned her head invitingly toward her friend, who, unsure, only cringed at the edge of the thicket. Panther never ventured a step farther. His lot was to watch Poto happily licking up the white cream—while the hens were away.

We saw and heard no life except the animals. There were wild birds in the trees outside the window, and at that time a long-tailed mare with a foal had descended from the mountains to keep close to our walls. But they were both extremely nervous. Our greatest surprise, however, was the first time we saw large crabs rattling across our clearing, miles from the sea. They were not the famous coconut crabs known in the atolls farther south, and we could hardly have been more surprised if lobsters had come crawling out of the pools or if flying fish had come sailing through the rain. This was something new to zoologists, and we managed to catch some to include in the collection for the Oslo University museum. The feeling that our cabin was sailing away in a deluge of mud and water was strengthened by the presence of the crabs.

It was the mosquito that became our only truly hated enemy. We could no longer leave the cabin door unprotected by shirts and shorts—and hemp sacks intended for the human skulls under our bed were pulled up over our leaf-covered legs. Endless swarms of these buzzing little devils were drawn to us like iron filings to a magnet the moment we opened the bamboo door. We flailed about helplessly with our arms until we were behind the door again. Now a cloud of pursuers would dance against the window netting trying to join us inside. Stupidly, they would fumble with their long noses through the nets but at the same time straddle the meshes so widely with their long legs that they could not get through. Yet gusts of wind would sometimes push them right through the netting in dozens. This was no more than we could cope with while awake, but when we slept it was good to have the second net hanging over our bunk. For if the day mosquito was bad, the one that came at night was ten times worse.

It was the nocturnal mosquito that carried the horrible germ of the disease we dreaded most: elephantiasis. The filaria of elephantiasis is a tiny parasitic worm transmitted into the human blood stream in its larval stage by the bite of the female nocturnal mosquito. Both types of mosquito were unknown on these islands prior to the arrival of white men.

No matter how well we bound up the netting, we could never prevent half a dozen or more of the aggressive nocturnal mosquitoes from finding their way inside, and we would wake up bitten all over. We knew that the itching of the bites was caused by the gastric juice the mosquito emitted to dilute our blood in a sort of extra-abdominal digestion. Whenever a mosquito had poked its nose into us at night, it was already too late to kill it, and we let it drink freely in the hope that it would suck back again any possible filaria together with the diluted drop of blood. If the mosquito had infected us with elephantiasis, our first warning would be a fever.

Captain Brander had told us that, if we escaped to a cold climate before any of our limbs began to grow, the disease would not develop. But once a leg, an arm, or any other part began to expand in size, nothing could be done except the removal of surplus flesh by surgery. But, said Brander, this would not stop the growth.

During those days when we lay stretched out under the mosquito netting, suffering the savage pain of *fe-fe*-infected legs, the mosquitoes seemed to grow to fill our whole existence. We were blinded with hatred for them and filled with an evil desire for revenge. We got really mean. When the hungry devils had sucked enough through our skin to fly away like tiny red balloons, barely able to stay airborne, then *their* problems began. They had to get away, but were now too fat to get out through the netting they had somehow tackled when inbound, with empty bellies. They fumbled and struggled to get out, each one dancing drunkenly with its inflated red rear turned temptingly toward us. With sadistic delight, we pricked the red balloon with needle-sharp thorns until it was punctured. But we got even more sadistic. When a cloud of hungry mosquitoes hummed and buzzed in front of the net, searching in vain for a passage in, we would put a finger close to the net as a sort of bait. A choir of little devils would immediately descend on the net, struggling to poke their noses far enough in to reach the finger. First we enjoyed the sight of the greedy little devils eagerly but vainly twisting their noses. Then, with two fingers, we would grab one by the nose, and the sprawling resistance of the poor devil was of no avail: he was pulled in, brutally executed and fed to the ants, while the rest outside stupidly lined up, poking their noses in, each one eager to be the next in turn.

We could never spend more than a day or two in bed before we had to leave the cabin in search of food. Limping around with sore and swollen legs, we found to our surprise that there was suddenly very little to harvest. The breadfruit season was coming to an end, and all the mature trunks of banana and *fei* that bore fruit had already been chopped down. There were coconuts and some taro roots, but we were very hungry.

One day, Tioti came with the tail end of a swordfish. We baked it in leaves and ate and ate and ate, tingling all over with sensual delight and enjoyment. Again we realized that hunger can pave the way to a sensation a man will never experience who says that he is hungry merely because he has worked up an appetite.

A few days later, we were to learn where all our fruit was going.

Ioane, our former friend, was seen before sunrise one morning with a company of *vahine* and young boys. They stole downhill through the thickets beside our hut, lugging sacks and baskets filled with the fruit we had paid for by renting the land. We knew they had enough to harvest elsewhere, and we knew all too well that they would report us to the chief for theft if we were forced to resort to land that belonged to others. Tioti had just told us that Pakeekee had been reported to the chief for the theft of *fei* which he had never seen or eaten. Pakeekee was the last person who would steal. Or even lie.

This was a planned stratagem. Looking up, I noted that even some of the tall palms on our very terrace had been stripped of coconuts. This was a desperate situation. Furious, I staggered empty-handed down the trail and caught up with the heavily laden party down by the river, where they were about to load part of their burden onto a pack horse. They were carrying away large quantities.

"Ioane," I said, "that fruit is mine."

"*Aoe* [No]," the man lied boldly. "We have picked it on the land next to yours."

Both of us were equally angry. I got nowhere. He had the chief and the village people on his side.

Then, one day, we woke up to see Ioane climbing down from a coconut palm on our very own terrace. I was out of the door in a flash. I was furious.

"This terrace is ours," I said.

"But the coconut palm is mine," Ioane shouted.

"You have leased both land and fruit to me, Ioane."

"The fruit, but not the coconuts," was the reply.

"All the food, and the coconuts. We cannot survive without the coconuts. Besides, the land is stripped of fruit, too," I added, and felt I was about to lose my self-control completely.

"Coconuts are not food; they are the money of Ioane," he shouted back.

I could not have restrained myself longer if Ioane had not turned his back on me and departed, remarking that the damned nuts he had left could be ours.

There was not much we could do. We were alone among the islanders. When a schooner finally arrived, we could send in a complaint to the French authorities. It would take months before the cause was in the hands of the proper authorities, and years before a settlement was reached under such out-of-the-way conditions. And in this case it was our word against theirs, all the natives sticking together. Besides, it was quite customary for the white men to be the ones defrauding the poor islanders. Ours was perhaps one of the first cases in reverse.

We had no choice; we ate coconuts, and tried to catch some prawns in the river. But the prawns seemed to have all gone with the flood, and only mosquitoes were left to move upon the face of the waters. The jungle mosquitoes became such a menace that finally neither Ioane nor any other natives ventured into the interior of the valley, not even to harvest copra. Now we were merely sitting in our cabin waiting for some ship to come and take us away from the island, away to just any place where we could breathe without swallowing bamboo dust and mosquitoes, away to where we could fill our empty stomachs with all the food we no longer dared even to think about.

Hunger drove us on a visit to Pakeekee. We learned that the whole village was waiting for a ship to call. A woman had stepped on a fishbone and got a slight cut. But the sore began to eat its way in every direction, and now her whole foot was raw. We suspected what later happened: She had to be transported to Tahiti, where her entire leg was amputated to halt the further spread of the disease.

We waited for a ship until we fell asleep, and we started waiting again as soon as we opened our eyes. And, late one evening, as we sat on our stools on each side of the bamboo table, chewing nuts, we heard the faint blasts of a distant steamship's siren. The deep, hoarse sound was carried across the jungle from the far sea. That night, we slept little. Long before dawn, we dragged out from beneath our bunk our hidden suitcase with the clothes preserved for our possible departure, and we pulled on these unaccustomed garments.

I almost had a fit as I looked into the suitcase mirror in order to knot the ridiculous tie around my neck. For it disappeared entirely behind a wide flow of chestnut-colored beard. My shaving kit had gone long before as payment to Ioane. I was facing a tanned and savage-looking Viking with blond hair flowing down across the collar of a modern white shirt. Liv unquestionably made a more favorable impression when she brushed her hair down over a smartly tailored gown. But the sight of our sun-baked faces above this type of white man's attire was so extraordinary that we both doubled over with laughter.

We were in the best of spirits. We pulled our hemp sacks up over our knees as protection against the jungle mud, tied them on, and limped happily down the valley. Before we reached the first house, we pulled off the sacks and paraded in all our white man's elegance through the village, down to the sea. The village spectators were terribly impressed. We felt once more on top of the world.

But, down on the beach, the bluest blue ocean stretched on to the bluest blue horizon, dotted with its usual pattern of white-crested waves. There was no sign of a ship. Not even a modest schooner.

"We saw the lights last night," reported Pakeekee. A steamship had passed far out at sea.

Pakeekee, too, was depressed. Life was not easy for this islander whose faith was as unshakable as Father Victorin's, with the great difference that Pakeekee had all his own compatriots against him. They hunted him all the time. They had just moved the stones that marked the boundary of his valley property, and the chief had punished him with a fine. I told Pakeekee about Ioane, who had stolen all the fruit on our land and lied by claiming he had taken it from the land next to ours.

"*C'est pas bien* [it is not good]," said Pakeekee laconically in his finest French. "For the land next to yours is mine."

Before we left, we were tipped off by Tioti that Haii with the big legs had just gone up the valley carrying his hoard of scorpions. We hurried homeward. As we reached the last huts of the village and began looking for the sacks to pull back over our legs, we discovered Haii in front of Veo's house. He watched us with a madman's smile from behind a huge empty wooden bowl that still smelled of *poipoi*. As I snatched a photo, he rose on his mighty legs and lifted both arms, wielding an ax and a long machete knife. His gestures were the very opposite of "come and eat." We hastened up through the forest. No naked footprints as big as Haii's could be seen around our walls. And if scorpions had been dropped inside, Garibaldus would have eaten them or chased them away, for he sat in his usual lookout position and greeted us with a purr as we came back.

In the village, too, conditions now began to be precarious. The local families were accustomed to a modern diet of rice and flour, and felt at a loss if they ran out of this imported provender. Trusting to the supplies from Willy's store in exchange for coconuts, they no longer bothered to hoard large supplies of fermented breadfruit, *poipoi*, in their ancestral storage pits to carry them safely from one breadfruit season to the next. It was a common complaint that the digestive system played up if pork or fish were

eaten on their own. It was therefore regarded as a catastrophe
when Willy's little cellar store was suddenly empty. No rice, no
sugar, no flour. The reason was that the supplies on board the
Tereora on its last call had been quite inadequate. In Hanavave,
too, all supplies were exhausted. The little Chinese had locked his
door and taken to the mountains, goat hunting. Willy had just
paddled to Hanavave but come back with an empty canoe.

Everybody waited for a schooner. But none came.

The days passed. Weeks went by. A month. Two months.
Three. . . .

Certainty began to grow in us about what was going on. The
last news we had received from the outside world was now six
months old, and at that time a terrible civil war was raging in
Spain. Another war was raging in China. War. I had always said so:
Modern man had learned nothing from the great World War.
Never before had so much money and human effort been spent on
armaments and further progress in ingenious means of slaughter.
The spectacular progress of the modern world had not reached an
inch below the human skin. It was abusing the theory of evolution
to make ourselves believe that the brain of a man behind a type-
writer had advanced beyond that of a man behind a wooden plow
or a fishing line. It was just as absurd to fool ourselves that a man
behind a machine gun had higher ethical standards than one behind a sling or a spear. I was convinced that a second world war
was bound to occur, because modern man had learned nothing
from the first. The architects of peace were still building with gun-
powder. Perhaps the outside world was in flames right now.
Teriieroo had told us that years had passed before the news of
the Great War had reached the Marquesas. At Tahiti, Papeete's
wooden houses had been shot to pieces by a German battleship. But
nobody had brought that news to Fatu-Hiva. It was probable that
a second world war was raging at this moment.

When the third month had passed and no copra schooner had
been sighted by those who kept a constant lookout, conditions for
the village population became intolerable, and more so for Father
Victorin, who wanted to get away from the island at any cost.

The distance from Fatu-Hiva to the next island was about one
hundred kilometers, about the same as from Italy to Corsica. Not
even the biggest dugout canoe on the island was considered safe
for the trip.

The largest vessel on Fatu-Hiva was an old, discarded lifeboat once obtained by Willy for loading sacks of copra aboard schooners that anchored in the bay. It now lay cracked and weather-beaten under some palm leaves down by the sea. Willy had dismissed it as useless and had for some time been looking for another. On instructions from Father Victorin, a few of the natives dragged it out from the palm leaves and began patching up the hull by replacing the rottenest parts with new bits of wood. The shabby little craft was pulled out into the bay and left afloat, tied to a stone anchor, to let the planks swell. A few slender trees were felled near the village, and from these the men made a mast and rigging that seemed fit for a vessel far bigger than a little, open lifeboat.

On Fatu-Hiva, no other land could be seen from sea level. But on clear days in the high mountains the hazy blue outlines of rugged mountains could be made out at two points far to the north. These were the lofty peaks of Tahuata and Hivaoa, the nearest islands. In the prevailing, cloudy weather, they could not be seen at all, even from our highest peaks. This was the worst season, and the dark sea was as angry as a shoal of fighting sharks; its whitecaps flashed in endless rows like greedily snapping teeth. But the strong east wind had veered and was blowing from a more southeasterly direction, favorable for a north-bound trip, toward Tahuata or Hivaoa.

At last, on a morning that was as cheerless as all the rest, Father Victorin made his decision. With a chosen team of native rowers, he was conveyed by canoe to the anchored lifeboat, and a few moments later we all saw the fragile craft heading into the boundless ocean. The black figure of the little Frenchman sat motionless amid his crew. We had to admire his courage. The frail boat rose and fell on the huge swells and shot ahead as soon as the big sail was hoisted. Sail and all else were swallowed up completely at intervals by mighty jaws of water, and we held our breath in fear that the departing group would never emerge again. But, a moment later, they would ride high on top of the next towering swell. They emerged and vanished and showed up again, until the white sail became a tiny speck that was lost from sight entirely. We shivered. This could never end well.

Exciting days were to follow. Little Father Victorin with the big legs was to be landed on Hivaoa, the main island in the southern part of the Marquesas group. His Fatu-Hiva crew would come back to the Omoa village with rice, flour, and sugar. For a full week, expectation and excitement dominated the feelings in the village. We were greeted as before, and Pakeekee and Tioti were seen chatting with the others while sitting on the boulder beach watching the horizon. Then a lookout signaled that the lifeboat was in sight.

On the verge of complete exhaustion, the men and their open boat were washed ashore by the roaring surf. They had rowed back across the sea. The mast was broken and gone. A bottom plank had been smashed in and all the rowers had bailed for their lives while the hole was patched. The father had been set safely ashore in Hivaoa, but a tiny sack of soaking-wet flour was all they had managed to rescue from the billows. Dripping with sea water, each man staggered to his own hut, and none of them opened an eye for twenty-four hours.

For all of us, now, conditions grew even worse. No schooner arrived. The radio operator on Hivaoa had said that there was no world war, only copra speculation.

The natives ran out of their fermented *poipoi;* the stinking pits were empty, and even Tioti complained that he could not digest fish or pork without rice or flour, in spite of the fact that his ancestors had never known any form of cereal, but had been accustomed to eating *poipoi* with everything.

Now that the natives were more friendly, we came down for sea food and began to feel less fearful of disease here than at our inland, jungle home. In the village area down by the beach, there was a constant sea breeze, which drove away most of the mosquitoes. But the beach water was obviously filled with invisible germs from the polluted outlet of the river. The slightest scratch even of the very surface of skin of our feet resulted in ugly, *fe-fe* wounds. Our own feet horrified the apparently more resistant natives, although the woman with the completely raw foot was even worse off than ourselves.

On advice from Willy, Liv and I began to strip the newly healed skin from our feet. This was because our wounds were not healing from around the edges, but were forming an island of skin at the center of the wound, and as this island grew, the raw ring around it widened correspondingly. Thus, increasingly wide hoops of raw flesh threatened to flay our limbs completely, like the foot of the poor village woman.

After his futile visit to the Chinese in Hanavave, Willy was conspicuously interested in resuming our earlier chats about Paul Gauguin. Willy's Swiss father, Grelet, had had no other friend in the Marquesas group. Although Gauguin had lived and died in the distant bay of Hivaoa, where Father Victorin had just been

landed, they had been in contact whenever possible, and Paul
Gauguin had more than once come with the schooner to stay for a
while in the little bungalow inherited by Willy.

Was it true that Paul Gauguin was so very famous in Europe
and America? I could tell Willy that anything left by Gauguin had
a great commercial value. Not only paintings, but letters. Anything.
In Tahiti, we had heard of an American visitor who had bought
an old window, because a local informant had told him that Gauguin
had crawled through it once when he was drunk.

Willy wanted to know more. Prices for Gauguin's possessions?
Enormous, I said. And not knowing what I was speaking about,
I made it abundantly clear that any identifiable Gauguin property
was worth a real fortune. Priceless. I added that I had met both
Gauguin's sons, the Tahitian one as well as the European one.
Gauguin's Tahitian son was a tourist attraction. His Danish-born
son, Pola Gauguin, was a noted art critic in Norway. He had called
on me, when he learned that I was going to the Marquesas, to ask
me to search for anything concerning his father. He was particularly
interested in verifying or disposing of recent rumors indicating
that his father had been poisoned by the islanders. Willy could
only confirm what I had already heard from an old native eyewitness
on Hivaoa: Paul Gauguin died while falling backward off his chair
during a meal, but he was not poisoned. He was afflicted by a
terrible disease.

On the day following this discussion, Willy was gone. Gone for
two days. Then he showed up again, coming by canoe from Hanavave. He had been back visiting the Chinese, and although that
shop was as stripped of food as his own, in Omoa, Grelet came
back with an acquisition: an old gun—an old and rusty Winchester
rifle. I was no expert on guns and did not understand Willy's
triumphant mien until he turned the wooden, butt end toward me.
It was hand-carved in low relief the whole length of the left side.
It showed a big man with a raised beaker, seated riding backward
on a little chariot drawn by what looked like oxen. Over and around
the figures were undulating scrolls suggesting clouds. A deity in a
heavenly cart? None of us could tell. Only Paul Gauguin could
have explained. For the gun had been his, and the smoothly worn
relief was one of his extremely rare wood carvings.

While still alive, Paul Gauguin had presented his favorite gun to
Willy's father. When old Grelet died, the gun was bought by a
local native, who sold it to the Chinese in Hanavave. He had still

been using this old rifle for goat hunting until a couple of days before. After his conversation with me, Willy had paddled to Han-avave and for a trifle had bought the gun back. Now he told me he was planning to go to Tahiti by the next schooner, to sell his precious booty there.

I was neither an art dealer nor a collector, but I was fascinated by this old, decorated gun from the very moment I saw it.

"I shall save you the trip to Tahiti," I said tentatively. "How much do you want for it?"

"Lots of francs," said Willy. "You told me yourself that Gauguin's possessions were worth a real fortune."

I could not go back on my own words. This was ridiculous. I offered ten times the price Willy had paid some hours before. Willy shook his head. I offered a hundred times the price he had paid to the Chinese. Willy hesitated. A fortune was evidently smaller on Fatu-Hiva than in most places.

"Liv," I said, marching up the jungle trail like a proud soldier with Gauguin's gun on my shoulder, "we shall no longer be able to return to Europe first class, but we shall travel with the world's most precious goat-hunting gun."

One day, we were sitting with a little group on the stone ledge around the huge banyan tree down by the beach. Still no boat. With Willy, I was making a decision. We had no choice. The naked flesh in Liv's wounds had begun to emerge from her legs like a stump of speckled salami. She was able to take it calmly, but not I. We had come to a dead end. We had to take the same trip as Father Victorin, away from the island. Willy and several other men from the village were planning to try another voyage in an attempt to bring back rice and flour, and we decided to go with them.

The bamboo cabin was abandoned. We would have to return somehow for all our zoological and archaeological treasures, but how, we could not tell. Meanwhile, we were worried that they might be stolen. Our bottles of bugs, the skulls, and the large collection of stone adzes and other ancient tools would hardly interest anyone. But we had obtained things that every native knew to be of high commercial value: a king's crown of white conch and brown turtle shell carved as rows of squatting *tiki;* a priceless royal costume of black human hair knotted together with thread made from the fibers of coconut husks; hollow sections of human thigh-bones carved into little figures to be threaded on as hair ornaments; earplugs carved from human bone, as groups of small single- and double-headed *tiki;* and now even a European gun, the dream of every islander.

I decided to try my luck as a medicine man. Some of the less trustworthy youngsters from the village followed us as we went on our last visit to the cabin. I opened a jar of formaldehyde, used for the preservation of zoological specimens. In turn, the young men sniffed eagerly at the bottle, then, with burning nostrils, began to leap about, grimacing and sniffing. I turned over a number of big stones until I found one of the large banana-colored centipedes of the poisonous kind that would crawl about even if cut into a dozen segments. If dropped into water it would wriggle about like an eel. I dropped it into a jar of formaldehyde, and the eyes of the spectators grew big as they saw the creature stiff and dead in a moment. Now I splashed some of the liquid upon the bamboo floor and jumped out, shutting the door with a bang, bolting it with poles and cord. In a moment, the deadly vapor would fill the room, we explained, and until we came back with a neutralizing liquid, no one could enter without suffering the fate of the centipede. The four hitherto hopeful visitors stared at the closed cabin with a mixture of disappointment and awe, and hurriedly followed us as we left, pursued by a cloud of mosquitoes. But I did not dare to leave the gun behind. We took it with us, together with a copper casket containing our camera and a bag holding the few garments we had hidden in reserve for possible departure.

That night, we slept in Willy's house. There was no swarm of mosquitoes dancing to get at us. We had almost forgotten that quiet nights existed. It felt as if we had spent all our lives up in the Omoa jungle.

It was still dark when we were awakened by dogs barking and saw the lights from lanterns coming from the forest. Noisy groups of strong men gathered outside the door. Everything had to be prepared for an early departure. They all gazed at the weather. The clouds sailed wildly across the night sky. Surely the sea was rough out there. Better to wait and see.

It was cold at that hour of the night. Willy put a kettle on the wood fire. Orange tea warmed our sleepy bodies. We felt more awake. It was strange to sit among former antagonists. Neither Tioti nor Pakeekee was there, but Ioane was sipping his tea from a bowl and throwing quick side glances at the weather. There was a light drizzle.

The rumble of the surf seemed particularly sinister that night. It had never before affected us like that. We shivered from drowsy chill and suppressed fear. One or two of the men tried joking, with chattering teeth. The rest remained silent.

It seemed to get slightly lighter, as if dawn were on its way, the very first indication that the black night was loosening its grip. Willy rose and gave an abrupt order: "*Hamai!* [come!]"

This was it! We were about to embark on a lunatic sea voyage. There was nothing I dreaded more than another confrontation with the sea. But it would be still worse to remain behind. With fresh banana leaves wrapped around our legs, we staggered after the others, waddling down to the boulder beach, where there was no more time to think: Our ears and minds were filled with nothing but the rumbling, thundering surf on slippery boulders.

Experienced paddlers took us out by canoe to the dancing lifeboat, which was anchored at a safe distance from the rocks. Then the canoe returned to bring the second group through the witch's caldron. As the canoe came out for the third, and last, time, one person remained on the beach, wildly and angrily waving his arms: the Chinese, who had come from Hanavave and also wanted to escape. But there was no more room, and the poor chap had even brought with him a large pig and a flock of live chickens which he wanted to take on board. Our last picture of Omoa was the tragicomic Chinese standing on the beach with his pig and his fowls, desperately waving to be picked up. But the lifeboat was already loaded far more than made sense. There was frighteningly little of it above the water, and we were still only in the bay, where the long swells rolled in smoothly until they stood on end above the shallows. The scanty freeboard would have made the enterprise seem quite crazy but for the fact that our brown companions had made the voyage before.

Quantities of *fei* and bananas lay stacked up under the thwarts, on which the crew doubled up in pairs, and a barrel of water was stored in the bow together with green coconuts. If all went well, with such a wind the voyage would be accomplished in a single day. But we had neither compass nor chart to give us a course. We could only steer into the empty ocean in the general direction of the other islands, and stick to one course until the summits of Hivaoa rose above the sea. If we ran into fog, we had no chance unless the weather cleared before we drifted away from the whole island group.

Fully laden, the old lifeboat rolled perilously in the swells. The Polynesian crew took a last look at the weather. The strong southeast trade wind was at our backs.

We were thirteen. Old Ioane was the captain and sat high astern with an oar serving as a rudder. At his feet, in the bottom of the canoe, lay Willy, Liv, and I, leaning against a pile of shabby suitcases and sacks. In pairs on the four thwarts in front of us sat eight rowers waiting, the eight best from the village. With deeply marked, almost brutal faces, which seemed to defy any kind of weather, and with muscles rippling under their coconut-oiled skins, they sat ready. One man was in reserve, with a big, wooden bailer. A hammer and some rusty nails lay ready beside him, in case a plank should come loose when the waves struck the bottom.

Ioane sat waiting impatiently, dressed as usual in a straw hat, white shorts, and singlet. He looked as if chiseled from stone, as with wrinkled face he grinned toward the drifting clouds and studied the course of the rolling waves.

Then all was ready. Ioane rose to his feet and uncovered his head as he crossed himself first at his forehead and then at his chest. Tough and serious, the rest sat with bent heads while, in the Polynesian tongue, Ioane slowly said the sailors' prayer. As he finished, everybody crossed himself and the ceremony was over.

It was as if a thunderstorm had suddenly hit the little craft. Ioane swung his arms and shouted his orders. The others leaped from the thwarts, yelled and bawled; the stone anchor was hauled on board and the huge sail was hoisted with terrific hullabaloo, while the whole vessel threatened to capsize. All aboard went completely wild. Even the taciturn Willy began shouting and giving orders.

Like a bird on the wing, we shot across the waves. The natives beamed excitedly and shouted like savages as the large Polynesian sail was properly lashed and caught the wind fully. This was the life of their ancestors, something that made the blood rise in this drowsy, sleepy, modern tribe. They cheered and rejoiced while Ioane sat grinning, hunched over the steering oar, his unshaven face bristling and beaming with the joy of living.

This was fast going, and for two tired jungle dwellers, too, something to make the blood course through the veins. But if only the entire trip could be passed in the shelter of Fatu-Hiva! For we knew that we were soon to find ourselves in wilder surroundings: The waves would rise high as soon as we left the lee of the island.

As the lofty island slid astern and was left behind us like a rock, jagged and wild, we were to get familiar with the ocean at the closest range. Foaming, towering waves rose on end above us. In a moment, we were whipped up to the top, the lukewarm sea drenching our bodies and slapping salt spray against our faces until we could hardly see for the burn of salt and sun. No sooner was the frail boat at the top than we looked down into another green and glassy valley, followed by another white and hissing crest. And then we were suddenly once more deep down, looking up again in awe at the water fumbling high above. This was sea wild enough to toss about a vessel much larger than ours. We had no idea that at this very moment the *Tereora* was pitching north-ward in the same waters. The schooner was badly battered by the seas, which crashed over the whole vessel, bursting through the galley door and causing havoc and destruction below. But our little Fatu-Hiva vessel with the large sail had more room in the dancing, watery valleys. We shot up onto the wave crests and rode the heaving mountains in a dizzy race.

At the steering oar, Ioane was incredible: Crouching and grin-ning, he was on the alert for every chasing comber that threatened us, and he rode it off. If it burst and sent the breaking surf crashing into the whole vessel, he clung to his steering oar with almost diabolical determination, and not for a moment did he let his attention wander from the next wave that rose up in pursuit. While sea water streamed down his face and salt burned his eyes, he clung tightly to his oar and was on his guard. He was a truly magnificent captain.

Two of the younger men soon lay huddled in the water at the bottom of the boat while the others growled ironically and made jokes about their seasick companions. Drenched in sea water and with the banana-leaf bandages long since washed overboard, Liv began to look terrible, her legs swollen as if from elephantiasis. Raw flesh was literally bursting from her wounds. At the height of the day, she passed out and lay lifeless against our bag, while I held her tight each time a sea broke over us.

Several times, the boat was almost filled with gushing water, and it was as if we were sinking into the sea. But soon it rose once more, the bundles of bananas floating in sea water, while all the rowers bailed for their lives. The excitement was hectic, without a moment of repose. Time and again, I abandoned all hope as we raced along the wall of a breaking swell that rose on end and tumbled down upon us in massive cascades of water before we managed to sail clear, or when we raced crazily over a tall crest and took a leap down into the valley so hard that the planks creaked and columns of water tumbled away on all sides. I was also increasingly worried about Liv, who lay against my legs with her eyes closed, not even reacting when heavy cascades of water pounded over us.

I was still a sworn landlubber, but I began to digest a few lessons from the sea. This was my second experience in a small craft on the open ocean. The first had been in Tioti's dugout canoe. I began to wonder why the ancient boatbuilders had stopped building buoyant log rafts and begun to produce sinkable canoes instead and boats with frail, planked hulls. In this lifeboat, as in the canoe, we were struggling for our lives, bailing all the time. I was clinging continuously to the hope that there was some invisible power behind the wonders of nature that could respond to my intense desire for help and mercy. How stupid to make a boat of thin planks, no more than a receptacle for the breaking seas. Early people floated on rafts, and any water that entered ran out by itself. I wished we had been sitting on a raft. A raft would obviously have been quite safe between these same waves. But man long ago changed marine architecture, preferring precious speed to security.

Our speed was breath-taking, but our lives were at stake. For a long, long while, we saw no land in any direction, even when we rode over the highest crests. Fatu-Hiva, with its lofty mountains, had vanished, but Ioane steered on as confidently as if he had a compass.

Not for a moment did it occur to me that we had run into an exceptionally rough sea. I was greatly impressed by the height of the waves around us, but I thought that any ocean wave would look as scaring when seen from a tiny vessel like ours. Not until we heard of the seaworthy trading schooner *Tereora*'s troubles in the same area did I understand that there was something exceptional about the seas we rode. Not knowing this yet, one thing was clear to me: It was thanks to its small size that our open lifeboat kept afloat. There was room for the whole vessel between the waves; if it were a little longer, it would have stretched from one wave to the next, either the bow or the stern cutting into the walls of water around us. It was a landlubber's misconception that the perils at sea are greater the smaller the vessel.

I cannot remember how the hours passed. All I can recall is that a truly burning sun dazzled our eyes and struck our skins like hot sparks between the cold and heavy cloudbursts. The copper-colored backs in front of us turned almost as dark as those of Negroes during the trip, whereas the salt spray and radiation from the sun and the gleaming waves made our own skin rise in blisters. Our

flowing hair was our only protection from sunstroke. I recall the
puffing of a shoal of glittering black porpoises that emerged on all
sides, dancing about us in a wave trough; then we were all lifted
up by a mountain of water and parted company in the confusion
of waves as we ourselves raced on in a wilderness of water.

Farther and farther we sailed. By now, it must have been late
afternoon. The distance we had covered had been increased by
sailing up and down and by zigzagging between the waves. Half
asleep, I heard a shout from Ioane: "Motane!" Motane was a small,
uninhabited island to the north. Ioane altered course, for we had to
pass to the west of it.

New life seemed to have been injected into the brown backs.
The men on the thwarts, too, were sitting half drowsing, guarding
the long boom of the sail to prevent it from breaking in collision
with tumbling waves. There seemed to be more things happening
now. To the far north, we kept seeing the dark table mountain of
Motane rising like a whale's back whenever we traveled across a
high swell. We climbed and we leaped and we skirted alongside
the wave walls just as before, but now at least there was something
in sight. Only Liv did not open her eyes.

After a while, the contours of Tahuata Island rose indistinctly
from the sea to the left of Motane, with haze obscuring what
seemed to be patches of jungle or green valleys running up the blue
mountainsides. This inhabited island froze to a sort of mirage that
seemed never to come nearer. There was a long way left to go, for
although not quite as high as those of Fatu-Hiva, the mountains of
Tahuata rose to more than three thousand feet above sea level
and could be sighted from afar.

Like a thin veil, Hivaoa at long last emerged to the far north,
outlined as a long and grayish-green ridge between the other two
islands, but much farther behind. I shouted to Liv that we could
see our destination, but she heard nothing.

The day went on. The most dangerous stretch of water now lay
before us. Our traveling companions all knew that a strong ocean
current forced its way through the narrow passage between Tahuata
and Hivaoa. The wide Humboldt Current was forced at increased
speed into a sort of huge funnel as the first land masses since South
America impeded its westward drift, and a mad reflex of waves
and rushing water chased up angry billows far out in the ocean at
each end of the channel.

We had to cross this area to reach our destination. Willy was
admittedly afraid to venture into the treacherous belt in the existing

weather conditions, and was deliberating with Ioane, but they could find no alternative. The best Ioane could do to reach Hivaoa was to hold as far to the east of the channel as possible. The sea would be worse the closer we kept to the coasts of Tahuata. This was my second lesson from the sea. I had always heard from anthropologists that primitive people could travel at sea only by hugging the coasts of continents and islands. Experience showed me that no-where is the danger of ocean navigation in a small boat less than at the farthest possible distance from any treacherous coast.

We darted at full speed into the marine wilderness swept up by the confused current. Ioane sat crouching astern with all senses and muscles alert, like a puma ready to spring. Everything now depended on him.

Far ahead, to the left, was the long headland leading in to the largest valley on Hivaoa: Atuona. This was a sort of capital, at least for the southern islands in the Marquesas group, the only competitor being the Taiohae Valley, on Nuku-Hiva, to the far north. We knew that some two or three hundred Polynesians lived in Atuona Valley. And the French governor had at one time lived here, for this was the place where the statues of Tukopana and his daughter had disappeared. We also knew that this same valley, which now opened up indistinctly behind the headland, had been the final home of Paul Gauguin. His tomb was on a hillock in there somewhere. I sat in the dancing lifeboat with his gun. We began to be tossed about so wildly that I tied our few possessions to a thwart for fear that we would lose them, should the boat turn keel upper-most.

Black clouds and dark cliffs covered the evening sun as we came abreast of the headland leading into Atuona Bay. Exposed to the ceaseless east wind, the cliffs blocked the freedom of the high rollers we rode, and a continuous belt of white cascades and geysers was flung skyward along the steep rock face.

Drenched, exhausted from bailing, and stiff from salt and sun-burn, we came through the area of mountainous seas and prepared ourselves for a hazardous landing. The swells still rose high as we turned in close to the rocky shore, and the hoarse commands from many voices mixed with the thunder of the surf as the sail and mast were lowered.

The black sandy beach of Atuona lay in front of us; we had reached the journey's end—almost. Yet none of us felt the slightest relief, as we could see and hear the inferno that separated us from land. Wind and waves came straight in from the agitated ocean

to the unsheltered beach. This time, we were not to land on the
leeward side of an island, as we had on Fatu-Hiva. Four thousand
uninterrupted miles had brought the surf in front of us from the
Pacific coast of South America to this island.

The eight strong rowers shoved their oars into the rowlocks and
Ioane set the course straight for the center of the long beach. The
sandy bay was incredibly shallow for hundreds of yards in front of
the beach. Row upon row of towering breakers raised themselves on
end with irresistible force, and although we saw only the long
sequences of sloping wave backs, we could clearly visualize the
glass walls of water as high as houses that fumbled and tumbled
in across the shallows toward the land. The white streamers and
the roar of the water left us in no doubt. And on this day the surf
went beyond the sandy beach, flooding the green meadow at the
foot of the coconut palms. There was still light enough to see a
group of natives gathering as if to watch the mighty display of
nature's forces.

Liv was fully conscious now, but she watched the surf in front
of us with tired indifference, as if it did not concern us. All the
men were seated with oars ready, waiting for the slightest com-
mand from Ioane. The two who had suffered from seasickness
were sharing one oar in this last effort. Time and again, we rowed
slowly toward the edge of the surf area, but some disturbing wave
then rose behind us and the rowers backed the oars as fast as they
could, while the rising crest tipped the stern into the air like the
tail of a sea bird. Then we ventured forward once more.

Ioane sat grimacing like an angry devil and yelled his orders until
his voice cracked. He was watching every oar. Crouching almost
double, he seemed to be alight with fight and fury. At this moment,
we all looked to him as the leader with dictatorial rights. His brain
served for all.

The right wave came and caught us from behind just as Ioane
shouted, "Row, row, row, row!" as if in ecstasy.

Creaking oars rumbled in the rowlocks: the dark men rowed
desperately, clenching hands and teeth, eyes sparkling with excitement.

As if we were all on one surfboard, we were carried by the
racing, fumbling wall of water all the way in across the shallow
area with rows of breakers thundering in front and other rows
rising one after the other behind us. We were in the middle of an
inferno. We grabbed the gunwale with cramped fingers, clinging to
the unsteady boat. Then the grip of the two young men with the

same oar slipped. Ioane raved like a madman, and in two bounds Willy passed over us and grabbed the loose oar, while the two men sprawled on their backs on top of the fruit.

But it was too late. The lifeboat turned sideways and Ioane had not the slightest chance of taking hold of the chasing wave with his steering oar. The crew tossed away the oars and, like acrobats, they sprang onto the gunwales. Then they all threw themselves overboard and disappeared into the sea.

I grabbed hold of Liv, and together with Willy, we jumped away as the boat rose on end and turned bottom up.

It was due to no effort of my own that I rotated, helpless as a starfish, in whirling water until I realized the sea itself had delivered me seated next to Liv in shallow water. A pursuing glass wall was on its way in to get us, and we felt the suction as the backwash came like a river, pulling us seaward. But, clutching hands, we fought our way up onto the foaming beach and the safe grass beyond.

In the wild surf we noticed all our traveling companions clinging like ants to the dancing lifeboat, which had rolled over time and again in the surf. They did not want to lose it, at any cost, and while boat and men completely and repeatedly disappeared in the frothing water, not one of them let go. More under the water than above it, they came swimming ashore with sacks and suitcases. Finally the boat, filled to the brim with water flowing in and out, was tilted up and pulled out of the ocean. To put it beyond further risk, the old and battered lifeboat was carried up onto the turf and well inland between the palms.

The oars, the fruit, some straw hats, and other trifles were politely delivered by the sea and saved.

We had landed on Hivaoa.

7. ON HIVAOA

Moist grass without wheel tracks covered the wide trail that led straight inland from the coal-black sand of the beach. We felt as if we were walking out of our own coffin onto a soft temple carpet stretched down a lofty colonnade of coconut palms. Once more, we were back to life, and we were filled with peace and gratitude.

It seemed as if we walked straight through the temple and out through the open back wall, where the only building in sight was the little shack of the wireless operator. Beside it was a well-trodden clearing with linteled posts at each end, obviously a football field. We were clearly back to civilization.

A step away from nature was also reflected in the attitude of the handful of natives who stood calmly between the palms, watching our landing. Slightly indifferent to our unconventional arrival, they stood with their bare feet planted in the grass, their straw hats carelessly tilted at an angle, and cigarettes dangling from the corners of their mouths.

This was Hivaoa. Atuona Valley, on Hivaoa. Obviously the main port of call for the occasional yacht that cruised through this remote part of the Pacific. Even here, however, the number of calls were very few, for the Marquesas group lay beyond the shipping lanes, and globe-trotting yachts were discouraged by the lack of a harbor and the need of government permission to stay for more than twenty-four hours. But more frequent than elsewhere were the calls of trading schooners from Tahiti; they anchored in a rocky inlet behind a high promontory east of this sandy lava beach.

Indeed, we were not the first foreign visitors to this bay, although we might have been the first white couple to arrive upside down. The little group that watched our landing studied Liv and me with the eyes of experts. They knew the white breed of mankind, and divided them categorically into three species: uniformed personnel, whom they admired; tourists, whom they laughed at; and copra workers, whom they despised.

To them, a uniform meant power and authority. Inside it was a man who made laws and could send people to prison in Tahiti.

A tourist, on the other hand, was respected only for his wealth, as he was a crazy fool. He spent his life moving about from one place to the next, spending money. He was a Christian, but would offer his shirt and any sum of money to get a heathen image, and the worse it appeared, the more he would pay for it. So, to get a better price, the island wood carvers left their fine new products in a river until they looked old and shabby. A tourist was ignorant; nobody could pose more stupid questions. He did not know when the rainy season would start, he did not know how to make *poipoi*, and he could not see the difference between *fei* and banana. When he came to look around, he walked straight past the fine new village houses and stopped instead to gaze at barren rocks and sheer wilderness, saying that this was beautiful. Some tourists even wrapped *pareus* around their waists and wanted to dance *hula*, for their ideas of progress were entirely deranged.

But a tourist was at least a millionaire, while the worst of all foreigners was the copra worker. He, too, was a white man, but he was as poor as any islander. He had more brains than the tourist and did not ask all those silly questions. He could even climb a coconut palm and take as much rum as any drunken islander. But he was out to gain and not to give. Tourists and government officials also treated him with scant respect; they did not accept him on quite the same level as themselves, and he must therefore belong to an inferior kind.

As we staggered up the grassy trail, scorched by the sun and drenched by the sea, with our legs in a miserable condition and with no other property than a rusty gun and a shabby, water-dripping bag, there was no doubt in the minds of the spectators: We belonged to the third category.

This is surely how we were classified by the French *gendarme*, Monsieur Triffe, too, when we lined up behind Willy and Ioane as they knocked on the door of the village *gendarmerie*. We remembered what Captain Brander had told us. Very few white people remained in the Marquesas group. Except for two on Nuku-Hiva, they all lived here on Hivaoa: the *gendarme*, Triffe; the wireless operator, Belvas; "Mister Bob," who ran the local store; and a

Catholic mission with priests and two nuns. There were also a
Chinese with his large family; and two white men lived on the
other side of the island. One of them was the Norwegian copra
planter Henry Lie. Captain Brander had warned us that any
white man who had spent a generation ashore among these islanders
would become like them: He would "go native" mentally.

The thin white man who opened the door of the *gendarmerie*
glanced at us apathetically over Willy's shoulder. Keeping his tropical helmet on his head and his right hand in his trouser pocket, he
stretched out his left hand to Liv. Then he turned his back on us
and invited Ioane and Willy into his home, in case they had no
other place to sleep. He did not give us a second look. Well, we
were certainly not dressed for a royal ball.

We left.

Atuona village consisted of a few scattered plank houses and
abandoned government bungalows, and was considered a major city
by the island population. For those who had never seen Tahiti,
this was the apex of beauty, a real foretaste of heaven. There was
not one old-fashioned hut. Every house was built of planks painted
gray and corrugated iron.

A hard-beaten track led from Triffe's *gendarmerie* down through
the core of the village. Farther along this main village road, we
found the double-decker house of Mister Bob, with the village
store at ground level and his residence above. Mister Bob, pronounced Popé by local tongues, was not known by any other name.
Stout and ruddy, he stood smiling in the doorway, with his feet in
carpet slippers, wide apart, and his arms folded. Thin, hairy legs
emerged from his blue shorts, and thick, tattooed arms from his
white singlet. A big blue anchor on his right arm was in keeping
with the rest of the figure: a delightful version of a once marooned
British sailor.

But there was no lodging and no shelter to be had under his
roof. We were told that two photographers had come to visit the island, and the house was full.

Mister Bob turned around and shuffled into his house with a
casual remark about the bad weather. Actually it was starting to
rain again and it was getting very dark.

Gradually it dawned upon us that something was not quite right.
It was not proper to come to Hivaoa barefoot and looking like white
savages. We were in the suburbs of our own world, a world that
was fighting for progress from nature. We insulted the local white
people by coming here disheveled and unshaven, as if we thought

we were outside the boundary of Western civilization. We hurt their pride and their desire to be part of the modern world rather than outcasts in the wilderness.

While we were standing in the dark outside Bob's closed door, we heard Willy's voice. Unlike Ioane, he had not accepted Triffe's invitation, because he was heading for the home of Atuona's chief, a close relative of Willy's Polynesian mother. Behind him came the whole crew of the lifeboat. As when they brought Father Victorin across, they were going to sleep in the Catholic mission. Lucky men. Reluctantly, we called to mind what Pakeekee had told us: On arrival, we should ask for the trail leading to the house of the native parson, telling him we were Protestants. Hesitantly, we followed Pakeekee's advice.

Far over, on the other side of the valley, lay what seemed to be a dark and dirty barrack. It was larger than most of the native huts, but equally gloomy. It was night as we fumbled our way to the door. These were the Protestant quarters. Anyone who cared to share in the faith of the Protestant parson was welcome to stay in his lodging. And here lived the most peculiar collection of local characters—Polynesians and individuals clearly of mixed blood.

A smiling, brown parson, wearing nothing but a black dinner jacket over a rosy-red loincloth, came padding out barefoot in the mud and bade us welcome to his congregation. I can only recall a shrill choir singing psalms as Liv and I collapsed into a deep sleep on a mattress left by somebody else.

When we opened our eyes, the sun was shining. It shone through a broken glass window high up in the wall. The rays fell on heaps of red coffee berries laid out to dry on the dusty floor of the big room. We were alone in the room, but coughing interrupted by groans and loud lamentations from an adjoining room gave us the creeps.

Liv bit her lip. We could not remain here.

We opened our waterproof bag and splashed out the contents. Everything was drenched. Our finest city garments were salty and heavy with sticky sea water. Nevertheless, we pulled on our fine clothes and hurried out into the hot sun.

As the two of us limped in a sort of mannequin parade down the village trail, we felt promoted: she on high heels below a crimson silk dress, I in a dark suit, with a hat, a tie, and black shoes. We were creased and crumpled, but that did not matter: we had suddenly turned into tourists for all the spectators.

Inside the little village shop, we detected Bob busy with a group of island customers. He was selling hair lotion, strawberry jam, and caps with lacquered vizors. A corpulent *vahine* was just buying a length of elastic; Bob stretched it as much as possible along his wooden yardstick, then he cut it off and gave his gaping customer the shriveled lump.

"Mister Bob," I said. "We need some provisions."

Now Bob's eyes nearly popped out of his head when he saw us.

"Yes, Mister," he replied with a little bow.

"Do you have any more strawberry jam?" I asked, as the other customers grabbed their two jars.

"Yes, Mister, how many jars do you want?"

"I'll take all you have. And all your corned beef, too," I added hungrily after a quick look at the poorly stocked shelves.

"Are you crazy?" whispered Liv in despair as she saw Bob coming with one armful after the other of cans and jars.

"Be quiet," I whispered. "We've got to show off."

"This is all I have," Bob mumbled in deep respect as he began to pile a tower of comestibles on the counter.

"Don't you have any sweets?" I asked.

"Candy and chocolate," he answered as he wiped his forehead, his eyes sparkling with respect.

"We'll take the lot. Do you have any tobacco?"

"What kind do you smoke?"

"I don't smoke. It is to give away."

The shop was gradually filling with islanders, who looked upon us as celebrities. We felt like a Rothschild in a country store.

"Some hair tonic from Tahiti?"

"Of course. All of it."

When I figured we had won the battle, I pulled out my largest traveler's check and signed it with Bob's pen.

"There is no hurry, there is no hurry," Bob said, and snatched the check happily from between my fingers.

Turning toward the door, I told Bob with a loud voice that we wanted the goods delivered later. Where to deliver them remained as much a riddle to us as to Bob, but this we did not tell him. Two things were fixed in my mind: We had to find someone to attend to our legs, and we had to sit down somewhere and eat the cans of corned beef I had tucked into my pockets.

On the road in front of the door, we ran into Bob's two lodgers. They were French. He was thin and timid, wore bracelets of boars' tusks, and had cameras hanging all around him; she was tiny and cute, as energetic as a little lioness, and had bushy, red hair.

It was like stumbling into an oasis in the desert. Our friendship was spontaneous. Madame Renée Hamon was a French journalist and had come to the island with her photographer only the day before, a few hours before we did. The trading schooner *Tereora*, which had brought them from Tahiti, was still riding at anchor behind the promontory on the other side of the beach.

Madame Hamon was a lively person of the type who can manage everything. She became like a barrel of high explosive when she caught sight of our troubled legs and learned where we had spent the night.

"*C'est une scandale!*" she shouted. "You are in a colony of my country, and tonight you will sleep in a proper bed even if I have to leave my own!"

We learned that these two had been given the whole of the former governor's bungalow, now locked up and abandoned. In Bob's house they only took their meals, and they would leave for Tahiti again by the *Tereora*, as soon as the copra was loaded.

"And from Tahiti we go to France!" exclaimed the slender cameraman happily. "I would trade you a thousand palms for a single pine needle beneath the snow."

We were all heading for the *gendarmerie* when we saw Triffe coming down the road toward us as if he were sleepwalking, surrounded by a swarm of native consorts. Madame Hamon winked at us and rushed toward the poor *gendarme* like a storm cloud; he pulled his hands out of his pockets politely and saluted.

A few moments later, his team of brown attendants was seen lugging along bed frames, mattresses, white sheets, and long brooms to a bungalow next to the one where the two French visitors were staying. Empty, like that of the former governor, this bungalow had once housed an official island doctor. Today the doctor and the governor were combined in one person, but he lived on Nuku-Hiva, far to the north, with little or no access to this southern part of the group.

With our bag and our gun safely stowed in our new bungalow, we staggered as fast as we could to the only bamboo cabin in the valley. This was the island hospital, run by a most winning and cordial young male nurse from Tahiti, named Terai. Terai was one of the rare Tahitians still of pure Polynesian blood, and his countenance, his mighty corporation, and his proud bearing reminded me of a younger version of Teriieroo. When Terai learned that we had been adopted by the chief and given the name Terai Mateata he shook my hand as a namesake. Thus we found another valuable friend on Hivaoa.

Only in his twenties, of medium stature and yet with a massive 250 pounds crammed into his brown skin, the crew-cut Terai was a fervent sportsman and incredibly agile. Born in Tahiti, he had spent some years assisting at the hospital in Papeete, where he must have used his time well. With a mere glance at our troubled legs, he identified our wounds as tropical ulcers. If we had come a couple of weeks later, he said, Liv's infections would have reached her bones and she would have lost a leg by the time he could have arranged her transfer to the hospital on Tahiti. This proved to be the sad price paid by the Omoa woman who had refused to follow Father Victorin or ourselves on the lifeboat crossing to Hivaoa.

Surrounded by a group of islanders suffering from ailments ranging from toothache and venereal problems to the fresh loss of a finger, we took turns to stretch out on a bench while the corpulent Terai selected tools from a box of knives and pincers.

A week later, we could look back on the first visit to Terai's bamboo hospital without feeling pain flashing from head to foot. Terai had used his instruments well. He had cut and poked, he had pulled out toenails to stop infection from reaching the bones, and he had smeared on thick coats of a magnificent yellow-green ointment scooped out of a big pot. We were feeling better already.

Some of the provisions bought from Bob were transferred from our bungalow to that of our yellow friend Chin Loy, the Chinese who ran a tiny restaurant behind a low screen in his own exotic family kitchen. We never saw any other clients, but Chin's whole family kept us company and served us extremely well.

At the end of the week we learned that the *Tereora* was ready to weigh anchor, calling at Fatu-Hiva on its way back to Tahiti. Terai would not permit us to return to our own island, for he insisted that our feet were still in danger unless we continued his cure. We staggered to the rocky cape to get a glimpse of the *Tereora* and to wave to Captain Brander, who never came ashore. Farewell to all our friends. Vivacity and energy seemed to sparkle from the bushy, red head of the little French lady as she shouted a last *au revoir*. Holding the apparatus-loaded photographer by the hand, she jumped from the cliffside into the *Tereora's* dancing lifeboat, both of them falling like drunkards into the waiting arms of experienced brown seamen.

Then the *Tereora* hoisted her canvas and sailed away. On her deck we saw Willy, Ioane, and all our other friends from Fatu-Hiva, well provided with sacks of food. Willy's old lifeboat had

been patched up once more and taken in tow behind the white
schooner. Our thoughts went ahead of them, and for a moment,
once again, we were sitting looking out at the splendid view from
the window of our little bamboo cabin. Then we shook the memories away as we seemed to inhale the scent of bamboo dust and
feel our bodies itching. We returned to Terai's bamboo house to
have our endless yards of bandage changed.

Opposite:

THE PUAMAU VALLEY, ON HIVAOA, with Henry Lie's bungalow and
the little Frenchman's shack. Afflicted by spreading *fe-fe* wounds,
or tropical ulcers, on our legs and feet, we were forced to embark
in a discarded lifeboat and sail into the ocean, out of sight of
land. We landed on Hivaoa, where a Polynesian male nurse cured
our legs and rode with us across the mountains to the lonely
Puamau settlement of the Norwegian planter Henry Lie.

Overleaf left:

TOP LEFT: STONE GIANT IN THE PUAMAU VALLEY. The little Frenchman on top of the statue had access to few of the blessings of
civilization apart from Henry Lie's fine collection of books. They
were both absorbed by the mystery of the origin of the Puamau
giants, since nothing like them was found elsewhere in the Pacific
hemisphere, except on Easter Island, Raivavae, and South America.

TOP RIGHT: STONE GIANT IN SOUTH AMERICA. Our two hosts in the
Puamau Valley gave me the first piece of a puzzle which was
later to occupy my life, when they showed us a book with photo-
graphs of statues of unknown origin in the jungle of San Agustín,
in South America. Did these stone giants, separated by nothing
but an open ocean, have a common origin?

BOTTOM: PRONE STATUE IN SOUTH AMERICA. In San Agustín, together with the standing giants, there were some monuments
representing a creature that was half man and half animal in a
swimming position. They had stunted arms stretched forward
on each side of a wide, grinning mouth.

Overleaf right:

PRONE STATUE IN THE PUAMAU VALLEY. The little Frenchman is
sitting on the outstretched legs of a swimming monster which is
resting on a pedestal that extends from the belly into the ground.
In the entire Pacific hemisphere, there is nothing similar to this
sculpture, which closely follows the prone statues of San Agustín
in all its basic ideas. Had the unidentified artists on this island
come with the winds and currents from South America?

Above:

A HEADLESS GIANT ON A PEDESTAL, found hidden in the under-brush. Like their South American counterparts, these statues had flexed arms, with their hands placed on the belly, and thick, stunted legs supported by pedestals sunk into the ground. In the Marquesas group, stone statues of human size or larger existed only in the Puamau Valley, on the eastern extremity of Hivaoa; and in the Taipi Valley, on the eastern extremity of Nuku-Hiva; in both cases directly facing South America.

Opposite:

LARGE-EYED PUAMAU STONE HEADS were sometimes carved as sepa-rate monuments, a feature also shared with Easter Island and South America.

THE PRONE PUAMAU STATUE lacked its left arm when we first saw it. The arm was found in the soil nearby and fixed on when I came back with my archaeological expedition in 1956 and started excavations.

FACELESS PUAMAU STATUE, unfinished or eroded.

HEADLESS PUAMAU STATUE, damaged by hostile tribes or by mis-sionaries.

Above:

BACK TO FATU-HIVA. Heading first for the Hanavave Valley, the schooner set us ashore in Omoa, where we were determined to resume our interrupted life in the jungle cabin.

Opposite:

HENRY LIE AND FAMILY offered us great hospitality in the Puamau Valley. The unusual observations of this alert settler made me turn from Asia to America in my search for the early oversea routes of the first settlers of Polynesia.

CAPTAIN BRANDER, a white-haired Englishman, and Théodore, his supercargo on board the schooner *Tereora,* were the chief culture-bringers of the Marquesas, introducing civilization in the form of wooden planks, corrugated iron, flour, and refined sugar from Tahiti.

FELLOW PASSENGERS ON THE SCHOONER when we left Hivaoa to return once more to Fatu-Hiva.

PAUL GAUGUIN'S GUN had been given by him to a friend in Fatu-Hiva before he died on Hivaoa. I managed to buy the gun, but the metal part was confiscated by the *gendarme* on Hivaoa, since I had no license to carry arms. I unscrewed the wooden butt, which had been carved by the great painter, and brought it with me to Europe.

By now it must have occurred to Triffe that I had carried a gun when we had knocked at his door. I was duly asked if I had a license to carry arms.

I proudly exhibited the old rifle, showing him that Gauguin had carved the stock. I had bought it as a piece of art; I did not even have a cartridge.

To the *gendarme*, a gun was a gun, old or new, carved by Gauguin or by Rembrandt. I was armed and without a license.

The gun was confiscated. I could get it back if I obtained an arms license from the government headquarters on Tahiti.

With the *Tereora* gone, it would obviously take at least a year to get any kind of license from Tahiti.

Triffe had taken my gun. I had lost my precious souvenir. Then an idea occurred to me. I asked him for a screwdriver, and to his bewilderment I detached the wooden stock from the metal part. Holding the wood carving in one hand and the rusty barrel with the firelock in the other, I asked him which part was the weapon. Triffe did not hesitate, and pointed to the metal mechanism.

"Then you take the weapon and I'll keep the wood," I said, and leaving Triffe speechless, I returned to our bungalow with the carving under my arm.

What I suspected, happened. I never again saw the mechanical part of Gauguin's rifle, despite years of attempted correspondence. Possibly, or even probably, a less able artist than Gauguin has added a new piece of wood to the metal part, and for all I know,

Opposite:

VEO was a fine man, who became one of our best friends on the island.

TAHIA-PITIANI was his wife and the beauty of the island.

"COME AND EAT" was the normal greeting to a passer-by. Not knowing that it was not meant literally, we at first got involved in undesirable meals around family *poipoi* bowls. We later learned that the correct reply to this greeting is, "No, thanks, I'm full."

UMBRELLA LEAVES was the name we gave to the leaves of these plants, which were always handy when it rained.

THE HANAVAVE VILLAGE was the only other community on Fatu-Hiva besides the Omoa village, both of them being clusters of huts near the beach. The interiors of these valleys and all mountain regions were uninhabited.

the old rifle may still take its toll of mountain goats in the Marquesas.

Not much happened during the weeks that followed. We staggered back and forth between Terai's bamboo house and the screened compartment of Chin Loy's exotic kitchen, where we drank in the gentle atmosphere of age-old Chinese culture and ate our fill of every delicacy Chinese master recipes could concoct by combining Bob's tins with the rich products of the island soil.

Due to the great distances and the lack of proper water transport, Terai was never able to visit other islands in the group, but once a month he saddled his horse and rode on an inspection tour to other mountain-girt valleys of his own island. In spite of his corporation, he was a born horseman, and his tiny Marquesan stallion galloped as if it were carrying nothing but a balloon tied to its back.

Terai never walked a step. He kept his horse tied to his bamboo wall when not required, and when he visited the sick, with nothing but a sack for a saddle, he dashed along all the village trails. When the day came to start his monthly expedition around the island, two extra horses with hand-carved wooden saddles were lined up beside his own. With much persuasion, we had got his consent to join him on the trip. Our legs were improving, and in his company we could better continue attending to the wounds.

Long before the sun rose, we started the long climb to some winding mountain ridges that were to take us to the remote Puamau Valley, near the eastern cape of the island. Once more, we felt the surging of happiness at entering virgin wilderness, while we filled our lungs with clean, cool mountain air. Large palm valleys opened below us. Green, jungle-wrapped pyramids of mighty dimensions rose into sight in the island's interior, united by ridges as sharp as horses' necks. The winding trail led up to these inland ridges, because the wild coast permitted no passage. As on Fatu-Hiva, the entire shoreline was eaten away by the ferocious ocean, which had transformed volcanic slopes into vertical walls, leaving only canyons and deep sections of crater valleys to open seaward between the overhanging cliffs. White birds sailed deep below us, outlined against the blue sea and sky, and a menacing white snake, the unbroken surf, wound along the whole coast, marking the boundary between the little island and the vast ocean. Wild cocks crowed in the dark valleys where the sun had not yet risen, and others answered high above in the sunlight. The horses neighed merrily, their unshod hoofs trampling upward and ever upward along the red trail.

Reaching the central crest, we stopped as we suddenly found ourselves on top of everything hands or hoofs could climb. There was nothing more above us. The trade wind tore at our hair and at the manes of the horses, and the beasts reared restlessly. We began to scan the now far more distant horizon for a glimpse of Fatu-Hiva. Tahuata was all wrapped up in thick cloud banks, and others hung at intervals and cast black shadows on the blue ocean. As we were high up, vast expanses of hidden ocean had risen above the former horizon. There, to the south, blurred by haze where the world ended, were the rugged contours of a very little island. Only the upper crests emerged indistinctly above the water; it looked like the unrigged wreck of a burned ship sinking below its own thick cloud of smoke. It was still raining down there on Fatu-Hiva. Fatu-Hiva was far, far away.

The world of Ioane, Tioti, and Pakeekee was so tiny when seen from a distance. With the eyes of the universe, mankind is reduced to microscopic proportions, and our quarrels assume absurd dimensions compared with the invisible trifles we fight about.

"*C'est joli*," said a voice behind me. It was Terai sitting on his rearing stallion and gazing over the valleys below.

"What is beautiful?" I asked, surprised, and looked at my Tahitian companion.

"The mountains, the jungle, all of it. I realize that nature is beautiful."

Terai surprised me. He really did resemble Teriieroo.

"But isn't Papeete the ideal of beauty for all islanders?" I asked.

Terai spurred his horse. "Not for everybody. Some of us understand better. Tahiti was good enough the way our ancestors kept it."

We rode side by side along the wind-swept ridge.

"But don't most Polynesians move to Papeete if they can?"

Terai agreed. It was the tragic fate of his people, he said. All young girls are drawn to Papeete for the white men's wealth. The island boys then follow, to get their share of the amusement.

I did not know it then, but many years later, when I led a scientific expedition back to these same islands, we could not find on Tahiti a single Polynesian of guaranteed pure stock for blood-group studies. Chief Teriieroo was dead and a generation of white immigrants and islanders of mixed origins had inherited the land. We even had the greatest difficulty in finding more than a handful of pure-blooded natives on Hivaoa.

Terai anticipated all this as we rode along the roof of an island world which his own people had once discovered without our help and had kept as a garden home until taught by us the life philosophy of progress.

We reached a beautiful mountain forest, where the horses trotted in a row along a soft, grassy trail. Terai started singing the familiar tune composed by the old Tahitian king: "I am happy, *tiare* flower from Tahiti." The sun flickered between the crowns of the trees and we had to duck to avoid the lianas and low branches that hung across the trail as the horses began to gallop on the soft carpet. Rare birds, some of them splendidly colored, fluttered or ran among the foliage.

Suddenly Terai halted his stallion and pointed to the trail in front of him. We had reached a hillock with low ferns, and a bird without wings was standing in the middle of the path, watching us. Then it ran faster than a little hen along the trail and disappeared like lightning into a sort of tunnel between the dense ferns. We had heard of this wingless bird, a strange species quite unknown to ornithologists. The islanders had often seen it but had never managed to capture one, as it always disappeared into holes and tunnels at great speed. Wingless birds in the Pacific are known only in New Zealand, represented by the kiwi and the now extinct, twelve-foot-tall moa bird. We searched a labyrinth of galleries crisscrossing the fern-clad hillock, but we failed to see this mysterious bird again.

Half the island lay behind us as we paused for a picnic lunch by a spring before we rode into really wild terrain. The forest suddenly came to an end and, emerging from the trees, we felt as if we were heading into empty space. No more foliage, no more earth before us, only a dizzy precipice. We heard a strange, distant sibilation from the surf far below, and the deep rumble of the wind as it rose up the huge wall, threatening to seize us.

As we followed Terai, who turned his horse onto a narrow shelf cut into the cliffside by the islanders long ago, we saw the world raised on end. Dizzy, we turned our heads to face the rock wall while our horses slowly, very slowly, followed behind the stout horseman before us. His mighty corporation seemed to fill all available space, like the rump of the horse beneath him.

Suddenly the shelf ended as the trail turned sharply to the left through a short pass which brought us out on the other side of the ridge and we faced a new precipice, this time on our left instead of on our right. Here, too, air currents roared up from below. The

island was not very wide at this point: another bay with white
surf lay below us, with a drop as horrifying as the one we had just
left on our other side. It was better to turn our noses the other way
now, facing the wall on our right while the horses moved as cautiously as before.

Then the rock wall opened again. There was no wall to face on
either side. It was like riding on a Pegasus, without visible foothold.
There was a mountain peak in front of us and another behind.
Between them passed an edge so sharp that the trail filled it completely. Terai turned his head, giggling. On either side, our feet
dangled above slopes that ran into nothing except the bands of
surf far below. The surf seemed to advance in slow motion and
was inaudible from this height; all we could hear was a general hiss
carried up from the depths. Even the horses seemed nervous at this
passage. With heads raised and ears pricked, they proceeded
slowly along the ridge. The irregular blasts of wind from down below seemed to scare them. I held my breath, for there was nothing
to jump down upon should the horses stumble.

We were across. The trail looped around the peak in front,
crossed another narrow edge, and then we rode into trees and were
at once engulfed in dense jungle. When we next emerged from the
foliage, we had reached the Puamau Valley. One misstep and we
would have arrived at our destination in a matter of seconds, falling
three quarters of a mile through the air. We were on the rim of
the mightiest crater valley we had seen on the island, opening only
toward the sea. Steep and sterile as the walls of a fortress, the
naked rock rose horseshoe fashion to enclose the huge jungle valley.
The last red rays of the evening sun skimmed the dense rows of
palm crowns lining the beach.

The sun sank quickly as we started our descent, and black rocky
walls swallowed even the last light of the red sunset clouds. We
could see nothing more. Only the emptiness transmitted to our
ears through the faint hiss from far below our feet told us we
were riding along the wall of a precipice. And the slanting of the
horses' backs, rump up and head down, told us that we were
descending. There were countless hairpin curves. The small, Marquesan horses had an incredible ability to put their hoofs in the
right places in the dark. They were tired, having carried us over
rugged terrain all day, yet they patiently moved on, slowly because of the dark, but rarely stumbling. As for ourselves, Liv and I
were so tired, so painfully stiff in our sore legs, so drubbed on our

behinds, that we felt the descent was the one to Hades. We did not care where the horses took us, so long as we could get off the wooden saddles. We did not see the horses' hoofs or the shelf we rode on; all we heard was pebbles that rattled and sometimes fell over the edge. We lost sight of each other in the dark, but we kept together by frequent shouts which carried so strangely into the emptiness above the mountain-girt valley.

At long last, the slanting backs of the horses leveled again and the animals began to jog-trot on grass. Next we heard the splashing of hoofs in water, accompanied by the sound of a gushing stream. Clearly, we were down in the valley. The surf, too, began a rhythmic rumble, and it came from our own level.

A spot of light pierced our blindness and began to dance and to grow bigger between the horses' ears till it took the shape of a window. The thunder from the surf was close beside us, and a fresh sea breeze suddenly struck our faces. We approached a house near the beach: our destination. We were scarcely able to alight from the horses and tie them to some trees. The door. A gorgeous smell of fried eggs filtered through it. I knocked and listened.

The door was brusquely opened and a muscular, but not big, middle-aged man of Nordic appearance held a kerosene lamp above us. With sharp blue eyes, he scrutinized his uninvited guests. Months, even years, passed between the occasions when this man received white visitors. And when they came, they came from the beach.

"*Bonjour,*" he said quickly.

"*God-dag,* Henry Lie," I answered in Norwegian, saluting him in the language I knew he had once spoken.

The man backed, totally bewildered; then he recognized Terai behind us.

Yes, indeed. More fried eggs were cooked over the fire while the corks popped that night in the lonely Norwegian cabin in the Puamau Valley on Hivaoa.

Henry Lie had lived a strange life. He had come to the Marquesas group as a young boy, thirty years earlier. He was then a deck hand on an old sailing vessel. The captain was a drunkard and there were daily fights and trouble on board. As the ship anchored off Hivaoa, young Henry was sent ashore with some of the crew to fetch water. He managed to run away and hide in a cave. He did not come out again until the angry captain had given up the search and the ship had sailed away from the island. Falling in love with a Polynesian girl, he married her, and when she became the heir to a local valley, he started a copra plantation. His wife died but left him with a son, and, moving to the large Puamau Valley, he worked up the finest copra plantation in the entire Marquesas group.

Henry Lie saw nothing of the outside world except the trading schooner from Tahiti whenever it called to fetch his copra. His life, apart from work, was his fine son, Aletti, and his books, of which I was surprised to see he had an impressive collection. His big, one-room bungalow was filled with beds and books, witnesses of hospitality as well as considerable intellect. I was puzzled to see that Lie had so many books, since I knew that Gauguin had never made the long trip across the mountains, so he had apparently been the only local intellectual.

Enough books and periodicals were cleared away from the surplus beds to give sleeping room for all.

Morning came. Henry Lie went to work before the sun rose, but young Aletti and Lie's second Polynesian wife, a stout but pretty *vahine* from the Tubuai Islands, were left to ensure us a good Polynesian breakfast. Terai attended to our legs and ordered Liv to stay in the house. Then he mounted his horse to visit the sick of the valley.

As on Fatu-Hiva, the entire native community lived down by the sea, where the breeze drove away most of the mosquitoes. There were very few houses for so big a valley, however, and the handful of families living there all seemed to be squatting at leisure in front of them or stretched out on floor mats inside. There was a marked contrast between the busy Henry Lie, who was always at work expanding his large plantation, and these relaxed Polynesians, who wanted nothing but to fill their stomachs and make love. Aletti explained that they were just sitting there waiting for their coconuts to fall down of their own accord. Then they split them with an ax and sun-dried the kernels for sale to the schooner or for barter for canned goods from Henry Lie, who had a tiny store like Willy's on Fatu-Hiva.

Except for the birds singing and Lie working, there was silence and no sign of activity anywhere. I saw Terai's horse tied in front of one of the huts, and strolled inland to see the beauty of the valley with young Aletti as a guide.

Suddenly we saw them. The giants. Aletti had been silent as we approached, and merely pointed as he held the foliage aside.

They stared at us from the thickets with round eyes as big as life belts and grotesque mouths drawn out in diabolical grins wide enough to swallow a human body. Bulkier than gorillas and nearly twice the height of a man, they had impressed every one of the few travelers who had so far been lucky enough to visit the locality. The giants of the cliff-girt Puamau Valley displayed such a contrast to the lazy people down on the beach that the question inevitably came to mind: Who put these red, stone colossi there, and how? They must have weighed many tons.

I had read about large stone monuments in the Marquesas group, but it is one thing to read a couple of lines and another to stumble unexpectedly on large stone monuments in human form standing among the forest foliage.

We approached the tallest, which stood on an elevated stone platform. It took two of us to measure its fat belly, and with a deep pedestal sunk into the platform masonry the image was some ten feet tall, carved entirely from one block of red stone, a kind of stone that did not exist anywhere locally.[1] Aletti told us that the quarries were far up the valley, where some unfinished blocks of this very same tuff had been discovered, together with the hard basalt adzes used in carving them.

The red statues had obviously been raised on some outdoor temple ground. We found that there were walls and terraces everywhere, as we began looking around in the underbrush, and a few statues lay half buried in the ground, their heads or arms broken by force. There were also huge, round heads gazing at us from between creepers and ferns, heads that had been carved as independent stone images without busts or bodies. The strangest of all the sculptures was a bulky giant carved as if in a swimming position, with stunted arms and legs stretched out fore and aft, the whole resting on a short pedestal extending from the abdomen into the ground as part of the same piece.

Aletti had read in his father's books that this temple site had been used until only fifty years before for cannibal festivities, when

[1] A detailed description with illustrations of this and all the other monuments of the Puamau temple terraces is to be found in T. Heyerdahl, "The Statues of the Oipona Me'ae, With a Comparative Analysis of Possibly Related Stone Monuments," in *Reports of the Norwegian Archaeological Expedition to Easter Island and the East Pacific.*—Ed. Heyerdahl and Ferdon, Vol. 2, Report 10, Monograph of The School of American Research and the Kon-Tiki Museum, 1965.

Kekela, a Hawaiian missionary, had converted the three local tribes to Christianity and planted coffee shrubs at the temple site. In fact, most of the underbrush that had overgrown the image area was still sprinkled with red coffee berries.

Three scientists had visited these images. F. W. Christian and K. von den Steinen in 1894 and 1896, and Ralph Linton in 1920, when Henry Lie was already living there. They had all been told different tales and been given different names for the statues by the local natives, who admitted to Henry Lie that they actually knew nothing. All they knew was what they had admitted also to Linton: the statues were already there when their own ancestors had arrived on the island and driven an earlier people away into the mountains. Who these earlier people were, nobody could tell, although certain traditions maintained that the old Naiki tribe had absorbed their blood.

There are incidents in everyone's life that may be casual and yet prove to have vital consequences in future development, even to the extent of sidetracking an entire life. My introduction to the Puamau stone giants during an attempt to return to nature later resulted in switching me onto a new track that was to guide my destiny for many eventful years to come. It set me asail on rafts, led me into continental jungles, and made me excavate Easter Island monuments as high as buildings of several stories. All in an effort to solve a mystery that puzzled me from the day I began to suspect that an enterprising people with the habit of creating stone colossi had reached the eastern headland of Hivaoa before the Polynesian fishermen arrived. The Polynesians, too, were full of vigor in earlier times, but their bent was generally to the sea, to the warpath, and to wood carving. These stone monuments seemed to have a different story to tell. It made good sense that the people down on the beach did not give the credit of carving them to their own kin.

In the evening, Henry Lie was back with us and, placing a stack of books next to the bright kerosene lamp, he began to turn pages that I had read before but to which I had not given adequate attention. He reminded me that throughout Polynesia there were persistent traditions to the effect that another people had been living on the islands when the ancestors of the present population arrived. Everywhere within the Polynesian triangle, which extends from Easter Island in the east to Samoa and New Zealand in the west and to Hawaii in the north, the learned men of the tribes agreed: an industrious people with reddish hair and fair skin, claiming descent from the sun god, were found on the various islands and were expelled or absorbed by the newcomers. The traditional memory was still so vivid that the first Europeans were mistaken for returning groups of this early fair people. Captain Cook lost his life in Hawaii when the mistake was finally realized. He was not as lucky as Cortez and Pizarro, who conquered the vast Aztec and Inca empires in Mexico and Peru due to the same strange belief in an earlier visit by white-skinned culture-bringers who had taught sun worship and erected giant stone statues before they left for the Pacific.

"The old Polynesians were ancestor worshipers; therefore they were addicted to genealogies and knew the names of their forefathers back to the day of their landing," said Henry Lie. "Here in the Marquesas they even had their genealogies preserved by a complicated system of knots on strings, like the *quipu* of Peru. There is no reason to doubt their claim that their ancestors found these islands already inhabited."

"But by whom?" I asked. "There are four thousand miles from here to South America and twice that far from here to Indonesia; so, by whom?"

Henry Lie ran his hand through his thin, blond hair. "Not by the Vikings," he laughed. "And not by people walking on imaginary land bridges which every geologist knows never existed in the Polynesian part of the ocean. But by sailors who came from a treeless country where they were used to quarrying rocks and to carving in stone. The Polynesians themselves must have come from forest-covered coasts, since they were great wood carvers. They carved totem poles and sculptured the bows and sterns of their canoes. They would pick up a pebble, and chop and grind it into a tool or a little image, but no man ever saw a Polynesian heading for a cliff to detach a monolith and carve it into human form. No indeed! And they have never claimed to have tried. Would *you* like to try?"

I admitted that it was not easy. And besides, it evinced something more than mere expertise. I knew of no stone-age people in any European country who had even tried it. Nor in Africa either, apart from Egypt.

Aletti interrupted us, coming with an invitation from the only other white man in the Puamau Valley. We had forgotten he existed. He turned out to be a tiny, friendly Frenchman with bushy eyebrows and a giant mustache hanging down on either side of his mouth. Lie introduced him simply as "my friend." The two of them used to sit up late in the evenings discussing politics, art, and the sciences. If they disagreed, the little Frenchman would poke strong tobacco into his nostrils and bang his fist on the table: Who knew the world better than he? He, who had cruised as master cook on a luxury yacht, hunted bears in Canada, herded sheep in New Zealand, and dug for gold in Alaska.

We were received by him in a tiny hut resembling the kind of card-house we built as children. Proud and happy, he made us stoop to enter his home-made castle. The roof was made of bundles of grass, and the walls were of boxes, odd pieces of driftwood, and old planks. We had never seen such a small residence with as much room in it for ingenious devices. If the old man pulled a rope or turned a nail, the most unexpected things would happen. When he wanted to go to bed, he pulled on one cord, and if he wanted to bring out his table, he pulled on another. From a single spot on the floor, he could reach the various compartments and accessories. If the wrong rope was pulled, a saddle might descend from the ceiling, or a box might open that contained the most delicious home-baked bread, which the old man had made himself over an open fireplace of corrugated iron between the bed and the table.

There was not room for all of us inside, so when we had seen it in turn, Lie called us back to his roomy bungalow, and his friend followed us with a warm and fragrant fresh loaf under each arm. I was never to forget the little man who lived in this tiny Pandora's box. I turned around to get a second glimpse of the amazing structure, crooked and strange from the bamboo floor to the tufts on the roof, surrounded by a tidy kitchengarden and dwarfed by giant coconut palms. This was all he had. But never did I encounter another white man more contented and genuinely happy.

The old man became really keen when he saw that we had been busy with a pile of books. While Lie's food-minded *vahine* began laying the table and slicing the loaf, he headed for one of the beds and pulled out a thick book he seemed to know well.

"You were discussing our statues," he said. "Look at this."

He found the page and pointed. I was amazed. He was showing me the picture of a giant statue of the same type we had seen that very morning, similarly standing unroofed among the jungle foliage. The colossal head, making up a third of the total size, the ridiculously stunted legs, the intentionally grotesque round face, with huge eyes, a flat nose, and the enormous mouth grinning from ear to ear, were strikingly similar.

"And look at the arms with bent elbows and hands clasping the belly: every single statue and image on this island has that special pose," the little man added enthusiastically.

I closed the book to look at the title. It was a book about travels in South America. I read the caption to the picture carefully. The large statue was from San Agustín, in the northern Andes, due east of the Marquesas. There were numerous other, similar statues in the same area, and I knew that large stone monuments in human form were scattered from there in a continuous belt down to Tiahuanaco, the main pre-Inca cult center near the shores of Lake Titicaca. Some of them were found right down on the Pacific coast below San Agustín. None had been carved by present-day Indians in any of these localities. The European conquistadors had discovered these bulky stone men abandoned everywhere in the jungle or on the pampas as relics of lost and unknown artists. The greatest concentration was at the main pre-Inca cult site of Tiahuanaco. Here the primitive Aymara Indians living near the ruins told the Spaniards, when they arrived, that the sculptures had not been made by their own ancestors, but by white and bearded foreigners resembling the Spaniards. Preaching the worship of the sun, these people had followed their leader on a final migration northward to the Pacific coast at Manta, in Ecuador, where all Inca traditions confirmed their arrival from Tiahuanaco and claimed that the foreigners had embarked on balsa rafts and disappeared forever, westward into the Pacific Ocean.

I looked at the three men beside me around the kerosene lamp. The young and refined, island-born Aletti, who had never gone to school but had been taught to read and write by his father. The happy little Frenchman, who greedily piled corned beef and onions on his bread while he licked his thumb to turn pages of learned books. Our calm Norwegian host, leaning over the table in a singlet revealing a workman's muscles and a pink skin except for the shoulders, which were coffee-colored from upright exposure to the tropical sun. There was nothing in Lie's appearance that seemed to match his great devotion to books. How he had assembled his stacks of fine literature since he stole ashore with empty hands and scanty schooling remained a mystery. He had never been away except for a short visit to Tahiti to select his present wife. Here he and his Robinson Crusoe friend were sitting in a hidden corner of a remote island expounding to me interesting observations that no professor had pointed out.

One by one, I examined the other pictures of San Agustín statues which showed some peculiar resemblance to the abandoned monuments up in the valley.

South America. But it was too far away for oversea contact. Yet Indonesia was double that distance in the opposite direction and showed no similar relics. Not even the mainland of Asia beyond could muster anything to match the Puamau images.

The old Frenchman snapped the book shut triumphantly, as if closing a jewelry box after letting me admire the treasure. I did not know what to believe. It was safest to believe in my own trained teachers who followed the textbooks written by accepted authorities. They all agreed that, before the days of European sailing ships, no craft could have reached these islands except from Asia and Indonesia, since American Indians had no real boats. I was trained to believe in the authorities. Yet I believed in my own eyes too. And the authorities could not always be trustworthy, for they did not even agree among themselves as to where in Asia to locate the Polynesian origins. Some proposed Java, some China, India, or even such distant places as Egypt or Mesopotamia. Even Scandinavia. Yet, in fact, none of them had found a single trace of Polynesian passage through the buffer territory separating Polynesia from Indonesia: the island world of the hostile and very ancient Austro-Melanesian and Micronesian tribes which alone was four thousand miles wide, or just as wide as the open ocean space between South America and the Marquesas group. Besides, who was to say for sure that only one landing had taken place on these islands?

When Terai came back from the last of the village houses, we all went to bed. Early next morning, he was on his little stallion ready to return into the highlands for a descent into Hanaiapa, on the north coast; the many other valleys were no longer inhabited. Henry Lie insisted that we should remain with him, and I was too fascinated by the developing riddle of the stone giants to want to leave. Lie was familiar with Terai's ointment and took charge of our treatment.

I spent a whole week up at the temple terrace, known as Oipona by the natives. No nook or cranny in the area was to be left unchecked. A huge, finger-shaped rock known as Toeva hovered high above the image site, reminding me of the taboo pinnacle we had climbed on Fatu-Hiva. Henry Lie said he was the only white man who had tried to reach its summit, but he had stopped one step short, at a wobbly slab that formed a bridge to the top.

Guided by a fine boy from the village, Aletti and I began the climb. It was easy to crawl up to a lookout point formed by a

roomy masonry platform, with a spectacular view of the valley down
to the distant beach. Here real climbing began, facilitated by a
shallow vertical cleft that gave a good grip and foothold up the
otherwise smooth pinnacle. The crevice closed to form a short
tube near the very summit, and climbing up through this chimney
we reached the point where the peak was split and a very wobbly
slab spanned the gap. We ventured carefully across, and as we rose
to our feet, we had a magnificent all-around view of the valley, with
the red stone giants visible among the greenery below us.

The summit had been artificially leveled off and paved with
slabs. There was not much room, but a wall of big blocks had been
built as a breastwork, and in niches between the boulders we found
an abandoned supply of fine sling stones. Like certain ancient
people in the Middle East and Peru, but unlike any nation in
Indonesia or East Asia, the early Marquesans used the sling for
warfare. Two slanting tunnels outside the parapet lay packed with
human craniums and other bones.

A connection between the temple site and this defense position
seemed obvious. In the event of enemy invasion, the king with
his priests and nearest followers would be safe on this summit,
their defenders holding out on the larger terrace below. If the
enemy managed to defeat the defenders and pass on, they would
have to climb one at a time through the upper tube. Before they
managed to balance across the wobbly bridge, they could easily be
pushed off the pinnacle and down to the stone images below. Only
thirst and starvation could force the people at this summit fortress
to surrender. And this had probably been the fate of the image
makers when the ancestors of the present tribes invaded the valley
after alighting from their canoes in the bay.

It would be tempting to consider the masses of human bones
stacked like rubble into the crevices on the summit as the remains
of the vanished stone-carvers. But this could hardly be so, since
the bones, although stained green and eroded, could hardly date
back more than one or two generations. That would place them at
the end of the nineteenth century, when the last cannibal ceremonies
took place in front of the grinning images. Lie had known people
who still recalled the last of these cannibal feasts. Conspicuous at
the image site was a large altar stone with the face of a one-eyed
god incised on a projecting corner, and its flat surface dotted with
cup-shaped depressions. Our companion insisted that they had
been filled with human blood during sacrifices.

The prone image, looking more like a swimming beast than a

human being, was particularly fascinating. It represented perfection of design and workmanship in stone. Only the best professional stone sculptor could create a work so masterly and so symmetrical, streamlined, and polished. I knew of nothing similar, since I had not personally inspected the hundreds of statues abandoned in the South American jungle at San Agustín. Not until I got there, years later, did I come face to face with two big stone statues of the very same, remarkable type: beastlike images with diabolic human faces, stretched out on their bellies in a swimming position, with stunted hands reaching forward along the face. The South American statues were identified as representing the swimming cayman god. But in Polynesia there were no caymans or other large reptiles.

To check every detail, I tore away the turf that obscured the short ventral column supporting the prone image. Aletti helped me with his knife. To our surprise, the reliefs of two squatting human figures with hands above their heads appeared, and between them, two large quadrupeds in profile, each with an eye, a mouth, erect ears, and a tail.

Two quadrupeds! Here was something for a detective. Every student of Polynesia knew that the Polynesians had no quadrupeds other than dogs and pigs, and that dogs for some reason were not present on the Marquesas Islands when the Europeans arrived. But this was certainly no pig, as it had a very long and thin tail standing straight up, with only a slight curve at the top, just as the tail can sometimes stand erect on a cat. A cat? No, for there were no felines in Polynesia. Not in any part of Oceania, Australia included. A dog, then? The early artist must have known the dog. And yet, the Polynesian dog had a bushy, curly tail, not a thin stick standing erect like this. Anyhow, it was a new discovery, and even the local people came up to gaze at it in amazement. They had not observed these reliefs when they had re-erected the statue, which, until a few years before, had been lying at an angle upside down, obviously overturned.

Not until years later did I find the sequel to our discovery. More than forty years earlier, Von den Steinen had removed the finest of the large, loose stone heads and taken it to the Völkerkunde Museum in Berlin. I had in fact seen it there during my studies before I went to the Marquesas, but the head had not meant enough to me to take a second look at its neck. I did, when I came back years later, and then I noticed the relief of two squatting human figures and two long-tailed quadrupeds, corresponding exactly to my discovery on the island. Von den Steinen had noticed these animals only on the head he brought with him, and here they were, so well preserved that one could see long claws on the feet and tuftlike whiskers at the snout, increasing the resemblance to a feline. But as cats were unknown and neither dogs nor pigs had such tails, Von den Steinen concluded that the animals were meant to be rats, the only other mammal known to the Polynesians.[2]

Rats? But no artist, however bad, would depict a rat with an erect tail and with a head raised proudly above the level of the back. Pairs of rats are depicted nowhere on ancient monuments of deities or heroes, but a pair of lions was the royal symbol carved at the base of the oldest statues of the Hittites and other early cultures in the Mediterranean world. And a pair of pumas is carved in relief at the very base of the red stone statue at Tiahuanaco, representing none less than the white and bearded sun king, Kon-Tiki, the South American master stone sculptor, who, according to Inca traditions, left for the Pacific. Felines yes, but not rats.

As the curious natives came up the valley with Henry Lie and the little Frenchman, they all had to revise their former belief that the swimming statue represented a woman giving birth to a child. According to Henry Lie, until quite recent years women had secretly brought food offerings to place before this image when they were expecting a child. The local people had re-erected this statue only a few years earlier, as it had been lying capsized in the bushes, overturned either by their own ancestors or by the missionary, Kekela. The three scientists who had been here before had therefore seen the statue upside down and had not recognized the reliefs. They had interpreted the projecting ventral cylinder as the child coming out of the womb of a struggling goddess, although they were unable to detect either a head or limbs on the cylindrical baby, which, besides, emerged from the region of the navel rather than from between the groins. Linton, in fact, began to doubt the natives' words, and claimed that this image differed so much from all the rest that it could scarcely be identified as human. He had no alternative suggestion, however, but admitted: ". . . It is evident that the artist worked on a preconceived plan and was a master of design and execution."[3]

Henry Lie and the old Frenchman both realized that stone statues of any form had a very limited distribution in the hemisphere

[2] K. von den Steinen, *Die Marquesaner und Ihre Kunst*, 2 vols. (Berlin, 1925–28).

[3] R. Linton, *Archaeology of the Marquesas Islands*, B. P. Bishop Mus. Bull., No. 23, p. 162 (Honolulu, 1925).

covered by the vast Pacific ocean. Such monuments were present only on a few islands, which happened to be those directly facing South America: Easter Island, the Marquesas, Pitcairn, and Raivavae. The biggest and most numerous were on tiny Easter Island, all alone in the vast ocean space, halfway between South America and the other Polynesian groups. Since nothing similar was found on any of the tens of thousands of islands elsewhere in the Pacific, the distribution was so specific that it called for some explanation. And since the people who had erected these stone monuments were thought to have come from the part of the Pacific where there were none, the idea was interpreted as an innovation on the islands farthest from Asia. Finally, since Easter Island was farther from Asia than even the Marquesas group, the idea was thought to have originated in the Marquesas and been spread by aboriginal seafarers from there to that last outpost before the American mainland. There, on Easter Island, the statues had reached enormous proportions only because the island was treeless and the Polynesian wood carvers had been obliged to look for another material. Although starting as a theory, this explanation was accepted by almost everybody when it was published as "the simple truth" by the leading authority on Polynesian culture, Sir Peter Buck, even though he had never seen any of these statues.[4]

Lie and the old Frenchman did not trust any authorities. They did not want to discard evidence they themselves could see and touch, in favor of postulates made simply to suit a theory. Had I been close enough to see the landscape of Motane, the island we had passed coming from Fatu-Hiva in the lifeboat? No? Well, that island was today completely treeless too, and yet, not long ago, it had been covered with forest, like Fatu-Hiva and Hivaoa. Man had caused the island to turn into a desert. How could we know that Easter Island had always been as treeless as it is today? Crowded with monuments, that tiny island must once have been overpopulated, and the forest could have been cleared away. Besides, argued Henry Lie, there were hundreds of treeless islands off Norway as well. Even Iceland and the Shetlands were barren, but this did not inspire the settling Viking wood carvers to erect stone images. And who could say, even without looking at them, that the group of stone statues up in the Puamau Valley were older than the hundreds of gigantic monuments on Easter Island?

[4] P. H. Buck, *Vikings of the Sunrise*, p. 232 (New York, 1938); A. Métraux, *Ethnology of Easter Island*, B. P. Bishop Museum Bull., No. 160, p. 308 (Honolulu, 1960).

Until a riddle is solved, every piece of evidence deserves a fair
trial, the old Frenchman said wisely, and with a raised finger he
added pompously that there was one thing worse than ignoring
facts and that was to try to explain them away because they did
not fit in with foregone conclusions.

"Easter Island is just as far from this island of ours as it is
from South America," he went on. "If anyone could cross the empty
ocean from here to Easter Island with the knowledge of how to carve
stone monuments, they could have crossed as easily from South
America."

Aletti handed him a school atlas. Nobody protested, for he was
right. Besides, it was getting late.

When the lamp on the central table had been blown out, I lay
awake for hours on Henry Lie's iron bed, trying to collect my
thoughts in the midst of a snoring choir. It was my dream to
come back to Hivaoa one day, properly equipped, and start professional excavations up in the valley. No archaeologist had as
yet thought of digging in any part of the Marquesas group, not
even on famous Easter Island or in any other island of east or
central Polynesia.

Dreams are like seeds; they remain as nothing more unless taken
into the field and cared for. My dreams in Lie's bungalow were
nursed until they grew into reality, and many years later I was to
drop anchor in the Puamau bay with my own expedition ship. Together with me on board, all gazing into the mountain-girt palm
valley, was a team of professional archaeologists. We had come
from Easter Island. We had spent six months excavating in the deep
soil which in bygone centuries had accumulated up to the necks
of the local stone colossi. Precious, new scientific information had
been harvested from below the turf of this, the most remarkable of
all Pacific islands. Three different culture periods had been uncovered, deposited in layers one on top of the other. With new
and solid information on the age and evolution of the Easter Island
stone busts, we had now come to the Marquesas to look for comparable data. From the bridge, I scanned the curving black beach
for the familiar sight of the big bungalow and the tiny shack among
the palm trunks. Nothing. All was gone.

We learned from natives ashore that the two houses had been
swept into the ocean by a terrific deluge. Furnishings and everything else had been lost. Gone were Lie's books, and gone was
his newly started collection of ancient images and relics. The old
Frenchman was no more. Lie had moved to the next valley to live

as a hermit. We found him there. He had already cleared the jungle and started a big, new plantation, finer than the old one, although his walking was hampered by elephantiasis in both legs. Aletti was his pride and joy; he had grown into a fine young man aspiring to become a supercargo on one of the Tahitian trading schooners.

Only the bulky red stone giants up in the valley were the same, immobile and unaltered in pose and expression, but again partially hidden by the jungle and the coffee bushes. How long had they been standing like this? How long a time had passed since they were inconspicuous parts of a lichen-covered mountain wall, demanding vision, energy, and skill from the men who quarried them into blocks and lugged them through a jungle—full of wood—to shape them into stone men, carved according to a preconceived plan? Venerated by their creators, feared by their enemies, detested and harmed by the missionaries, and still admired and marveled at by the few modern travelers who had found their way up to look at them, they themselves remained as mute as the jungle trees. But, a few months later, the expedition's archaeologists could speak on their behalf. They excavated carbon from burnt wood inside and under the stone platform on which the monuments had been raised. The structure could thus be dated by a radiocarbon analysis, just as we had been able to date the three superimposed culture periods on Easter Island. The date for the erection of the Hivaoa giants proved to be about A.D. 1300. At that time, the stone workers of Easter Island's Middle Period had long since been at work erecting the giant busts that were to make the island famous. Before then, however, the Early Period Easter Islanders had left behind a large number of much older stone men, which, down to the last details, were replicas of the oldest statues from Tiahuanaco, in South America. Stone statues were therefore raised on the island nearest America centuries before any statues had been erected in the Marquesas. What was more, pollen deposited in layers in the Easter Island bogs proved that the island had formerly been wooded, like all other islands in the warmer zone of the Pacific. The first human settlers had destroyed the forest to get space for their vast stone quarries, fields of American sweet potatoes, and extensive villages consisting of non-Polynesian houses of stone. No sooner were excavations attempted on these islands than the whole picture became the converse of all that had been supposed previously merely to conform with vested theories.

None of this was known to any of us as Liv and I saddled our horses and bade farewell to Henry Lie and his family after our first encounter. We rode over to salute the cheerful little Frenchman, then we followed in Terai's long-since-obliterated tracks up the winding cliffside path into the highlands.

We were so busy chattering, enjoying the spectacle, and looking for another glimpse of the wingless bird, that we took a wrong turning on one of the fern-covered hillocks. And we did not realize the mistake before we found ourselves about to descend into the deep Hanaiapa Valley, the place Terai had left for, and the only one of the three local settlements we did not yet know. Heavy clouds darkened the sky, evening was not far away, and night would fall upon us before we got back to the right trail for Atuona. We therefore decided to ride down into this unknown locality.

There was a somber atmosphere about the whole valley as we started the descent around the usual hairpin bends and lost sight of the open highlands. Unlike the crescent-shaped crater walls enclosing the other two inhabited Hivaoa valleys, this one was shaped like a deep and dark canyon, with overhanging walls running northward to open as a gate straight into the rumbling ocean. There was no sign of life.

As we reached the bottom and the rim seemed to lean top-heavily over us, we came to a gloomy hut of the usual kind: imported planks, window glass, corrugated iron. We knocked and peeped cautiously in through a broken window pane. It was empty. Abandoned, to judge from the lack of fiber mats and other chattels.

Farther along the path, we reached another house of exactly the same type. Also empty but for cobwebs and lizards. It was all very gloomy. Not until we reached the clearing in the forest near the beach did we see people in some of the huts. But even here most of the houses were empty and abandoned. We saw the outlines of three churches. It was difficult to decide where to ride.

While we were hesitating, I was seized by my leg by a rather queer and shabby person, who held on and tried to communicate something I could not at first understand. It was getting too dark to see well, but the little we could see left the impression of a most unhealthy individual.

"*Venez*," I heard him say. "*Pluie tomper*." In pidgin French, he predicted rain and wanted us to come to the house of the Protestant parson.

"*Merci*," I said. "But we shall sleep in the open tonight."

The fellow did not let go of my leg, shook his head vigorously, and pointed into the air. The black clouds were accumulating over our heads; their gray fringes rolled like steam along the edge of the canyon wall. It started to rumble somewhere up in the mountains. Thunder! This was most unusual on these islands and invariably foretold really bad weather. Yet we were imperturbable until the first electric explosion opened a cannonade right above the canyon, shooting at us with straight, hard rain. It was a real cloudburst. Then we took refuge up on the roofed balcony of the local parson's house. Night was fast descending over Hanaiapa. Water flooded, and the darkness was repeatedly split by blinding flashes of lightning, while the thunder was tossed back and forth in deafening explosions as between fortress walls. There was no escape.

Motaro, our well-meaning host, briefed us patiently about the valley we had involuntarily entered. There were only thirty inhabitants left. All Polynesians. They were harassed by tuberculosis. The people were so superstitious that they refrained from burying their dead in the ground; they placed them under the floors of their homes. In such houses, everybody died who tried to go on living there, said the parson. Elephantiasis and leprosy were also more common here than in the other two valleys, and two of the thirty left alive had lost their wits.

Whether we were half asleep or fully awake, the valley seemed to us a nightmare. While the lightning flashed and flared and the thunder cracked and banged and rumbled, we sat the whole night on the balcony floor. We bluntly refused to go inside and share beds with the rest of the parson's guests. We could not help it, although they felt insulted by our behavior. But we would rather have gone straight out into the pouring rain than dared to join them. The coughing, the moaning, the whimpering that reached us through the open door between thunderclaps made us shudder right through to our bones.

In the middle of the night, we leaped to our feet as something seemed to loosen in the rock overhanging the valley. First a slight purring and rolling of pebbles, then a heavy thump, and a whole section of the cliff rim came thundering down the valley. The hut was alive with desperate people trying to escape as the avalanche, with deafening booms, crashed into the valley stream, making the whole house quake. Then nothing more was heard, as the echoes died away; only a few boulders and small stones dropped and rolled in the wake of the main slide, and the lightning flashed as before. Everyone squatted on the balcony for a long time, then they calmly returned to their beds. A landslide was no extraordinary event in Hanaiapa.

Next morning, the weather improved and the heavy clouds de-

parted, rumbling away for some time, out across the sea. The naked
scar from the avalanche shone wet in the morning sun, from the
very edge of the cliff down into the thick forest, where everything
had been swept away, leaving a wide, stone-filled causeway. The
little stream had grown into a mighty river, filling most of the
valley bottom. Like molten chocolate, it wandered slowly toward
the bay.

Without hesitation, we saddled our horses. We had acquired unexpected company. Against our will, we found ourselves riding
behind the queer person who had stopped us the evening before.
He wanted to lead the way and would not let us pass. We had in
fact seen very little during the descent in the dusk. And our guide
was therefore able to lead us skillfully off the right path.

There was enough to see along the trail to keep us distracted.
Old walls everywhere. A large stone was covered by the familiar
assemblage of cup-shaped depressions, and beside it stood a slab
with a large lizard in high relief. Very old. I found it strange that
an ancient artist would depict a tiny creature which he neither ate
nor worshiped, and that he would carve it so very much larger than
its natural size. And there were no caymans or alligators in any
part of Polynesia. The largest reptile we had seen was our little
roommate Garibaldus, the gecko. No Polynesian would bother to
immortalize him in an enlarged version on a slab. It was strange.

Strange also that the trail never seemed to start climbing. What
was going on? I realized we were being led astray when I suddenly
saw hundreds upon hundreds of human craniums on the ground
in front of us. We had reached a clearing in the sparse forest, fully
paved with large stones. The whole area was packed with human
heads, large and small, white or green with mold, complete or
broken. They lay side by side, grinning in all directions, with big,
empty eye sockets, seeming to sniff the jungle air with fleshless
nostrils. I turned my horse abruptly to get an explanation. Our
strange companion only laughed sluggishly, exposing a pair of almost toothless jaws. He was clearly one of the two lunatics mentioned by our host. I got down from my horse and took a closer look
at the myriad skulls. Some were very long and some were very
broad. If cranial shape had any thing to tell, these Polynesians had
not all descended from the same stock of progenitors. A mixture
had taken place, either right here on Hivaoa, or before these Polynesians had left their unknown fatherland. One other thing was no
less apparent: Cannibals or vegetarians, the ancient islanders had

at least maintained rows of perfect teeth for chewing their own kind of food.

I mounted my horse and spurred it, galloping with Liv and the madman at my heels, until I detected the narrow side path up the cliffside. Here we left our giggling companion behind and rode as fast as the horses could trample up the steep, hairpin curves.

On the rim, we paused and took a last look at Hanaiapa, where new clouds were beginning to assemble over the valley with its thirty living souls, three churches, and a thousand skulls. We rode slowly into the freedom of the open highlands, and down into the broad, crescent-shaped valley of Atuona.

A smiling Terai removed our bandages for the last time. Our legs were shaping up perfectly, although Liv, especially, would never be rid of the scars. The horses were left with Terai and we walked to our Chinese friends, who received us with joy and steaming pots. We had nothing to do but eat and rest and wait for the next schooner.

Some days passed. One afternoon, we were sitting with bowls of green tea on the Chinese's balcony when we saw Belvas coming down the road. The stout and friendly wireless operator always marched as if he were walking on the springs of a mattress. He halted before Bob's store and unfolded a telegram. Bob, Triffe, and a dozen Polynesians gathered around him as he read the text out loud in a dramatic voice. A new governor had been appointed for French Oceania. A naval vessel had already left to bring him on a formal visit to Hivaoa and Nuku-Hiva before he settled in the Governor's Palace at Tahiti.

A great commotion followed as soon as Belvas put his telegram away. In a few minutes, the whole village was informed. A messenger was sent by horse to the Hanaiapa and Puamau valleys to summon everybody who could walk or ride to come to Atuona, where Triffe announced that a great reception would be organized for the Governor.

The people who counted in the valley were gathered in a council. This was a unique opportunity to improve local conditions. Here was a chance to speak to the Governor in person. Concessions and amendments to be proposed were eagerly discussed by the reception committee. Bob wanted to end prohibition for the natives. At present, he was allowed to sell only one bottle of wine per person each week. Not that he was keen on making more money, but as things were on the island, people were brewing their own liquor from green coconuts and drinking themselves to death. This had to be stopped.

Belvas rose and voted against Bob. Any white man could buy as much as he wanted from Bob's store or from the schooners. That was only fair. But if the Government lifted prohibition for the islanders, they would indeed drink themselves to death. Surely they drank much less now, since they had to go to the trouble of climbing the palms for coconuts and making their own brew. Bob was voted down.

The request for a drainage ditch across the village road was unanimously agreed on. And a generator for electric lamps along the village walk was also everybody's dream. Tahiti had one.

One voice spoke in favor of getting a nurse stationed in Fatu-Hiva, like Terai. He had relatives there and they had no medical care. Others objected. Conditions on Fatu-Hiva were already too bad to be improved. The proposal was voted down.

Triffe was concerned about the program for the reception party. Hula dancing, said Bob. All Europeans like to see girls waggling their bums. Everybody agreed. But as there were not enough girls, men should dance too. But what about costumes? Grass skirts were suggested by Belvas. Wild opposition. The Governor would think he had come to visit savages. New white garments for all the dancers, said Bob enthusiastically. He had a stock of just what was needed. An islander supported Belvas. Grass skirts were used by modern dancers in Tahiti. European visitors always demanded them.

A heated discussion followed. Why receive the Governor like savages when they could receive him properly dressed? The majority voted for white: long white gowns for the women, and for the men white shirts with long sleeves to match long white trousers with sharp creases. The grass-skirt party, however, would not surrender. A compromise was therefore inevitable.

When the Governor was set ashore from his gray cruiser and proceeded up the village track with his uniformed followers, all in

Opposite:

NATURE TAKES OVER. During our absence on Hivaoa, the jungle crept back into our clearing on the royal terrace, and even the four poles rammed into the earth to support our kitchen roof had grown long branches covered with foliage and turned into trees again. Our bamboo cabin had been devoured by insects and we were left without a home.

Opposite:

THE TAUAOUOHO MOUNTAIN RANGE ran from north to south and isolated the entire east coast from the rest of the island. The other side, almost inaccessible, was uninhabited but for an old hermit who lived alone with his adopted daughter. We wanted to reach the unspoiled coast on that side by crossing the mountain region, where only wild horses and other animals reigned.

CROSSING THE OMOA RIVER with gifts for the old hermit, we set out once more for the highlands.

FERNS AND FERN TREES had recaptured the last part of the mountain trail before the jagged ridge.

Above:

SHEER CLIFFS fell away into the deep Ouia Valley. At this point we had to leave our horses and follow our guide onto a narrow shelf that had long before been cut into the wall of a precipice.

Opposite:

TEI TETUA was the last survivor of the entire east-coast population. A former chief, he had survived his twelve wives and was the last Polynesian known to have participated personally in cannibal ceremonies. More content to give than to receive, the hospitable old man accepted only a pipe brought from Hivaoa, refusing the tobacco, showing us that it grew wild in his valley.

Above:

TAHIA-MOMO was the old cannibal's adopted daughter, who was always laughing or smiling. The two of them gave us a most heartfelt welcome when we came to settle in their lonely valley.

Overleaf:

OUR POLE CABIN AT THE OUIA BEACH was our home during our happiest time in the South Seas. The perpetual trade wind, blowing straight to our cabin from South America, drove all mosquitoes deep into the thickets of the forest.

spotless white, he was received by a double row of hula dancers, also all in spotless white. But over the men's trousers and the women's gowns, loosely tied around the dancers' waists, hung long grass skirts with their fringes dangling merrily fore and aft. Everyone was satisfied. When the gray cruiser left, white man had admired his own shadow, and the sun could shine on another step up the ladder to nowhere.

Somebody had left a wreath at the modest little tombstone of Paul Gauguin. Somebody who appreciated his colors. Gauguin was a missionary in reverse, I thought. He tried to civilize us with the warm colors of the island people. Instead, we have succeeded in convincing their descendants of the advantages of a white collar. I had one around my own neck in honor of the Governor. I went home to our bungalow and tore it off. I reckoned the Governor had done the same when he was alone in his cabin. It was hot. I wrapped my green-and-red Polynesian *pareu* around my loins and made myself comfortable on a pandanus carpet on the balcony. It was decent and airy, and nobody could mind so long as I was in the house.

I began to long for Fatu-Hiva. We were nearer to nature there. It would be stupid to give up without another try. Liv, whose wounds were healing, had refused any thought of asking for a lift to Tahiti on the cruiser. As we watched it move away, guns fore and aft, we were as certain as ever that if we returned to civilized Europe we would get back just in time to see modern society collapse under the burden of all its tanks and guns and battleships. We had no idea about who would fight against whom. On Fatu-Hiva, we had no enemies except the mosquitoes. And we were prepared to confront them once more. It was better to be bitten than bombed. The stings of a thousand insects did not penetrate as deep as a single bayonet.

We were longing for our bamboo cabin on Fatu-Hiva.

Opposite:
PLAYING A BAMBOO NOSE FLUTE. Tei Tetua entertains Momo and Liv on the stone platform in front of his two huts. Tahia-Momo has adorned herself and Liv with tiaras of wild red fruits.

8. ISLAND OF ILL OMEN

I woke to the rattle of heavy chains, and as I opened my eyes I saw a beautiful Polynesian girl lying by my side. She had not been there when I fell asleep. At my feet, the sun swung slowly to one side, low on the horizon, but disappeared as a big boom passed over my head. I was about to sit up, but I had to lie down again in a hurry so as to avoid a blow on the head from the heavy boom. The unknown beauty laughed, her black hair blowing all over her face, and wrapped herself up to her nose in a blanket. Liv was on my other side, sound asleep, and there were other people wrapped up in mats and blankets on each side of us.

Pitching turned into heavy rolling, and I remembered that we had embarked the night before on the Tahitian trading schooner *Moana* while it was anchored beside the Atuona promontory. A couple of weeks had passed since the warship had made its hasty call, and now the *Moana's* captain had come to look for copra. The other passengers must have embarked during the night or just before sunrise. We heard loud voices from down below, while those who shunned the nauseating odor of copra and merchandise had gone to bed, like us, on top of the hatch, with the long boom of the mainsail swinging just above our noses.

The sail was being hoisted now, as we had just weighed anchor, and the *Moana* began to glide like a white eagle out of the green bay. With the wind-filled sail forcing the boom steadily to starboard, we could safely sit up and enjoy the last glimpse of the broad Atuona Valley before it dwindled and disappeared. Farewell, land of Terai and Mister Bob; tombstone of Paul Gauguin, your fate will remain unknown to us. One day, perhaps, there will be streetlights and liquor for everybody; perhaps other people, like Terai and Madame Hamon, will help you back into the sun.

As we rounded the point of the promontory, we saw the ruins of a few bungalow-type houses. These were the foundation walls of a former leper station. The buildings had recently been set on fire and razed to the ground, in order to kill the bacilli and arrest contagion. The remaining inmates, we were told, were sent home to their huts, except some who were interned in the leprosarium on Tahiti.

The never-failing trade wind hit us with full force now, and we sniffed salt-fresh air coming in from across the endless ocean. Some frozen islanders withdrew below deck and the rest of us wrapped the blankets more closely around us. It was chilly at sea before the sun rose higher. The three young girls on my left were itching to make acquaintance, wriggling and giggling in the Polynesian fashion, but they became calm and serious when the latest news spread from mouth to mouth.

There was a madman with us. Below deck, we learned, was a dangerous prisoner on his way to Tahiti. He was cursed by the taboo, and the Tahitian captain had all the details.

A group of islanders had tried to resettle a valley close to Atuona. Two of them had come all the way from Tahiti, intending to start coconut cultivation on this island where so much land lay deserted. In the valley where they had come to work, there was a huge old tree which was known to be taboo. The two young fellows from Tahiti were not frightened and went to inspect the tree, which they found to be hollow. They peeped inside and discovered three human skulls, described as being very big. They had never seen skulls so large. Their business sense got the better of them and they removed the skulls from the tree, as they would fetch a high price if offered to wealthy tourists in Tahiti.

They hid the heads in a suitcase, ready to be shipped with the next schooner bound for Papeete. But, on the very first night, the heads began to whimper inside the suitcase. At least this was the version reported to the *gendarmerie*. One of the two men repented and wanted to return the heads to the tree immediately. But the other man had refused. He wanted the money and did not believe in the taboo. The noise from the suitcase had finally become so loud that it woke up everybody around. The fellow who had prevented the heads from being taken back to the tree now became so frightened that he went completely out of his mind. He drew his long machete knife from its sheath and ran in pursuit of his Tahitian friend in order to cut off his head. A mad fight had followed before all the others had managed to capture and disarm their lunatic companion. He was dragged by force across the mountains and delivered to the *gendarmerie* in Atuona. Now he was down below, destined for the prison in Papeete.

Could it be, I wondered, that Marquesan fruit rats had taken to the habit of nesting in skulls?

Everybody sat up as the little island of Motane rose above the horizon on the port side of the bouncing bow. We remembered its hazy profile in reverse from when we came north. Then we had passed by at a distance, but now, to our surprise, the Tahitian captain ordered his dark helmsman to turn the wheel to bear straight down upon the uninhabited isle. We needed provisions, he said. Fresh meat.

As Motane transformed itself from a hazy profile into a three-dimensional landscape, we were astonished at what we saw. We had expected a green wilderness, for in any other area we had seen abandoned by man the jungle had returned victoriously. But that was not so here. And we called to mind what Lie and the old Frenchman had told us. The forests of Motane were no more, thanks to human interference.

We jumped ashore onto some rocks at the foot of low cliffs on the leeward side as soon as the *Moana*'s lifeboat had ventured in as close as the restless surf permitted. Ashore with us came half a dozen Polynesians, crew and passengers, while the others took the lifeboat back into safety alongside the *Moana*, waiting for us to signal for our return.

Stripped but for colorful *pareus* knotted like perineal bands between their legs, some Polynesians dived with slender spears into the surging water, looking for spiny lobsters and fish. The rest of us climbed the coastal cliff and proceeded up the hot, sun-baked slope, where the sharp light blinded us as on a coral beach. The ground was as white and dry as dust, covered with sterile sandy soil, loose stones, and bare rocks. Scattered far apart were clusters of dry shrubs with thick, sapless leaves. The whole island was otherwise devoid of a green blade or tree. The sun scorched the dry ground, unhindered by any dense crowns of forest, which was all gone. The landscape was transformed into a desert. At considerable distances from each other, we saw some dead, white trees, as white and dry as bone, sapless and stripped of both leaves and bark, their naked branches stretched like ghost claws toward the blue sky.

Scattered everywhere were bleached bones and complete skeletons: twisted horns of rams, animal craniums, ribs, and leg bones. Everywhere we moved in the rolling terrain, we saw the same sight:

windswept stones, dry scrub, and distorted skeletons of sheep. In a dead tree inland a wild cock sat crowing, and another answered in the far distance.

Man had once lived here. In several places we came across nicely built *paepae*, the old Polynesian house platforms. In the Marquesas, the houses had to be raised above the jungle mud. There was no mud here now. But, in the gullies and glens, we saw vestiges of watercourses and potholes from former streams and rivulets. There was not a drop of water now, not even the dark shadow of humidity. The salty surf against the windward side of the island seemed to augment our longing for drinking water in this desert landscape.

We had no guide, nor did we need one to find our way around in the open terrain and to learn what had happened. The whole island was an arena, or battleground, where modern man had beaten nature. Elsewhere on these islands, he had lost. We had seen how he had tried to enter, intent on improving conditions for himself and his uncivilized local host. He had brought useful plants and domestic animals, but had also upset the whole balance of a life lived in accord with local conditions. Failing in his effort to help the islanders in order to benefit from them, white man withdrew from the islands as soon as he confronted his own shadow, and the encroaching jungle followed at his heels, often right down to the island shore, until everything it had lost was reconquered.

But not on Motane. The island was small and its landscape not big enough to win the uneven battle. Since the first Europeans came to the Marquesas, a kind of constant war had raged, and the casualties were high. Captain Cook estimated a local Polynesian population of one hundred thousand when he ran into the group in 1773. After him came European settlers, whalers, and missionaries. A good century later, in 1883, the total census was 4,865. The ethnologist Ralph Linton estimated three thousand in 1920, of whom many were then Chinese or European half-castes, and he reported that on the island of Tahuata there were said to be nearly a hundred deaths to every birth. Some of these numbers may well be exaggerated, but even so, the casualties in the losing battle with imported germs and European living conditions were shockingly high. Indeed, on Motane they were so high that not a single survivor had remained to tell the story of what had long since become a ghost island.

As we advanced to the higher terrain, in the center of the island, we saw the first sign of life on the ground. A few frightened sheep ran bleating with their lambs through some arid bushes. They were scraggy and undersized, with scanty wool. The three crew members in our company ran barefoot after them uphill and downhill, and the clearly feeble animals could not escape. The unarmed pursuers just threw themselves upon the sheep, grabbing them by the wool. Soon Liv and I were left alone, meditating on the tragic sight, while the three men marched back toward our landing place, each carrying a bleating sheep like a bulky stole around his neck. Laughing victoriously, the one forming the rear guard of the party turned around and told us to wait where we were; they were going back for more. Evidently there was very little flesh between the skin and the bones of their booty.

Never before had the sun, the very intensity of the sunlight, given me the same feeling as when a full moon shines on a cemetery. The ghostly-white trees stood like tombstones over a pillaged graveyard; there were skulls and bones everywhere. It was midnight at noon.

We found the stone platform of an old *paepae*. The walls of a house had once stood there. There had been a door in the wall, where children ran in and out, where men stooped to pass with their fishing spears and women welcomed them back to the smell of *poipoi* and baked breadfruit. Perhaps the ghost tree before us had once been heavy with starchy breadfruit.

Then a big European sailing ship had anchored down in the blue water behind the trees. Men with three-cornered hats and tight-fitting breeches had come ashore with blazing firearms to obtain water, fruit, pigs, and women. They brought strange animals with "tusks" on their heads, they brought rum and the recipe for brewing spirits far more potent than the innocent island *kava*. They brought a different living system, and they brought disease. The islanders accepted all of this with gratitude and admiration. The era of Polynesian savagery was ended. The Polynesian era was ended. On Motane, local history ended. Perhaps the last surviving Polynesian died on the family's pandanus mat on just this *paepae* where we were sitting. Perhaps the last desperate family embarked in their canoe to escape to Hivaoa, whose mountain crests could be seen in clear weather. Or perhaps the last survivor was a child left alone between the trees and the animals. We shall never know.

But we do know that when their masters were no more, the domestic animals ran wild. Those which survived were the sheep. Sheep were one of man's additions to nature's composition of a balanced life on the island. On a continent, carnivorous beasts would have helped to enforce nature's law of stabilization, permitting an average of two lambs to grow up for each pair of wild sheep. But with flesh-eating man gone, the sheep of Motane met no obstacles to breeding and multiplying far beyond the point of saturation. Hordes of wild sheep consumed all the grass, all the leaves within reach, and when famine hit them, they devoured the roots of the grass and the bark of the trees until even the last of the foliage high above their heads withered away and the island turned into a desert. Without trees to shelter the soil from the scorching rays of the sun, and without roots to hold humidity near the surface, every drop of rain sank deep into the arid ground and was lost long before it reached any glen or watercourse. The gushing streams lost all their supplies and the last little rivulet disappeared from the surface of the land. Motane's biological clockwork had not only stopped, but was set in backward motion, until the hands showed a visitor pretty much what our planet looked like before life emerged from the sea. If the *Moana's* crew managed to catch the last of the scraggy sheep, then the miniature world we saw from our hilltop would more or less match Planet Earth in the period when life was confined to the ocean and the air: the remote era when eroding rock had liberated the first salts and minerals ashore, which, dissolved in water, had combined with sunlight to fill first the ocean and then the air with creatures swimming and flying around the lifeless coasts. But if all the world were reduced like Motane, how many million years would we have to sit alone on our hilltop *paepae* waiting for algae to be washed ashore and develop into grass and trees once more, or for fish to jump ashore and acquire lungs and legs and fur a second time? The tiny fish we had seen jumping in the surf area on the cliffs of Fatu-Hiva had certainly jumped like that for hundreds of thousands of years, and not one of them was as yet ready to take the first leap on the long road toward kangaroo or monkey. Better to take care of the world we had. It would take a long time to get a new one.

We were almost asleep on the old *paepae* when the Tahitian crew gave up the hunt and we were all ready to return to the *Moana*. The clear waters around Motane were evidently still teeming with marine life. The great variety of sea food speared by our divers included several fat moray eels, which, cooked in the milk of coconuts brought from Hivaoa, provided passengers and crew with a meal greatly superior to that cooked from the skin and bones of the starved Motane sheep.

Before the sun set, we left the dead island, with all its sand and bones, behind us. It was like departing from a world far younger or much older than ours. As I wrapped myself up in my blanket and squeezed in between Liv and the giggling *vahines,* I was longing to get back into the world of our own times, the green world with purling water and singing birds. I was longing desperately for our cabin on Fatu-Hiva.

Nobody but modern white man, in his restless drive for change and progress, could manage to lay waste an island paradise of which an earlier population had taken such great care. Or was this quite true? I did not know then what I myself, with a team of scientific collaborators, was to discover: that Easter Island was another Polynesian habitat whose original, verdant forest had all been destroyed by man. But that island was laid bare by the people who had filled the local landscape with giant stone men centuries before Europeans came. The stone sculptors had chopped down and burned the trees and underbrush until every little creek had sunk into the ground and disappeared. But at least grass and low ferns survived on Easter Island, for when white man arrived and occupied the island for sheep farming, there was no shortage of people to play the part of nature's carnivorous beasts.

Not knowing yet the answer to the riddle of the barren landscape of Easter Island, my thoughts traveled from that mystery island to the barren regions of Mesopotamia and the Mediterranean world. It was common knowledge that the Middle East had been a fertile region in Sumerian and Phoenician times, and that huge forests had covered Lebanon, Cyprus, Crete, Malta, and even Greece with its countless islands, until man had destroyed everything, partly to get timber and partly to start cultivated fields. There were those who even claimed that the huge Sahara Desert was a man-made product caused by shepherds burning the jungle, and by the subsequent overgrazing of ever larger herds of goats and sheep. Modern research has proved this to be so. We know today that the Sahara is still expanding southward, with an average progress of from one to two miles a year, partly because of careless land utilization. In some years, the expansion is much more. In the Sahara Desert, recent expeditions have discovered large numbers of prehistoric cliff paintings showing jungle animals of various kinds, among which hippopotamuses are common. In the very heart of the desert, at three different localities near Djanet, in southern Algeria, these ancient frescoes include crescent-shaped reed boats of the very same type as those depicted on the cliffs in Upper

Egypt.[1] The Sahara, then, had been covered by swamps and forests until man turned it into sand.

Our visit to a doomsday island between the jungle-clad landscapes of Hivaoa and Fatu-Hiva was not easily forgotten. Perhaps this was what later spurred me on to drill for pollen samples on Easter Island. Certainly it kept me on the alert many years later, when I chose to settle in a medieval village hidden in thickly forested hills on the Italian Riviera. Every year, an endless number of disastrous forest fires rage on the Mediterranean coast of France and Italy. Once, they were started by shepherds, bird hunters, and careless tourists. Their numbers have lately been increased by building speculators evading green-belt regulations, and by pyromaniacs drawn to the area by the sheer pleasure of participating in the havoc. A cigarette butt under a dry cake of cow dung, a burning candle left in a carpet of pine needles: not much ingenuity is required to set fire secretly to the dry underbrush that invaded the forests abandoned by man when the shepherds and farmers became hotel personnel and beach attendants. No sooner do shrubs and small trees start to return than a second fire rages on the same ground, and then a third. Who cares for a forest that is assumed to have nothing but aesthetic value? Some nature lovers cry a warning and the handful of local fire wardens are overworked, while city people down by the beach watch the spectacular flames on the hillside and attend to their tourists.

In the meantime, the fate of Motane is creeping upon us faster than in bygone ages, from the arid areas of the Sahara and the Middle East, via Greece and the islands of the Mediterranean Sea. Where the forest has burned once, it slowly returns. Where it has burned three times or more in a decade, things begin to happen: The roots die and the creeks and rivers sink into the ground and disappear. The rain washes away all the goodness in the soil and carries it in measurable tons down to the valley bottoms and into the sea. Naked rock emerges and sterile sand remains. After rain, a chocolate-colored belt just off the coast reveals where the precious water and the richness of the land have gone. Back to where it all once came from: the sea. Today, Motane is not the only place on our blue planet where man, eager for improvement, is turning back the biological clock.

[1] Henri Lhote, *The Search for the Tassili Frescoes* (London, 1973).

9. IN THE CANNIBAL VALLEY

The tall palms seemed to be lined up along the queen's trail for the occasion. Not as stiff flagpoles flanking a royal parade, but as friendly personalities from the green crowd of Fatu-Hiva's forest, wishing to welcome us back to our own valley. We felt like waving back to them, for we knew them all, the tall ones and the short ones, and the crooked one that leaned across the trail before it realized its mistake and rose skyward like the rest. Every one of them was a familiar friend. And so were the nests of orchids riding on the gnarled branches above our heads. They seemed to be waiting for us, exactly as when we left. We knew also where lianas and aerial roots hung down from the tunnels of greenery. We greeted them in passing and left them dangling behind us.

This was our world. This was our valley. We were back where we belonged, heading once more for our yellow bamboo home. We were happy.

Barefoot again, and wrapped in our light *pareus,* we felt anew this provocative touch of real life, as nature played on us with all its instruments to keep our senses wide awake. The jungle caressed our skin and filled our lungs with a warm aroma. We were no longer on a dead planet. Motane had been left behind; it had sunk into the salt seas. We were re-entering a living world where birds and butterflies still survived to flutter at will in the sun or in the soothing shade under a protecting jungle roof. Here a deep padding of rich humus still covered arid subsoil and gave birth and a foothold to mushroom legs, tender stalks, and giant trunks. Here was no sterile sand, but a soil teeming with growing and moving creatures. This was a sample of mankind's fabulous heritage: nature on the seventh day.

We hurried inland, gay and filled with happy expectations, like children going to a birthday party. Once more, all this was ours to dive freely into, to grasp and possess with all our appetite and all our senses. It was densely overcast, yet the sun seemed to beam from above; the weather was independent of the clouds. The jungle air was as raw as when we had last inhaled it, but now we enjoyed any form of humidity. We even enjoyed the musty scent of mold and other fungi. All combined to reflect the abundance of fertility and life. On the day before, we had seen an island where nothing as worldly as fungi would grow. Overnight, we had made the leap from an extinct world back to a living planet. A planet where pearls of water still dripped from the leaves. Where chuckling rivulets tiptoed into dancing streams. And where busy insects scurried about among the greenery, searching for proper places to poke their nozzles, as if they had been paid by their boss to grease the complicated machinery that grew about us and gave us shade, air, and food.

As we gazed around us, the scales again fell from our eyes, and we marveled at everything like globe-trotting discoverers, although we were approaching nothing but our own former doorstep. Yet today, once more, nothing was obvious, and all we saw in nature appeared worthy of a second thought. The barrenness of Motane was still fixed on our mind's eye. Motane was, after untold millenniums, returning to the primeval dead condition of all these islands. Fatu-Hiva, too, had originally been just as naked. This luxuriant forest was here today, not yesterday, and tomorrow it might disappear again. It was a loan exhibition for an undetermined time. So where had all these millions of tons of sappy timber come from, this complicated mass of interdependent life? Only a few wind- and water-borne cells had arrived here and exploded into this profusion of living, dying, rotting, and reconverted species. Time alone had made imperceptible to the human senses this total change from barren rock to a forest kingdom; this fantastic outburst of organic wealth had been as invisible to the eyes of beasts and man as the silent miracle of the golden cluster of bananas which, in one season, crawled out of the black soil. Like all animals, man, for his own self-defense, is designed to react to sudden changes in the environment, whether they be sights, sounds, smells, or tactile sensations. Permanence, monotony, and quiescence tend to put us off our guard and make us inattentive. We do not see the ever-present tip of our noses, nor do we hear the constant drone from a street or a waterfall. A dog will sleep unperturbed under a growing apple tree and a bird can sit just as peacefully among its slowly extending branches; neither will notice the apples coming out, little by little, among the foliage until one of them suddenly falls to the ground. Nature has made all of us living creatures alert to rapid changes that take place in our immediate vicinity. They may involve danger. But we are left out of tune with the frequencies of slow change. It rarely threatens us and usually represents nature's silent way of granting us our daily fare and a livable environment.

The two leaps that had taken us in one day from a naked island into a veritable Garden of Eden had somehow left us out of tune with a spectator's normal frequencies. We felt as if we had witnessed overnight how a splendid environment had arrived to cover barren lava that had once been lifted above the sea. Indeed, the valley we penetrated had once been more barren than Motane, without one green blade, without a single spoonful of humus. Time had hidden from all eyes the process by which jungle scenery had come from nowhere, as if on a flying carpet of rich soil. The barren rock of Fatu-Hiva had risen from the ocean floor to be laid like a picnic table. The lizards and pigs that ran around in the underbrush took all this for granted, and so did our friends down in the village, who sat there waiting for the coconuts to fall to the ground. But, on this day, we were out of tune. Behind the pleasant greenery, we seemed to see a second landscape, Fatu-Hiva before yesterday. Red lava oozed down all the ridges and ravines, and glowing cinders and ashes rained into this molten and mobile valley as the island under our feet rose from the frothing sea. Born as a little, hostile inferno, killing any life that approached its shores, the emerging body of lava cooled off and solidified into the lifeless contours of Fatu-Hiva. While the patient work of surf and rivers molded the island into its present shape, and while man still slept in the chromosomes of his primitive predecessors, the first miniature colonists arrived on barren Fatu-Hiva. Sea-borne and air-borne, they landed equipped with chromosomes enabling them to develop roots and mouths and other effective organs designed for drilling, tilling, and fertilizing the sterile soil. What began as tiny seeds, and eggs of worms and insects, sufficed to lay out the deep carpet of fertile soil on which we walked, and to decorate it with the moss and grass and ferns and shrubs and giant jungle trees that now surrounded us.

When we reached our river, we sat down on a wide, smooth slab to look at the running water and enjoy its melodious, nonstop performance. The only other sightseers were some twittering finches on a moss-covered trunk, who seemed to tune their own performance to the music of the river. At the crossing place, the water streamed as

rapidly as during the heavy rains before we left. The soil in the valley was soft and moist. Beside my foot was a big mushroom, clean
and white, like a porcelain bowl turned bottom up. A few days ago,
it would surely not have been there and I should probably not even
have seen it in its infancy by digging in the ground.

Usually, the sight of a mushroom was nothing I particularly enjoyed in nature, unless it had pretty colors or a strange form. This
one was glossy white, plain, and probably inedible. I touched it carefully with my big toe. It fell over. So fragile, and yet it had been able
to push its way up through the compact ground with such speed and
force that lumps of black soil and stones lay tilted to all sides. The
white hat and white leg were as shiny and clean as a girl dressed for
Sunday church, and the neat creation pretended never to have
touched that dirty soil out of which it had come.

The fallen mushroom exposed the lips of its fertility organ under
its gown: a dense system of blades radiating around the single leg.
Not many days earlier, this living upshot had been the size of one of
its tiny pores. What stops a mushroom from growing to the size of an
umbrella, or a millstone, or a circus tent? On Motane, there was not
enough humus for even a tiny fungus, but here there were tons upon
tons of deep, rich soil, from the beach to the vertical cliffs of the
Tauaouoho Mountains. Giant mushrooms could have conquered the
whole Omoa Valley, overshadowed the jungle roof, devoured all
nutritious substances, and collapsed like balloons, like the sheep on
Motane, when there was nothing left to eat.

Why did the wild mushrooms that had spread to these islands with
the wind behave in a more civilized manner than the domestic sheep
brought to Motane by man? Why had none of nature's wild species
managed to upset the balance around us, conquer the island, and
transform it into a wasteland like Motane?

I was so lost in my own reveries that I hardly noticed the hungry
mosquitoes as I brushed them aside continually. They had begun to
accumulate in clouds around us, and Liv had risen to put on her
khaki shirt to protect her shoulders. She blessed the little finches as
she saw how they came to our aid by helping themselves merrily
from the hungry insect cloud. The most colorful of our jungle friends
landed in all its glory in a tree above us: the parrot-plumed local
cuckoo. Another ally against the insects had arrived, ten times the
size of a tiny finch. These birds had one thing in common with the
mushroom: No matter how much they ate, a finch could not reach
the size of a cuckoo and a cuckoo could never grow bigger than its

own kin. And there came a tiny fruit rat, too. Light as a dab of cotton wool, it sprang from one bush to the next and ran along the slenderest branches. With tons of fruit and nuts available, it was designed to remain little, never to grow as bulky as the jungle hog, which ate the same food.

Nature would have gone mad if each species had not been confined to its own allotted size. The chromosomes had always taken care of that, from the beginning of time. My professors had shown me through microscopes how simple it all is. In any kind of fertilized egg or seed, a single cell will divide itself, without outside interference, into two, four, even into a hundred billion cells of all sorts. But when the intended form and correct size have been reached, the cells will suddenly stop dividing. Automatically, and still with no outside interference, each of the innumerable cells will stop dividing as soon as horns and intestines, teeth and tails, all have reached their predesigned form and measure. A fly, a whale, a leaf, a coconut, any growing creature has its own allotted size today. An invisible finger has installed in every species an unknown mechanism, a kind of check or stopper, that never fails, and always says: Thus far but no farther; this big, but no bigger. The ingenious check was installed somewhere in that mushroom, in the tiny mosquitoes that danced around my head, and in the giant jungle trees groping for the clouds above us without ever reaching high enough to stop them.

Damn the mosquitoes! I, too, pulled on my khaki shirt so as not to be devoured. If only the sun could be given a chance to dry up the jungle a little, no more of these insects would be bred than the birds could cope with. According to Tioti, it had been raining off and on every day since we left. But this wet season could not last forever.

We picked up our light burdens and returned to the trail. To our delight, we found ripe guavas on the bushes flanking the path. There had obviously been little or no traffic up the valley since we left. Of course: Willy and Ioane had come back with rice and flour.

We approached our clearing on the royal site. Liv was thirsty and turned off to drink at the spring. As she stopped and bent away the umbrella plants, Poto, the wild cat, ran out from among the big leaves.

Nearby, the yellow bamboo plaiting was visible through the greenery. I loved this place. This valley. I had never been as happy as in this friendly and hospitable wilderness. I felt wonderfully relaxed among all the green foliage. Secure in what had become familiar surroundings, a realm where the perpetual clockwork of nature was master. But we had to be alert to such diseases as had been unknown in early Polynesian times.

There was the cabin. Beside it, the unwalled kitchen. The ground was still quite muddy. To my delight, no footprints!

But what a change!

Liv was now at my side, and with a cloud of mosquitoes around us, we hurried up to the front wall, which was partly hidden by huge, sprouting banana leaves and other fresh vegetation. The jungle had begun to recapture our clearing at an almost incredible speed. Everything seemed to have bounced straight out of the ground while for a moment we turned our attention elsewhere. Had we been away overnight or a year?

An exclamation from Liv told me that she had noticed what I was gazing at too. The four poles I had pointed and rammed into the ground to support the kitchen roof had sprouted long branches with green leaves.

I tried to open the door of the cabin. The whole frame yielded. Surprised, I tested the strength of the beautifully plaited golden wall. My fist went through it as if it were thick paper. I peeped inside. Tatters hung down everywhere from a caved-in roof. Spiders and centipedes ran away up the walls as we entered. And once more, the bamboo dust. It poured down upon us if we touched the feeble walls. Like a coating of snow or desert sand, it had covered our home-made furniture, our sleeping-bench, and all we had hidden under it: stone tools, images, and skulls.

Nobody had been in. Our archaeological and zoological collections were safe. But we ourselves had no home now but the jungle roof.

We pulled out from the wreckage of the cabin the case of craniums and all other property that we did not want anybody to find when the walls collapsed completely. We hid it in a dry cache among the rocks. We praised our good luck that the rain was not pouring down, and hurried to raise a crude shelter of sticks and large umbrella leaves on the clearing in front of our former home. With our old mosquito netting carefully stretched over us, we fell asleep on a thick mattress of ferns. Then the rain started to drum against the dark world around us.

We were wet when morning came. The rain had stopped, and mud and mosquitoes surrounded us. This was, after all, not a place to remain in. We could build a new bamboo cabin on the site of the old one, but the same things would happen again. Besides, it was too risky to remain here in the mud. We would get the *fe-fe* on our legs all over again, and any one of these mosquitoes could carry the filaria of elephantiasis.

"We shall have to do what the islanders do," Liv suggested: "Abandon the jungle and live at the coast, where the wind drives the mosquitoes away." I agreed, but then we must escape to some other valley. For, with all the diseases among the islanders, we could not live with them in the village down by the bay.

We resorted to Pakeekee and told him our problem, but he merely insisted that his home was ours too. Tioti seemed to read our minds. If we wanted to escape from the mosquitoes, he said, we should try to get across the Tauaouoho Mountain Ridge. For, on the other side of the island, the constant wind from the east always blew so strongly that the insects were chased far up into the thickets of all the valleys.

Neither Tioti nor Pakeekee had ever been across the mountains to the east coast, but Veo had been there. He confirmed what we already knew, that the Tauaouoho and Namana mountains join to form a mighty wall that separates the windy, east-side valleys from those of our sheltered, western coast. Since the needle hole through the ridge between Hanavave and Hanahoua was no longer accessible, the only passage for man was at one specific point on the central plateau, where a very ancient trail had once been cut into the cliffs leading down to Ouia. Ouia was the largest valley on the other coast. Landslides had carried away much of that passage too, but, with care, people could still get down.

Except for Ouia, the other side was uninhabited. All the tribes had died out. All the valleys were empty of people. Only in Ouia lived an old man, called Tei Tetua, all alone with his little adopted daughter. Veo had met the old man. Tei Tetua had once been the chief of four tribes, but had survived all his people and all his twelve wives. A relative in Omoa had brought him Tahia-Momo, Little Tahia, the young girl that kept him company. Otherwise, he would have been entirely alone.

"Tei Tetua is the last of the men from the past," Tioti explained, and Veo nodded. The old man belonged to the ancestors. He was the only one left of those who had eaten human flesh.

We knew that cannibalism had been practiced in the Marquesas group, at least until fifty years previously. A Swedish carpenter had been eaten on Hivaoa in 1879. The last recorded instance of cannibalism on that island was in 1887, during a ceremony in the Puamau Valley. Tei Tetua was a grown man then, and this island

and his valley were far more isolated than any part of Hivaoa. But even an ex-cannibal would long for company when left alone. At any rate, there was no choice of valleys on the other coast, for, according to our friends, Ouia was the only valley we could reach on foot. From there, one could get nowhere, as all the valleys on that side were isolated from each other by insurmountable cliff walls.

Veo could also tell us that the other side of the island was much drier. The clouds that build up over the Tauaouoho Ridge blew over onto this side. There were fewer mosquitoes, too, on the other side.

Tioti, and Pakeekee's agile son Paho, both volunteered to follow us across the mountain ridge. But not Veo. And he was the only one of them, the only one of all our friends, who knew the road. No gift, not even the coveted goods from Bob's shop on Hivaoa, could tempt him. Nor would he give us any reason.

The same evening, however, Paho suddenly reappeared from nowhere as we sat waiting for him around Pakeekee's kerosene lamp. He had found a guide. He would not tell us his name, but all Paho required was a modest part of our cans from Hivaoa, and we were to find the companion we needed the moment we started our climb into the highlands next morning.

It was still pitch dark and there was no sign of sunrise, when Pakeekee called us and we rose from the pandanus mat on his floor to start our little caravan. The village slept, and in the stillness we could hear from the distance, at even intervals, only the eternal growling of the surf. Our friends had already loaded all our possessions onto two pack horses. All we had to do was to roll up our rugs and put them on top. Our proud old mountain friend, the stallion Tuiveta, was carrying baskets with all that was left of Mister Bob's goodies: corned beef, jam, candy, tobacco, and chocolate. Paho had been allowed to carry away part of it during the night. We never regretted our wild wholesale deal with Mister Bob. The remainder was now to be a friendship gift to the old man and his little daughter.

Tioti warned us that nobody should know where we had moved to. He trusted no one. We whispered a farewell to Pakeekee and his hospitable household, and with Tioti, Paho, and the two pack horses at our heels, we walked silently down to the bay. A few dogs barked lazily, but we saw no one.

Where the familiar trail took off for the highlands, we found our third companion, a young man we had seen before but did not know by name. He waited till our caravan had passed and joined us at the rear.

The sun did not rise that morning, but the clouds turned from black to gray, and we gradually obtained good visibility as we followed the winding path through the glens and hills we knew so well in the central highlands. But, up here, our guide finally took the lead, and after some hesitation, located an overgrown trail that branched off from the main path and took us due eastward, in the direction of the highest peaks. The route we followed was often swampy and difficult. For a while, it led through a mountain forest where trunks of fallen trees occasionally barred all passage ahead. In the afternoon, we reached some bamboo thickets that blocked the road like bulwarks. We had to cut a passage, step by step, with machetes. Bamboo canes, thick and thin, yellow and green, were interlocked in a crisscross chaos where knife-like edges were pointed against us like drawn bayonets once the canes had been chopped off.

Tioti hurt himself rather badly when a thick bamboo pole slid down as he cut it, and speared his fist. As Liv sat down to attend to his bleeding wound with leaves and bands of tough bark, she caught a glimpse of his right ankle and was shocked. Without interrupting the bandaging of our friend's fist, she gave me a silent sign with her eyes, and I looked. It was clear enough. Tioti had begun to wear long pants, and the right leg of his trousers had been split at the base to make room for a colossal ankle. Tioti had started to grow in one leg with elephantiasis. He was obviously trying to hide it. We both were overwhelmed by this tragic discovery as we rose and continued eastward at the heels of the gay sexton. And we realized more than ever how important it was to escape from the clouds of infected mosquitoes.

The east wind struck us full strength as we reached the point where the cliff edge fell off in a vertical drop, down into the deep abyss of another underworld: Ouia. For the horses, there was no longer a foothold and we had to tether them, each to its own tree, where they could stay grazing while we proceeded on foot. Then our three companions cut carrying-poles and loaded the burdens onto their own, naked shoulders. At this point, we had to start climbing. The wall was no less than perpendicular, but, in ancient times, men had carved a narrow shelf toward the left, where it was possible to get a foothold. At several points, the old shelf had been destroyed by erosion and slides, but our guide was prepared and had brought a strong pole to lay across the gaps.

We were both admittedly scared. But we had very little choice. The schooner had left, the moment it had set us ashore; up here in the free highlands there was not enough food; and our former home in Omoa had been conquered by bugs and mosquitoes. It was clear to us that we had to get down this cliff, and therefore we did get down.

Down in the deep, dark valley, with the vertical abyss rising around us on three sides, we followed the course of a gushing river through a crisscross jumble of crooked hibiscus trees. The ground was covered, moreover, with a chaos of boulders, and we had to proceed as best we could without any kind of trail. Halfway down the valley, the entire river suddenly disappeared into the ground. All the gushing masses of water were lost, to the last drop, below the terrain. There were more stones than mud as we proceeded. Down by the mouth of the valley, the river suddenly reappeared, welling up from among the rocks, and we followed it as it danced on between boulders toward the sea.

Paho had run ahead down along the river, and the distant baying of dogs told us that he had reached the old man's hut. We had not far to go now.

The valley had gradually become much wider, and soon it became bright and open. The thick brush yielded to a beautiful palm grove, down by the glittering sea. The sun broke through. We inhaled a fresh wind from the open ocean. Down between the lofty palm trunks, we saw a cluster of low, sun-baked huts, built in the old-fashioned Polynesian way from sticks and thatch. A seemingly naked person came running toward us between the trees. The old man.

Tei Tetua ran like a young mountain goat. He was weather-beaten and sun-tanned all over and wore nothing but a bag around his loins, tied to a waist string of bark. The old man was muscular and agile, as if he were half his real age. His whole face seemed to grin as he laughed with happy animation, showing teeth as perfect as those of the ancient skulls under our bed. When I gave him my hand and said *kaoha*, he grabbed it, laughing and writhing like a shy boy short of words. His whole person was almost bursting with restrained energy. He just did not seem to be able to express all he had to say after years of loneliness.

"Eat pig!" he finally exclaimed. "When pig is finished, we eat cock. When cock is finished, we eat more pig!"

Then he bounded away like a young boy, down to his cluster of huts, and began shouting at his bristly, semi-wild boars. With the aid of Paho, he got a bark lasso looped around the hind leg of one of them and came staggering toward us with the huge black beast struggling in his embrace.

"Eat pig," he said merrily, and showed us the fat and shrieking hog.

To him, that was clearly the greatest expression of friendship. And until late at night, we were sitting on his earthen floor eating juicy boar baked underground. We sat squatting around a sparking wood fire with large chunks of hot meat in our hands, and devoured it greedily with the teeth and fingers alone. Close at the old man's side sat Tahia-Momo, his little adopted daughter. Barely a teen-ager, she was beautiful. With her large, sparkling eyes and long, black hair, she sat squatting like the rest of us, listening attentively to every word that was said. Tei Tetua, too, was as alert as a child, beaming with happiness at seeing people in his lonely valley.

"Remain here," he asked all of us insistently. "Ouia has much fruit. Much pig. Every day, we shall eat pig. The wind is good in Ouia."

Liv and I promised to remain in his valley, and old Tei and little Tahia laughed with joy and thought up the most tempting plans for the days ahead. But our three friends from Omoa shook their heads.

"Ouia is not good," said the sexton. "Ouia has much fruit, much pig, much wind. But Ouia has no copra, no money. Omoa is good. Many houses, many men. Much copra, much money."

"Tioti," I interrupted, "what do you want money for, when you can get enough food?"

The sexton grinned. "It is like that," he said and shrugged his shoulders. "Before, it was good enough without money. Not now. Now we are no longer savages."

The old man knocked out the fire and scooped ashes over the embers. Liv and I were shown from his open kitchen shelter into his stick-walled hut, where he left his own pandanus mat on the earthen floor for us to sleep on. He himself moved out to sleep with all the others in a separate hut beside our own. We were never to learn the original function of that hut. But the closely set sticks that formed the walls of both of Tei Tetua's dwellings were gray with age and of a very hard wood that might well have dated back to the days when he had other company than little Tahia-Momo.

We rolled ourselves up in our rugs. How marvelous it was to go to bed without mosquitoes! The surf was so near us, somewhere just beyond the airy walls. In Omoa, we had been used to hearing the distant breath of the ocean carried to us on calm nights above the jungle roof as a faint, rhythmic hiss. Here the boulder-beach surf rumbled and snored with the same slow rhythm, but with a strength that made it seem as if we shared a pillow with the ocean. It would take time for jungle dwellers to get used to this ocean throb.

What were the others chattering about? Tei Tetua was back with them. They stirred the ashes and remained squatting around the embers, talking in low voices so as not to disturb us. Tioti repeatedly mumbled our names and was probably telling our story. Old Tei had a long, exciting tale that seemed to keep the others spellbound. Perhaps they had asked him about the days of cannibalism. As for us, we should have plenty of time to hear his stories later. But not our friends; they were off in the morning. On our way across the mountains, our three companions had been deeply involved in the topic of eating people, *kaikai enata*. They knew from the missionaries that this had been perhaps their ancestors' greatest crime before Christianity had been introduced. Their ancestors had eaten people as a religious rite, believing that they obtained the strength of the person they consumed. But judging from the conversation of our friends, they seemed to have strange ideas about what was evil in cannibalism. The immorality seemed to them to lie in the act of eating unclean people, and the pagan people eaten by their ancestors were unclean. But our guide, as a Catholic, and Tioti, as the Protestant sexton, could not agree as to whether it was proper to eat Christ or merely to pretend to eat him in Church. They had descended all the way into Ouia without convincing each other.

Kaikai enata. In the intervals in the sound of the surf, I seemed to hear that phrase more frequently than it was probably spoken. Our knowledge of the Marquesan dialect was still rudimentary, but we had consistently added to our little home-made dictionary, and we were now familiar with most everyday words. However, trying in vain to follow parts of the subdued conversation, I was probably beginning to let my imagination get the better of me. So with Liv too, who lay motionless but wide awake. I could not help thinking of my father-in-law, who had run to his bookshelf and read about cannibal islands when Liv wrote to him about our plans. What would he have said now, if he had known we were lying on the floor mat of a formerly practicing cannibal, with the host squatting in the dark outside the wall. If this cabin was only as old as my father-in-law, somebody would probably have been eaten within these walls. Probably this was where Tei Tetua had participated in his cannibal rite. There was nothing cruel about the old man out there. If he had posed in a laboratory coat beside a microscope, he could have passed for a university professor. In fact, he reminded me of my own genial zoology professor, Dr. Hjalmar Broch. If Tei Tetua had eaten the flesh of some slain foe, it would have been in obedience to his own ancestors, who told him to do so out of religious conviction. In fact, beside him out there in the kitchen shed sat peaceful, modern Polynesians who would be willing to eat Christ. That might have been considered the utmost limit of obscenity to the pagan generations of Marquesans; they would have been willing to eat a foe, but not their own sacred *Tiki*.

The sexton seemed to be in no hurry to sleep, and each time he poked the ashes to get more light, a flickering flame created dancing shadows in our room, for there were as many open cracks as there were crooked bars in the walls. We noticed some large containers, made of brown bottle gourds, suspended from wooden hooks on the walls, and some bowls of coconut shell, black with oil, elaborately carved in geometric and symbolic patterns. A bundle of dried tobacco leaves hung in a corner. Some old stone adzes and a crude iron hatchet had been flung down beside us on the earthen floor, together with the old man's flint and steel. And down from the thick beams of the roof hung a long and strange wooden box. That was Tei Tetua's own coffin.

"If I get ill," the old man had told us quite cheerfully, "I shall just crawl into the coffin and shut the lid. If I should remain on the floor, the dogs would just break in and help themselves."

The old man had also dug his own tomb beside the house. He had put a gabled slab roof and a cross over it, and we often found him inside throwing out dirt kicked down into it by his chickens.

This was a new world to us. No schooner came here. At last, we were as far away from the grip of civilization as we could possibly get.

The last embers died. We fell asleep to the rhythmic thunder of the surf. Our friends in the kitchen shed, too, must have withdrawn to their hut. They had to get up before the sun the following morning and start their long return trip to the west coast.

We woke to find ourselves alone with Tei Tetua and Tahia-Momo. They were as happy as they had been the day before. The sun shone, the birds sang, and the valley was open and hospitable. This was the land of our dreams. This was where we should have come at the very beginning.

Tei Tetua was sole proprietor in the Ouia Valley: At least, there was none to contest his rights, and we were free to choose any site we wanted without paying rent. We were guests in the old man's kingdom and anything that was his was ours. Tei Tetua had no feeling of personal property.

Tei's own cluster of huts lay in the open palm grove at the southern corner of the bay. An old terrace had been raised here at one time to keep the ground safe when the river flooded, and a solid stone wall was built all around it to keep out the wild as well as the semidomesticated boars which abounded in the depopulated valley. The shallow river passed right below the wall and entered the ocean through a wide passage in the huge boulder barricade that the powerful trade-wind surf had piled up along the curving mouth of the bay. This high boulder barricade sloped steeply into the agitated ocean, where the wild surf droned against it uninterruptedly and invited no one to swim or launch a canoe.

Across the river, a stone's throw from Tei Tetua's huts, and as close to the sea as they were, was a little grassy plain, which boars and wild goats seemed to favor. There was plenty of space between the lofty coconut palms, and we chose the site for our new home. Here there was a constant sea breeze and healthy, unpolluted surroundings, where insects and germs would leave us in peace. Chas-

Opposite:

CARRYING FRUIT HOME from the mountain-girt jungle, Tei Tetua heads for his thatched hut, protected from wild boars by a stone enclosure. The vertical wall of the Tauaouoho Mountain Ridge cuts his valley off from the rest of the world.

ORANGES were exceptionally large and juicy in the Ouia Valley and were picked by old Tei Tetua in baskets he plaited from the leaves of coconut palms.

TEI TETUA'S TABLE MANNERS did not please Liv, as she said that, even when he ate sugar cane, it looked as if he were gnawing a human leg bone.

Overleaf left:

OUR OUIA HOME was beside the beach and separated from the old man's huts only by a stream. The peak above us was the first land ever sighted by Europeans in Polynesia, when the Mendaña expedition sailed straight from Peru to Fatu-Hiva, in 1595. Before then, aboriginal people had planted South American pineapples, which now grew wild near the top of this mountain.

Above:

A WILD GOAT was caught and kept as our first pet. Our little hut was raised on poles as protection against the numerous wild boars.

Overleaf left:

TEI TETUA ROASTING BREADFRUIT in his kitchen. He did not allow us to do our own cooking, but supplied us with excellent meals so ample that Liv finally started to slim, claiming that the old man was fattening us up intentionally.

Overleaf right:

IN WATER-FILLED LAVA FORMATIONS along the coast, Liv and Tahia-Momo collected good sea food, beautiful shells for jewelry, and rare specimens for my zoological collection.

ing across the Pacific from South America, the eternal trade wind had not touched land for four thousand miles when it jumped this high boulder barricade and made the trunks of the waving palms sway like grass, high above our heads. White man's little stowaway devils, the mosquitoes, were swept far into the inland thickets. It was a sudden relief to experience Polynesia as it was before the unintentional introduction of these tiny vampires which had eventually made life unsupportable for us in Omoa.

The old man disapproved of our plan of sleeping anywhere but in his hut, but since we had picked a site so close to his, he yielded and wanted to make sure that this time we built a home that did not collapse after a few months. He had been furious when, the night before, Tioti had told him of our bamboo cabin in Omoa, and his mouth was set hard when he thought of his modern compatriots. People were no longer as they used to be. Nobody cared for the old arts. Now everybody just sat waiting for the days to pass, for the coconuts to ripen so that the schooner could pick them up.

Tei Tetua's experience of modern times was rather meager. He had twice been across the mountain to Omoa, the last time to bring back Tahia-Momo, when he grew tired of being alone. Long before, a missionary had also come across to his valley and had given him a proper baptism and a bronze cross to put on top of his tomb. Someone had even tried to land from the sea to harvest the large quantity of coconuts that were now left for the pigs, but the surf had caused havoc with the launch, and Ouia, like the rest of the east coast, remained unprofitable for modern man. An old rack for drying coconut kernels was still standing near the beach, in memory of this attempt, and a little dugout canoe, old and weather-beaten, lay beside it. We never saw it launched, and we admired the courage and skill of those who must have used it in former times.

Opposite:
WILD BOARS came to fetch the leftovers from our meals, as the old man fed us so abundantly that we could not manage to eat everything. Sometimes they scratched themselves so much against the poles that the whole cabin began to sway. We could easily catch them with nooses of hibiscus bark.

Previous two picture pages:
THE OPEN WALL WAS THE DINING ROOM of our pole cabin. Civilization was so far away that I began to doubt my own memory when I thought about the existence of airplanes and skyscrapers.

Tei Tetua was full of pride and enthusiasm when he spoke about people and events of long ago. In this respect, he contrasted with our good friend the departed sexton. Tei was in fact one more of the extremely few islanders we had met who had remained unspoiled Polynesian in both body and mind. Like Teriieroo on Tahiti and Terai on Hivaoa. It took wisdom and a keen brain for one who had never been confronted with anything but the tempting side issues of our civilization to realize that progress is worth striving for only in fields where progress means improvement. Not one of the disease-stricken islanders on the other coast, whose lives depended on the calls of the schooner, was half as carefree and contented as this old man who missed nothing, at least now that he had company.

A climb at the heels of Tei Tetua took me next day across rugged coastal shelves and around the northern promontory of the bay into a tiny valley called Hanativa, an easily reached appendix to our own, major valley. Old, overgrown stone walls, tombs, and a few large-eyed images were seen here, too, covered with a complete jumble of *borao* and *mio* trees. We had come to fetch *mio* wood, which the old man said was the best for building. I was completely amazed when I saw the natural agility with which this old islander, who could have been at least a big boy's grandfather, swung himself into the crisscross of trunks and branches. I followed with much less elegance. We were searching for the straightest possible sections for poles and beams. When a large quantity of branches of the desired thickness had been cut into convenient lengths, we pounded their juicy bark off with smooth stones, and tied the resultant slippery, ivory-like poles into bundles. My naked shoulder was rubbed sore and my bare feet cut by sharp lava as I climbed with my burden along the rocks as fast as I could at the heels of the old man. For him, it seemed to be mere play, and he was audibly amused when I stopped at one point and clung to the rock wall as an outsized breaker sent a runaway cascade all over me.

Reaching the tip of the cape, we threw our bundles into the sea and returned for the next load. The surf carried the poles along all the way into the bay and threw them up on the boulder barricade in front of our building site.

Our second home was destined to be even smaller than the first. It was in fact nothing but a palm-roofed nest, open on one side and raised on poles high above the ground to avoid visits from the many boars. The three walls were made of sticks of *mio* wood lashed together, and were high enough for us to be able to sit anywhere, but to stand only under the central gable. The frame and everything else was tied together with tough strips of bark. The local species of hibiscus always provided a truly excellent rope. A sloping ladder led to the open side, and the interior space was just wide enough for us to sleep crosswise on a bedding of palm leaves piled up along the inner wall. Except for the waterproof palm roof, sun and moon could peep in everywhere through the chinks between the slender sticks, and small items kept dropping through the floor until we covered it with a freshly plaited pandanus mat.

During the very first night in our new nest, we were awakened by a grunting boar scratching itself so passionately against one of the main supporting poles that the top-heavy structure began to sway and threatened to capsize. In the morning, we strengthened our slender framework with a stockade that held all the supporting poles together and also prevented beasts from getting underneath.

Our next project was to erect a kind of open kitchen shelter over a stone oven, like the one we had had in Omoa. But this caused the most vigorous protests from Tei Tetua. We were guests in his valley, and therefore we were to eat his food. He just grabbed our black iron pot, which was the only kitchen furniture we had, and with his booty he padded over to his own, nearby house.

This was the overture to our happiest days in the South Seas.

Tahia-Momo—the old man called her only Momo, "Little"—immediately took to Liv. To have another woman in the valley was for her as if a mother had descended from the lofty rock enclosures; a mother or a female companion, someone to talk to who had other interests and opinions than those of the old hermit. Momo would soon be a teen-ager, and was therefore considered almost an adult. If Momo had much to learn from Liv, she certainly repaid her lessons. Tei and I would frequently find the two girls sitting together in the grass beside the refreshing stream. Momo was the teacher, showing Liv the old arts once known by every Marquesan *vahine:* how to make *tapa* by soaking and beating the inner bark of the breadfruit tree into a fibrous, white paper-cloth; how to weave artistic basketry from slender vines and coconut leaves; how to plait sleeping mats from thin strips taken from leaves of the pandanus tree; how to make strings and solid straps from the fibers of coconut husk; how to clean and roast the rind of bottle gourds to make them into waterproof containers; how to make glue from resins, and oil paint from earth, ashes, or vegetable components; how to extract perfume from plants; and how to prepare leis and wreaths from flowers, and necklaces from nuts and shells.

Liv never wore jewelry, but her little Polynesian friend resolutely took her to dress her up. They did not have to go far before Momo found her choice. At the edge of the forest, she knew where to find colorful nuts, seeds, and fruits to thread on strings. Her favorite selection was some glossy-red, bone-hard peas which looked as if they had been designed just for ornamentation. With shining red necklaces and bracelets, and with perfumed flowers behind their ears, the two young women returned from the outskirts of the forest while old Tei Tetua grinned and looked at me with an expression almost as if he realized that women had much in common all over the world.

Next day, Momo dragged Liv along for a change of fashion. The shoreline of rugged lava running seaward below the cliffs on each side of the bay was to Momo a regular shopping center, exhibiting small sea shells of every shape and color, all for the picking. Their green shopping bags filled with marine jewelry, the two artists returned to the soft grass to pierce their shells with bone needles and thread them on strings.

There was beauty on display in all Momo's shopping centers. No evil-smelling copra was needed for barter; she had a fortune in her bare hands. We never saw Momo's face without a smile. She knew what she wanted, she had a certain taste, and she never missed anything she could not get. Her taste and harmony must have come to her from the hills and the trees, hardly from the old man. She seemed totally free from problems about herself and her environment. She laughed when she came climbing up our ladder to visit us and she laughed as she left. She saw something pleasant in everything, even in the little, gray creepy-crawlies hiding beneath the stones.

Tons of smelly copra carried to the schooner on the other side would not make the women of Omoa and Hanavave radiate happiness like little Momo, even if it had sufficed to give them access to all the glass and metal jewelry in the shop on board.

There were times when Liv was too conservative to follow some of Momo's island fashions. One afternoon, for instance, the girl came climbing up our ladder, her white teeth laughing out of a yellow-green face, and with yellow-green paint shining all over her body. She carried a coconut shell in her hand, filled with the greenish pulp from a nut pounded in coconut oil, and she wanted to anoint her friend with genuine Marquesan cosmetics. How crazy! Yellow-green and with flowers in her hair, she looked like a charming fairy-tale elf born of a cabbage. The effect was not altogether disgusting and might well have caught on in a more modern society. But Liv felt she should stick to her more conservative use of pure coconut oil, to which she let Momo add the sweet perfume of some tiny white flowers.

As for myself, I spent most of my time with Tei Tetua, in the forest or by the huts. If old Tei had wanted to come and live with me in Europe, I could have taught him many lessons that would have improved his own existence. But I was not the right person to better his existence here. Here, in this environment, I was the one to benefit from learning rather than from teaching. I could tell Tei the Latin names of some of the mollusks along the waterfront, and how to classify plants by counting their stamens, but I found it more important that he could teach me whether the clams were edible and how the plants could best be used.

Perhaps, at the bottom of our hearts, Liv and I were a bit surprised at feeling that Tei and Momo were not closer to the ape men than we were, because they did not know algebra or letters. In our part of the world, we had been used to associating illiteracy with the brains of children under the age of six. If an adult was illiterate, it was because something was wrong with his wits. But this was not the case with our friends in Ouia. If anything, we often felt absent-minded and stupid, because they, at a mere glance, could see a solution to a practical problem that had dumfounded us. We enjoyed their company.

After all, we began to realize, there is more to learn in this fabulous world than any one person can cope with, so it is for each of us to make the wisest or most advantageous pick of what to know and what to ignore. An astronomer knows the distances to the stars, and a botanist the petals of a flower. But neither dismisses the other as an ignoramus because his knowledge is confined to a different field.

We began to accept our two neighbors as specialists. Specialists in how to live and adapt themselves in the best way to the environment in the Ouia Valley. They did not know the size of either molecules or stars, nor the distance to the moon. But they knew the size of booby eggs and ripe husk tomatoes, and they could tell me how far it was to the nearest site of mountain pineapples. We felt ashamed to admit to ourselves that, with all our training and despite white man's inherited conviction that he had been born to remodel the earth, we from the world of letters ought to tread far more carefully outside our own circles. There is still so very much to learn that is not yet spelled out in letters. How do we know that we do not kill it before we discover it?

Tei Tetua had no shoes. He did not even own a pair to put on when he was to crawl into his coffin. His only wardrobe was one strip of loincloth, which he occasionally wore as a perineal bag, but he was clean and behaved as if he owned the world. The old Greek philosopher Diogenes, looking in vain with lanterns for honest human beings in the crowded market place, would have found one in Tei Tetua. Diogenes would also have given him a place in the sun next to himself in the barrel, and no king, no merchant, no teacher from any nation could have improved upon his existence.

He accepted with gentle courtesy the cans and jars I handed him on arrival, but we never saw him use them. He took more pride and pleasure in anything he could pass on to us as a return gift. He sometimes smoked his own, home-made cigars, and the only one of our presents we ever saw him using was a pipe. But he refused to accept Mister Bob's supply of tobacco, as tobacco plants grew wild beside his house.

The dead island of Motane was far away, and so was the unfortunate community of Omoa, but not farther than for us to realize how lucky we were to have ended up in Tei Tetua's world. We should probably have taken things more for granted, had we landed here directly upon our arrival from Norway. This was Polynesia as we had expected to find it. It was a surviving fraction of a world that white man likes to dream about, and at the same time wants to improve.

As I began to roam the valley with Tei to harvest our daily bread, it was easy to see that, with more sun and less rain, there was not the same tropical luxuriance in Ouia as there was in Omoa. Nevertheless, here too the landscape was a successful blend of wilderness and abandoned gardens, enclosed by steep mountain walls. There was a superb variety of fruit, among which only the *fei* was lacking. There were breadfruit and banana. There were mango, papaya, guava, husk tomato, and mountain pineapple. Taro fields, lemon groves, and large orange trees loaded with a kind of juicy, yellowish fruit we never tired of. Tei also knew a number of edible leaves, bulbs, and some delicious roots and tubers. A few steps away from the houses, we could catch prawns in the river, collect the eggs of sea birds and chickens among the rocks, and we could snare the trotters of lazy boars.

We could fish from the cliffs, but the old man himself was not a keen fisherman. As so often in Polynesia, he left the gathering of coastal sea food to the women. When the ocean was not too ferocious, Momo and Liv would venture along the rocky promontory that projected from the southern corner of the bay. Here the dark lava had once hardened into strange formations: grottoes, tunnels, ridges, and depressions. At high tide, the spray from the sea would replenish all the puddles and pools with fresh, clear salt water. A myriad forms of life had assembled there through the ages. Each pool was a natural aquarium, as colorful as the tidal area on the Tahaoa reef, but the lava background was rusty-red and black, with no white corals. Among the myriads of little fish, octopuses, crustaceans, and mollusks, Momo knew what was virulent and what was worth catching.

To our surprise, Momo never worked in the kitchen. It was Tei Tetua himself who was the cook. They took turns in carrying the food to us. Tei and Momo ate by themselves in their own kitchen, and so we smelled the familiar smell of sour, black *poipoi* as Tei dug it out of his storage pit in the earth. Tei had to eat *poipoi* with every dish he prepared. Like so many of his compatriots, he insisted that he could not digest a meal without a fair helping of this fermented dough.

Liv had no objection to Tei Tetua's table manners, for he washed his hands before he ate and we ate with our fingers just as he did. But she said that whether he chewed on a sugar cane or gnawed at a bone, he would squat with his head tilted to one side just as if he were gnawing a human leg bone. The accusation was unfair and cruel, but once it had been pronounced I could not see our friend eat without the same silly associations.

Tei was not only a well-meaning host, but also a gourmet, a gourmand, and a truly capable cook. If we had experienced a scarcity of food in the Omoa Valley, that was far from the case here. Every day, in the morning, at midday, and at night, he or Momo came climbing up the ladder of our pole cabin with the most appetizing dishes. We even grew really fond of *poipoi*, so long as it had been blended with sufficient fresh breadfruit by pounding them together with water. Tei's specialties were pork baked in banana leaves, soft-shelled crabs boiled in coconut sauce, and raw fish soaked à la Tei Tetua. He selected his fish carefully, cut it into small cubes, soaked it overnight in strong lime juice, and served it in a mixture of sea water and coconut milk. Not the slightest taste of raw fish remained.

But no matter what Tei served us, we ate pork as a second course. At all meals. Juicy, hot chunks of jungle boar baked in big leaves between red-hot stones. We received an abundance of food at every meal and we succeeded only in making a clearly visible inroad into the prodigious helpings and then prepared to take the rest back. But this was not accepted by the old man. We had to save the leftovers for our next meal. At the next meal, however, Tei would sometimes show up with a whole baked chicken, together with taro, breadfruit, and still more roast pig.

"The old man is intentionally fattening us up," said Liv one morning when she had trouble tying on her *pareu,* and she went to a calm pool to take a look at her own face. I was never quite sure whether she had only been joking, for the simple reason that she actually went on a diet from that very moment. For a fortnight, she ate nothing but large piles of oranges and pineapples, snatching only an odd banana from the clusters hanging from our ceiling.

As darkness descended over Ouia, we dumped food from the top of our ladder. We could not persuade the old man to take it back. Bristly boars from the forest crowded around our pole cabin every night and grunted, smacked their lips, and shrieked so much that we were worried that they might awaken the old man across the river. When the fattest of these nightly visitors scratched themselves against the wooden framework below, the whole residence would still sway like a crow's nest.

But the bark-lashed pole cabin was solid. Even when a blast from a tropical storm threw unrest among the crowns of the jungle roof and flexed the tallest palms like archers' bows, we lay as safe as babies in a rocking cradle. Only if the storm was strong enough to hurl cascades of sea spray and rain against us horizontally did we have to get up and hang our pandanus floor mat against the seaward wall. The open side of the cabin, where the ladder came up, was on the lee side, where rain never entered. The moon, however, had nothing to stop it from finding us, right in the innermost corner, whenever it rose to hang as the sun's mirror over the black silhouettes of the palms. The moon was never too full to enter, yet not one mosquito came in through the open wall.

On many nights, the moon would rise to light up an empty cabin, while the four residents of the Ouia Valley sat together around a crackling campfire down by the beach. We were sitting in the parquet with a mighty stage in front of us. The stage was so big that people watched the same show from the Sahara, Greenland, the Amazon, and Fatu-Hiva. It was just about the only show that has united people from all over the world since time immemorial. When it started, Arabs, Eskimos, Indians, and South Sea islanders were for a while on the same flying carpet sharing a common universe, carried far away from the day's trivialities. It is not so strange that for many ancient people the moon was the goddess of love and the soothing mother of the universe, while the sun was the alert and industrious father. Only modern man has traded away the night sky in an attempt to obtain continuous day. He turns night into day in less than a second and puts on a million city lights until he sees nothing but his own world.

As if he did not want to dim the moon- or star-lit surroundings with his own light, Tei always made a very small fire. Just big enough for us all to get close to each other and enjoy just the right amount of light and warmth.

Nothing could beat the nights when the moon was full and hung patiently, scattering gold and silver over the Pacific Ocean before us, twinkling behind us too, in the walls of our thatched cabins and in the glistening palm crowns moving lazily against the stars. When the moon was full enough, it lit up the whole forest behind. Giant banana leaves and strange trees stood there in bizarre nightgowns, crowding inland as far as the black silhouettes of the tooth-edged mountain wall that shut us out from the rest of the world. Except for the wind, the surf, and our own voices, there was nothing to hear but a rare, occasional bleating of wild goats high above us. Sometimes we heard the grunting of boars, and there was, of course, the melodious chuckling of the river flowing nearby.

Tei Tetua possessed one extra-island invention: a flint and steel which some early European voyager must have brought to his ancestors. He rubbed fire between two hibiscus sticks only to show his incredible dexterity in this old Polynesian art, but it was faster and easier to knock the flint and steel together and catch the spark on some tinder.

One evening, after the old man had made his fire and knocked out the flames, he sat gazing into the glowing embers until he began to sway slowly but rhythmically to and fro. Then Tei, in his coarse, old man's voice, began to sing a song which at first gave us the creeps, because it seemed to come out of another world. But soon we were fascinated. There was no real melody and not many notes to his tune; it was almost like a liturgical recitation adapted to a musical play. Tei was singing about the world's creation:

"Tiki, the god of man, who lives in the sky, made the earth. Then he made the waters. Then he made the fishes. Then he made the birds. Then he made the fruits. Then he made the *puaa* [the pig]. Then he made people: one man, his name was Atea; and one woman, her name was Atanoa."

Tei interrupted his song with the remark that these two made the rest of mankind by themselves. Then he continued his liturgical recitation with a seemingly endless genealogical list of kings and queens who descended from Atea and Atanoa, down to the generation of Uta, Tei's father.

"Tei," I asked, "do you believe in Tiki?"

"*E*," said Tei. "Yes. I am a Catholic like everybody today, but I believe in Tiki."

The old man grabbed a stone and showed it to me. "What do you call this?"

"*Sten*," I said in Norwegian.

"We call it *kaha*," he explained. "And this?" He pointed at the fire.

"*Baal*," I said.

"We call it *ahi*," he answered, and then he wanted to know the Norwegian name for the god who created man.

"Jehovah," I replied.

"My people call him Tiki," was Tei's prompt reply. He insisted that his own tribe had immediately realized that the missionaries were referring to Tiki when they came and told them about their own god.

"But your people had more than one god. You believed in Tane, too," I ventured.

This was the overture to an interesting briefing. Important kings became like gods after death, but Tiki was the only creator. Tane was just like Atea, a divine progenitor created by Tiki. Atea was brown with black hair, and the *enata*, the common islander, like Tei and Momo, descended from him. Tane was white, with blond hair, and the *hao'è*, fair people like us, descended from him.[1]

Tei believed in one god; the other mythical heroes of the past were just superior people.

[1] This same explanation had also been given to the B. P. Bishop Museum by the ethnologist E. S. C. Handy, who collected Marquesan legends on other islands in this same group in 1920–21. (E. S. C. Handy, *Polynesian Religion*, B. P. Bishop Museum Bull., No. 34, p. 105 [Honolulu, 1927].)

"But, Tei," I said, "I have often seen Tiki in the jungle and he is just made of stone. Carved by your own priests."

"Tiki was not made of stone," Tei answered calmly. "Nobody has seen Tiki. The priests made images of Tiki for the people. I have been inside the church in Omoa. Your priests make sacred images too."

Tei grabbed his bamboo flute and began playing a melodious tune with one nostril. He did not want to discuss religion any further. He was a Catholic, but he maintained the old faith. To him, Tiki was Jehovah.

To judge from Tei's more worldly traditions, there seemed to have been early kings who had the privilege of borrowing the name of the eternal Tiki. Perhaps they represented him as delegates or incarnations on earth, like the sacred sun kings of Egypt, Mexico, and Peru. Like them, the early god-kings of the Marquesas always married their own sisters.

It was Tiki in flesh and blood who had led Tei Tetua's ancestors across the ocean to these islands.

"From where?" I asked, and was curious to hear the old man's reply.

"From *Te-Fiti* [The East]," answered the old man and nodded toward that part of the horizon where the sun rose, the direction in which there was no other land except South America.

I was puzzled. Every scientist had taken it for granted that these islanders had come from the very opposite direction. From Asia. But the Marquesans themselves had always alluded to their ancestral fatherland as *Te-Fiti*, literally "The East." Henry Lie had heard the same legend in the Puamau Valley. There, in fact, while collecting traditional memories for his book on Marquesan legends, the American ethnologist E. S. C. Handy had been given details about an actual human return voyage to Te-Fiti. From Atuona Bay, a local party of men, women, and children had once embarked in a vessel of extraordinary size, which was named *Kaahua*. They sailed east and finally reached the ancestral land of Te-Fiti. Some of the voyagers remained there, while others managed to return to the Marquesas group. Handy had been so puzzled about the unexpected travel direction for Te-Fiti, that he had to ask twice, and added, "My informant insisted that this land was toward the rising sun (*i te tihena oumati*)."[2]

[2] E. S. C. Handy, *Marquesan Legends*, B. P. Bishop Museum Bull., No. 69, p. 131 (Honolulu, 1930).

A generation before Handy, the German ethnologist Von den Steinen had been equally surprised to learn about the location of this legendary land, which was referred to by his informants as *Fiti-Nui*, the "Great East." This great land was not in the direction of the other islands, but "beyond the eastern cape of Mata-Fenua." Mata Fenua is the very long and slim headland forming the easternmost extension of Hivaoa and pointing like an outstretched finger straight toward South America.

I looked across the moonlit sea. America was indeed far away. Still, Asia was more than twice as remote, and winds and currents came continuously down upon us from South America. It dawned upon me that we were in fact sitting on the one island of all the isles and atolls in Polynesia that had been first hit upon by Europeans. This very island had represented the European gateway to Polynesia. And the first Europeans had come here from South America. In fact, the lofty Tauaouoho Mountain Ridge, behind our backs, must have been the very first sign of Polynesia to be spotted by any European eye. For when the Spanish Mendaña expedition discovered Polynesia, in 1595, they came sailing this way straight from Peru down upon Fatu-Hiva. It was the Incas of Peru who had told the Spaniards that there were inhabited islands far out here in the ocean. At that time, the Europeans had known the coasts of Asia for almost three centuries without learning of inhabited islands in the Pacific. But no sooner had they come to Peru than the mariners and historians of the Incas gave them precise sailing directions to Pacific islands inhabited by dark people of which the Europeans were totally ignorant. Magellan had crossed the entire Pacific half a century earlier without finding any land until he was right in front of the Philippines. But the Incas of Peru willingly told the Spaniards about the islands. This, according to Inca tradition, was where the white culture-bringer from Tiahuanaco had gone when he left South America. Others, they said, had explored the ocean after him. The last major visit to these islands recalled in Inca oral history was undertaken by Inca Tupac Yupanqui, the grandfather of the ruling Inca met by the Spaniards. His own merchant sailors had told him so much about islands inhabited by black men that he equipped a vast flotilla of balsa rafts on the coast of Ecuador, just where his legendary predecessor had once departed. But unlike the great culture hero from Tiahuanaco, Inca Tupac Yupanqui was away for only about a year, and then he came sailing back to Peru with his large flotilla, and brought with him black-skinned prisoners to prove his success. The old custodian in charge of the Inca's souvenirs from his island expedition was still alive when the Spaniards came to Peru.[3]

We knew the Spaniards had come to Polynesia from Peru, and we knew the Incas of Peru had given them the sailing directions; could it not be, then, that Tei Tetua and the other islanders remembered the truth when they said that their ancestors really had come from the east?

After all, the scientists who had studied the physical types in Polynesia had stressed that the Polynesians contrasted with the Malays and Indonesians in nearly every respect: head form, nose form, hair color, hair texture, stature, complexion, beard and body hair; everything was different. The only scholar who made a special study of Marquesan somatology, the noted American anthropologist L. R. Sullivan,[4] had found that these islanders were far closer to certain American Indians in physical composition than to any Mongols, and there was nothing at all to support an Indonesian parentage.

For the first time, I really started to wonder whether these islands could have been reached first by one of the many different cultures that had succeeded each other before the Inca dynasty in ancient Peru. All kinds of physical types were realistically represented in the ceramic art of pre-Inca Peru. Along the Peruvian coast, mummies had been found of people far taller than the Inca and with the same long head form as in Polynesia. Some of these mummies even had wavy red hair and confirmed the Inca traditions that blond and fair-skinned people with long beards had lived among the Quechua and Aymara Indians of Peru long before the Spaniards came. When Francisco Pizarro discovered and conquered Peru, his cousin, Pedro Pizarro, recorded that some of the people they saw were as white and blond as Europeans, and that these were said by the Incas to be the children of their own gods.[5] All the Inca traditions stressed that their main god, Viracocha, and the people who followed him into the Pacific were white and bearded, like the Spaniards.

When old Tei Tetua told me that Tiki had brought his people from "The East," I had not yet studied enough Peruvian mythology

[3] For further details on the Inca legends and sailing directions to Polynesia, see Heyerdahl, *Sea Routes to Polynesia*, Chapter 4 (London, 1968); also Heyerdahl, *American Indians in the Pacific* (Chicago, Rand-McNally & Co., 1968), pp. 556–69.

[4] L. R. Sullivan, *Marquesan Somatology with Comparative Notes on Samoa and Tonga*, B. P. Bishop Mus. Memoirs, Vol. 9, No. 2, pp. 227–29 (Honolulu, 1923).

[5] Pedro Pizarro, *Relation of the Discovery and Conquest of the Kingdoms of Peru*, MS from 1571 translated by P. A. Means, p. 380 (New York, 1921).

to realize that the full Inca name for their departed god-king was Con-Tici-Viracocha, and that while he ruled in Tiahuanaco his name or title was simply Tici, Ticci, or Tiki. If I had known this as I sat with the old man listening to the surf coming in from South America, I should certainly have been keener still in my inquiries about the traveling god-king Tiki who had brought Tei's ancestors from the east.

At any rate, the early Spaniards had found the black people the Incas had told them about. On their very first attempt, they sailed straight from Peru into Melanesia, in 1568. Quarrels on board had made them depart from the route obtained from the Inca historians as to the nearest inhabited island, which was a precise sailing direction for Easter Island. By interrupting their course, they passed south of the Marquesas and hit no land until they reached the Melanesian Solomon Islands. Returning to South America with much trouble, they left Peru a second time, in 1595, and as they now steered due west they soon sighted the high mountains of Fatu-Hiva. As they sailed around the island to anchor on the leeward side, Polynesians and Europeans were to meet each other for the first time. The Polynesians already stood on the shore, but the Europeans called themselves discoverers.

From the records of the chief pilot, Pedro Fernández de Quiros,[6] we gather that the Spaniards must have anchored their four caravels in Omoa Bay. They found the island they had hit upon "thickly inhabited." Four hundred islanders came swimming and paddling from the shore to greet them, and still the beaches and rocks were crowded with people. Forty came on board, "beside whom the Spaniards seemed of small stature." One was taller than the rest by a head and shoulders. Mixed among the others were some of very fair complexion and with "ruddy hair." Some were even described as "not fair but white." An old chief, carrying a parasol of palm leaves, had a long, well-ordered beard, and mustaches so long that he raised them with both hands when he shouted his orders. On the day after their arrival, Admiral Mendaña himself ventured ashore, accompanied by his wife, to hear the first mass said in Polynesia. The pilot recorded: "A very beautiful native sat near Doña Isabel, with such red hair that Doña Isabel wished to cut off a few locks; but seeing that the native did not like it she desisted, not wishing to make her angry."

[6] Pedro Fernández de Quiros, *Narrative of the Second Voyage of the Adelantado Álvaro de Mendaña*, The Hakluyt Society, Second Series, No. 14, pp. 15–29, 150 (Liechtenstein, 1967).

While the admiral's wife graciously abstained from sampling the locks of red hair, the admiral's soldiers pointed their arquebuses at the old bearded man with the parasol and killed him, along with seven or eight others.

Having thus discovered Fatu-Hiva, which they named Magdalena, the Spaniards sailed north and caught sight of Motane, which was then "an island beautiful to look at with much wood and fair fields." They passed on as they spotted the larger islands Tahuata and Hivaoa, and took possession of all four islands in the name of His Majesty their king. They taught one native to say "Jesús María" and to make the sign of the cross, whereupon they shot an estimated two hundred others. When asked why he sat as a guest in a native hut and fired at people outside, one Spanish soldier answered that he did it because he liked to kill. The pilot recorded that another soldier had a different excuse for killing a native who tried to save himself by jumping into the sea with his child in his arms: The Devil had to take those who were ordained to be taken, he said, and besides, he had to make a hit lest he should lose his reputation as a good marksman.

The admiral ordered the Vicar and Chaplain to chant the *Te Deum Laudamus* with all the people on their knees, three crosses were raised, the islands were blessed and all four given Christian names; whereupon the Spaniards weighed anchor to move on westward, as there was no gold in the Marquesas group.

Before they left, the Spaniards slept with the local women and showed their gratitude by sowing maize in the presence of the natives. Conditions were apparently more favorable for venereal diseases than for grain, for syphilis began to spread like wildfire, while no maize came up. The Marquesas Islands were left alone with their newly introduced diseases for 179 years, until Captain Cook rediscovered them, in 1774.

Old Tei Tetua had never heard of either Admiral Mendaña or Captain Cook. To him, Tiki was the discoverer, for he had brought the dark children of Atea and the fair children of Tane whom the Europeans had found ashore. My folks were wrong when they had told me that some Europeans had discovered the Marquesas Islands. It was Tiki who had first led Tei Tetua's ancestors to this place.

I began to look at things with Tei Tetua's eyes now. Of course, Mendaña and Cook were only visitors. But who was Tiki to us in Europe?

When we sat with the old hermit and his adopted daughter on the beach, and the full moon lit up the big, empty valley behind us, I sometimes wondered how these people could tolerate white men.

"Tei," I said attentively, "why have your people all gone?"

"The diseases brought by the double men," said Tei.

The double men, I thought. That was a new and very fitting name for us Europeans. First we come to the islanders as priests and tell them not to kill. Then we come back as army officers and teach them how to do it. We come with the Bible and tell them not to think of tomorrow. Then we turn around and hand them a money box for hoarding their savings. God made mankind naked, but we want to dress the natives up. We arm for peace, and we lie to protect the truth. Double men; that is just what we are, I thought, and a bit abashed, I asked Tei how he had thought up such a denomination.

Tei's answer was not exactly what I had expected. His ancestors had referred to the first Europeans they saw as "double men" because they had two heads, two bodies, four arms, and four legs. The islanders had never seen tight-fitting clothing such as was worn by these foreigners when they arrived. If they took off a hat or a helmet, they still had another head underneath; if they unbuttoned their clothes or opened their armor, another body appeared; and when they pulled off their boots, an extra pair of feet turned up inside. This had caused great surprise among the islanders.

But the double men had brought coughs, fever, and internal pain, and people died. Before, nobody died from sickness, Tei Tetua insisted. People got so old that they sat like dried calabash rinds in one spot and let others feed them. If someone died young, it was because he fell from a palm tree, was caught by a shark, or was hit on the head by a war club and eaten by an enemy.

"Eaten?"

Liv shook her head in horror at such a statement.

"Don't you make war in your countries?" Tei asked with a mien as if to say, "Now come on, tell the truth!"

I had to admit that, when we had left Europe, a very fierce civil war was raging in Spain.

"And what do you do with those you kill?" Tei wanted to know.

"We bury them."

"Bury them!" Tei was amazed and truly disgusted at such barbaric waste. Imagine killing people only to bury their flesh in the ground. Did nobody come and dig it up again when it was matured?

Was Tei being sarcastic or did he mean it? He seemed quite serious. Perhaps he looked at us as we look at a Hindu who leaves a sacred cow to bugs and beasts once it is dead.

Tei began to tell us about his father, Uta, who was the greatest and most savage warrior of the Ouia Valley. He rarely ate any meat but human flesh. But he did not want it fresh, the way most of his friends ate it. No, he waited until it was old and tender before he headed for the burial platform to fill his *poe,* or calabash bowl. Then he would enjoy his meal, eating *poipoi* together with the foul meat. Once, when a member of his own tribe had been killed in an accident, the widow came to present Uta with a pig. She wanted to safeguard her husband, and thought that Uta would make do with the pig until her husband was gone. But Uta ate the pig first and the husband later, when the pig was gone. Tei's mother was furious at her husband, Uta, and begged him to eat fish and decent food that did not stink. And Uta was kind, said Tei. For very many days, he did not touch foul flesh. But then he got very ill and skinny and had to return to his customary diet.

Liv was horrified, and Momo sat with huge brown eyes and a half-open mouth, looking, like us, at the peaceful old man who sat there calmly recounting these events as if he were telling us about a meal at a faculty cafeteria. Tei himself had only participated in a cannibal ceremony once, here in Ouia when he was very young. Human flesh was sweetish, like *kumaa,* or sweet potato. The victim was usually baked, like the pork he prepared for us; that is, rolled up in banana leaves between hot stones in an earth oven. Some people ate human flesh from hunger, as there were too many people then for all of them to have enough food. But usually human flesh was eaten as a religious ceremony, and as a sort of revenge.

The choicest piece was supposed to be the forearm of a woman. "A white woman," Tei added, looking at Liv with a grin. This piece of information was obviously meant as a joke for her benefit, but I doubt if it was very much appreciated by either of the two women. I threw another stick on the embers to get a bit more light. Tei was undoubtedly the finest man on the island, but, sitting there under the stars, hearing cannibal stories told in the first person, had a strange effect on me.

Whether Spaniard, Polynesian, or Viking, man has always been a strange mixture of saint and satan. One moment we can be so pious that we do not want to cut a lock of red hair from another person, and the next moment we murder, bury each other in the ground, or roast each other like pigs. Tei Tetua would probably have grabbed

a club even now, and run onto the war path to kill if a tribal chief
had ordered him to do so. I should also have shouldered a gun to do
the same if my government had told me to. Progress on the battle-
field seemed easy to define: We are educated to run a bayonet into a
living person, but not to run a fork into one who is already dead.

Tei Tetua could tell how wounded and crippled men returned
from the wars then as now. They rarely wounded the enemy's body,
but usually tried to break his skull. A long and beautifully carved
wooden club was the common weapon. Friend and foe had the same
kind of club: the same shape and the same length. The clubs varied
only in their decoration, but all were covered with carvings of their
common god, Tiki. Daggers, swords, spears, and arrows were beneath the dignity of a Marquesan warrior. Small versions of bow
and arrow were made, but only as children's toys or for hunting
the edible native rat. There had been no armaments race in the Marquesas group. Like most Polynesians, Marquesan soldiers always
maintained the kind of weapons their first ancestors had brought
along to the island: clubs and the sling. In this respect, they contrasted with the peoples of East Asia, who favored cutting weapons
of all sorts and were completely ignorant of the sling. Strangely
enough, the Polynesians thus favored the only two weapons universal
in ancient Peru, the club and the sling. The Marquesan sling is indistinguishable in type from that of ancient Peru, and an Austrian
ethnologist, Professor D. J. Wölfel, had described it as a sure proof
of cultural connection between the two areas.[7]

When the Spaniards came to Peru and pushed on from there to
Polynesia, they represented us, as the forerunners of our civilization.
First we shot down the local people who had received us with hom-
age and hospitality. Then we told them in the name of Christ, Thou
shalt not kill. Next we took their barbaric slings and clubs away,
gave them long-range guns and compulsory military service. Chief
Teriieroo had shown me his pride, the *Légion d'Honneur* decoration
he had received for fighting with Frenchmen against the Germans.

Tei Tetua had a deep, round dent in his forehead. "Did somebody
hit you with a club?" I asked.

No. Tei had got a falling stone on his head as a boy. A *taoa* had
cured him. Even one who was rather badly hurt in war could often
be cured by the *taoa*.

What Tei called *taoa*, we refer to as a medicine man or witch doc-

---

[7] D. J. Wölfel, "Die Trepanation. Studien Über Ursprung, Zusammenhänge
und kulturelle Zugehörigkeit der Trepanation," *Anthropos*, Vol. 20, p. 42
(Vienna, 1925).

tor. Actually, he was much more. The *taoa* was a bit of a psychologist and a truly capable surgeon. He knew how to obtain the confidence of the profane by unintelligible speeches and ceremonial hocus-pocus, but he deserved the confidence placed in him, for he performed true surgical operations, some of which had not been mastered in Europe at his time. He could cut, splice, and even trephine without causing infection in the wounds. Today it is different, said Tei. Today a mere scar or scratch can become inflamed.

We certainly realized that infectious germs of various sorts were rife on the island now, particularly on the other side, where the river outlets of Omoa and Hanavave were so polluted that we had to step on the boulder beach with the greatest care so as not to scratch an ankle. In Ouia, we had no such experience.

We had seen some of the *taoa*'s instruments. These old island surgeons had access to no other material than bone, teeth, stone, and wood for making their instruments; yet they had made themselves very functional knives, awls, drills, and even saws.

If, two hundred years ago, a *taoa* had lived in Europe instead of in Polynesia, his skills would have been on the level of any local physician, and his title *taoa* might well be translated as "doctor." A certain Taoa Teke, or Dr. Teke, had lived in Tei Tetua's own time. He died years ago, and an image near the beach of Hanahepu, on the northeast coast, carried his name and even his spirit, according to both Veo and Tei Tetua.

Tei had personally seen Dr. Teke cut open the leg of a man who had broken his shinbone, adjust it properly, and splice it with a piece of hardwood. The wound healed, and the man could walk as before.

More remarkable was Dr. Teke's skill in cranial operation, or trepanation, an art regarded by modern surgeons as extremely difficult until the second half of the nineteenth century. Tei had witnessed a native of Ouia being brought to Taoa Teke after having fallen from a palm and fractured his skull. After appropriate dancing and incantations, during which he made use of a bowl of steaming water, the surgeon went to work. He first washed the wound and removed all the hair from the injured part of the head. Next, he cut a deep, cross-shaped incision in the skin over the fractured part and exposed the skull bone itself. Splinters and edges were cut and polished till the opening was smooth and even. A thin and smoothly polished piece of coconut shell, carved to fit, was now inserted as a lid, and the four flaps of skin were bent back into their original posi-

tion. The skin healed, and the operation was visible in after years
only as a distinct scar in the shape of a cross. Tei knew this man,
who had lived for several years after the operation. But he had
turned a bit odd, Tei added. The *taoa* would never proceed with
this operation if he found that the brain below the bone was injured.

Tei Tetua's description of Taoa Teke's cranial operation made a
great impression on me. I knew that, more than a hundred years before, one of the early visitors to this group, C. S. Stewart, had recorded that the pagan Marquesan priests performed trepanning with
a shark's tooth in cases of injury to the skull. I also knew that Dr.
Ralph Linton had seen and photographed an ancient trepanned skull
on Hivaoa. His colleague and companion E. S. C. Handy, in recording this, also stated that he met the grandson of a famous native
surgeon on that same island, who told him that his grandfather used
to repair injured skulls by inserting a piece of coconut shell the edges
of which were perforated.[8] We, too, were told in Omoa that plaques
of coconut shell were sewn onto fractured skulls with fine threads of
coconut fiber, which sounds almost incredible. While we lived in
Omoa, Veo had one day brought me a fragment of a skull that had
been trepanned, and the edges of the hole had actually reproduced
new bone, showing that the patient had survived. Fine needle holes
had been drilled at intervals around the hole, but these had all been
pierced by Veo, who said he had only poked out the dirt to clean
the piece, as it lay half buried in a cave. We shall therefore never
learn if this row of perforations was original or had been arranged
by Veo to support the local belief that such was the ancient custom
during trepanation.

The amazing thing is that trepanation was practiced on quite a
number of widely scattered islands in Polynesia and Melanesia, so
many in fact that this rare and difficult art seems to have spread into
the Pacific from one, common outside area. In Polynesia, apart from
the Marquesas, the custom was particularly well documented from
the Society Islands. From ancient Tahiti, it is recorded that medicine
men mended broken skulls with the shell of a half-mature coconut,
just as in the Marquesas. In Polynesia, such operations seemed to
have been purely surgical, but where trepanation was known in

[8] C. S. Stewart, *A Visit to the South Seas in the U.S. Ship "Vincennes," During the Years 1829 and 1830*, p. 175 (London, 1832); E. S. C. Handy, *The
Native Culture in the Marquesas*, B. P. Bishop Mus. Bull., No. 9, p. 269 (Honolulu, 1923); for further details on trepanation in Polynesia, T. Heyerdahl,
American Indians in the Pacific (Chicago, Rand-McNally & Co., 1968), pp.
655–65.

Melanesia it seems to have been more of a magico-medical act to relieve headache or to let out evil spirits. On the island of Uvea, for instance, almost all men were trephined.

Trepanning was completely unknown in Indonesia and East Asia. It was practiced by some of the early civilizations of the inner Mediterranean, by the Berbers of Morocco, by the Canary Islanders, in pre-Columbian Mexico, and above all in ancient Peru, where pre-Inca surgeons have left us with a larger concentration of trephined skulls than is to be found in any other part of the world. The vast numbers of trephined craniums found in the ancient desert tombs all along the Pacific coast of Peru show that the custom there, too, had been both surgical and magico-medical, and had been performed in the very same manner as on the islands. A thin sheet of hammered gold was sometimes used in ancient Peru to cover the aperture in the cranium, but it is also reported that sometimes a thin disk of gourd or calabash shell had been fitted to close the opening.

When we sat above the rumbling boulder beach, with Peru behind the curving horizon, and listened to Tei Tetua speaking of Taoa Teke patching up a round aperture carved into his patient's skull, I could not help thinking of the hundreds of medicine men that must once have been sitting in the same manner, behind that very horizon, with bleeding human heads in their laps, performing the very same difficult operation. Perhaps because their patients had been hit by sling stones or by wooden clubs. I went to bed filled with speculations and fell asleep to the rhythmic drumming of the surf from the east.

Pineapple had always been one of my favorite fruits. We had often had the common big type when we lived in Omoa. But never had I tasted pineapples as good as those we found by climbing high up into the arid mountains above Ouia. They were smaller than the pineapples grown by the village people in Omoa, perhaps a little bit acid, and yet superior in fragrance and flavor. To find them, I had to climb with old Tei up the very steep and treeless slopes of Natahu, the lofty mountain pyramid towering on the south side of our valley. This peak rose like a verdigris-colored spire on the gable of the long Tauaouoho Mountain Ridge. It fell vertically off into Ouia, but could be climbed on its eastern side from the promontory south of our bay. The ascent to the lofty pineapple site offered a splendid view out toward the vast expanses of the Pacific Ocean, and the trade wind tore at our hair and loincloths as we crept up the naked mountainside to a sloping, stony terrain some three thousand feet above the level of the sea. Up here, in a sort of abandoned plantation among the rocks, and scattered over dry and windswept shelves, were masses of wild pineapples. Thirsty after our hot climb up the arid hillside, we literally reveled in consuming as much as our throats and stomachs would accept of this juicy product of the arid ground. It was delicious, although it left a slight burning sensation about the lips. We lay for a while relaxed, as if half drunk, and looked at the mighty ocean. There was also a splendid view of the jagged green folds and ridges of the rather barren, east coast, and of the eternal train of trade-wind clouds coming from the east like millions of sheep trying to jump the obstacles of the Tauaouoho Ridge. Above our heads, they huddled together as if in a slaughterhouse, sending all their tears of rain down upon the other side. We were dry. There was not a drop of moisture here except for the golden fruit juice we squeezed forth between our teeth.

Fatu-Hiva is in the midst of a floating river, I thought, half dozing. As always, the air and the sea flowed steadily down upon us. Peru had two major rivers, I continued: the Amazon, which flows eastward through the green jungles of Brazil, and the Humboldt Current, which flows westward through the blue Pacific Ocean.

I am getting like the Polynesians, I thought next. They have always thought of east as "up" and west as "down." Botanists had discovered that most of the flora on these islands had simply been transferred "down" from South America by nature. Not only the special kind of *pavahina* grass I was lying on, but in fact the great bulk of Fatu-Hiva's wild plants were already identified as American species carried here before any human being had arrived. Even the juicy pineapple in my hand was a strictly South American species, although winds or birds could not have transported that. The pineapple!

I sat up as if waking from a dream. The pineapples! The pieces of a puzzle began to float together in my drowsy, sun-baked head. I looked from the golden fruit in my hand to the windswept blue ocean. The Great East. Tiki's home. The clouds. The pineapple. The sling. Trepanation. The huge stone statues of South American type.

"Tei," I asked, "did the double men plant these fruits up here?"

Tei looked at me like a teacher having to answer a perfectly silly question. "*Aoe*," he said. "No. The double men never climbed up here to plant anything." This was *faa-hoka*, a very ancient fruit planted by Tei's earliest ancestors. *Faa-hoka* grew here long before any foreigners visited Fatu-Hiva. There was another and much bigger kind of pineapple near the village in Omoa. That had been brought by the foreign missionaries. But these had come with Tiki.

I found myself sitting on the steep hillside almost laughing, staring at the little wild pineapple in my hand. I had read about this little rascal. It now seemed more fragrant than ever. I recalled how my professors had made me deliver a lecture on the Marquesas for the biologists at my own faculty in Oslo before I left for this adventure. I had studied three volumes by F. B. H. Brown on the flora of these islands. The pineapple was a strictly American plant that could not spread across an ocean without human aid. Yet Brown had shown that the pineapple, *Ananas sativus,* was widely cultivated in the Marquesas group long before any Europeans arrived. He had recorded no fewer than six different names of cultivated varieties, all of which pertained to the ancient Marquesan culture and had developed locally from a single, South American species. For purely botanical reasons, Brown had deduced that this was rather positive evidence that the early Polynesians had obtained their original stock through direct contact with America, long before the discovery of the Marquesas by Europeans.[9]

The same botanist had in fact come to an identical conclusion with regard to the papaya, too. The papaya was another strictly tropical American plant, and two varieties grew in the Marquesas. The natives called the larger and more palatable type *vi Oahu* and said it had been introduced from Oahu, in the Hawaiian group, by the missionaries, whereas they called the other and smaller variety *vi inata* and recognized it as one of their ancient food plants brought by the original immigrants. Even a papaya needs human care to enable it to spread from South America to the Marquesas, and Brown had concluded that it necessarily represented another introduction by aboriginal man.[10]

Sitting there on a windswept slope covered with wild American grass and with a genuine American food plant in my hand, I began to wonder why I had not before been more alerted by these most startling botanical findings. And why they had failed to leave any impression on the anthropologists. Indeed, when I came to think of it, few if any anthropologists would read three volumes about flowers. Perhaps Brown's study had been read only by fellow biologists. Dr. Sullivan, the prominent authority on the physical types in the Marquesas Islands, had indeed found that all Polynesian

[9] F. B. H. Brown: *Flora of Southeastern Polynesia,* B. P. Bishop Mus. Bull., No. 84, Vol. 1, pp. 49, 137 (Honolulu, 1931).

[10] Ibid., No. 130, Vol. 3, p. 190 (Honolulu, 1935).

tribes showed a much closer affinity to various aboriginal peoples on the American continent than to those of Asia and Indonesia, but did he also realize that the same was true of the Marquesan plants? Brown had found that the great bulk of Marquesan plants had come from America, rather than from Australia or Indonesia. But he, as a botanist, had not dared to doubt the validity of the vague but widely publicized anthropological theories. Since these held that man must have reached the Marquesas from the west, from some undetermined part of Asia, he simply concluded: "Although it appears that the main stream of Polynesian immigration came from the west, just the opposite direction from which the indigenous flora came, undoubtedly some intercourse may have occurred between the natives of the American continent and those of the Marquesas."

From now on, I began to suspect that the Polynesian riddle could never be solved by a specialist who put his head into one narrow hole. It had to be approached by an academically trained investigator with a sufficiently broad platform from which he could work as a scientific detective who ignored no fragment of evidence but reconstructed an over-all picture by combining what those who dug deep brought to the surface. Man can create the same kind of stone tools twice, I thought, but he has to bring a pineapple with him.

Tei and I ran side by side downhill until my calves and thighs grew stiff from the effect of the steep descent, while the coarse grass and sharp sun made my feet and shoulders burn. I threw off my burden when we reached the area of the tiny, red husk tomatoes. This was Liv's favorite. As small as a cherry, but with a flavor and appearance like a minute tomato, this was another plant of definitely American origin found scattered over eastern Polynesia when the Europeans arrived. It was found growing from Easter Island to

Opposite:

OLD TEI TETUA AT HIS OWN TOMB. As nobody else was left to arrange his funeral, Tei had his coffin hanging ready in his hut, and he often crawled into his tomb to clean out what his chickens had kicked down. The bronze cross was a gift left by a missionary who had once visited the lonely valley.

FROM OUR CABIN LADDER, we had a splendid view over the ocean. We once saw a steamship passing off the coast.

A GREAT FRIENDSHIP developed between Liv and Tahia-Momo during the months they spent together as the only women in the Ouia Valley.

Above:

HOME FROM THE HUNT. Our good friend Veo finally came to look for us, with his team of dogs. He was accompanied by his wife and other relatives from Omoa. Veo was the best hunter on the island.

Opposite:

SPEARING FISH, OCTOPUSES, AND CRUSTACEANS was a favorite pastime of the new members of our community.

DIVIDING HIS BOOTY, Veo shares it with his dogs, who helped him catch the wild boar. His only weapon was a piece of bark rope.

OCTOPUSES abounded along the rocks, and even the children could provide these delicacies, with their three-pronged spears.

Above:

A GAY EATING PARTY went on for days in Tei Tetua's hospitable
home, until other visitors came over from Omoa and started
brewing alcohol from oranges. A tyrant named Napoleon was
said to have whipped two wives to death when drunk. When he
came over, and real orgies started in old Tei Tetua's home, we
decided to escape at night.

Opposite:

WITH A SHRIEKING PIGLET in her arms, Liv finds rest and shade
from the tropical heat in a cave as we flee up the steep rock face
out of the Ouia Valley.

Hawaii, although it belonged to the ancient cultures in America from Mexico to Peru. I picked a few handfuls and threw them in with the pineapples. Tei was already way below, but I hurried to catch up with him and we entered the coconut grove by our huts together. Coconuts, too, I thought.

Liv and Momo shouted with joy when they saw our harvest, but I was so deep in my own thoughts that I just climbed up the ladder and lay down on my back, with my head turned to look at the waving leaves of the coconut palms. They, too, I thought. Even the coconuts.

For over a hundred years, botanists had discussed the problematical origin of the coconut palm, since all, related genera, including about three hundred species, were found to be American. Most scientists believed this palm had spread by drifting by itself in the current from tropical America to Polynesia, and thence right on to Southeast Asia. But some scholars had started to doubt that the absorbent husk and soft "eyes" of the coconut would allow the kernel to maintain viability after months of exposure to waves and boring marine organisms. Yet it was not until a few years later that independent experiments on board the *Kon-Tiki* raft and in tanks ashore showed that coconuts really need to be carried dry to survive a crossing of long duration like the one from South America to Polynesia. So far, I had noted only that among the hundreds of waterlogged and rotten coconuts I had seen on the beaches there had never been one with live shoots. And if the pineapple and the papaya had come with man, he could have given a lift to the coconut too. Not one other of its hundreds of American relatives left behind was as perfectly suited as the coconut itself, filled as it is with a cool drink, to be chosen for an ocean voyage. Captain Porter had

Opposite:

CAVE DWELLERS waiting for a ship. The last weeks, we spent in hiding on a lonely beach, keeping a constant lookout for a ship that could take us away from Fatu-Hiva. Apart from a few pineapples brought in secrecy by Tioti at night, our diet was the sea food we could collect with our hands among the rocks and a few coconuts from a couple of palms growing by the beach.

Previous two picture pages:

ALONE WITH THE OCEAN as refugees on the solitary Tahaoa beach. At high tide, the sea almost reached the mouth of our cave, and we had to barricade the opening to protect ourselves from moray eels, which crawled among the boulders.

been told by the Marquesans more than a century earlier that their ancestors had brought the coconut from a distant land specifically said to lie to the east. An eighteenth-century missionary had recorded the peculiar detail that the coconut was brought to the Marquesas in "a stone canoe." The word *paepae* has a double meaning in the Marquesas: the missionary would know it as the everyday term for the stone platform on which all Marquesan houses were raised, but elsewhere in Polynesia it is the term for "raft," and in fact it means "raft" in the Marquesas also.

I began to look around me to see if there were any other possible ties with ancient South America. Yes, the bottle gourds that hung from the rafters in the roof. As in every Polynesian household, we used fire-baked rinds of gourds or calabashes with rope handles for buckets and water containers. This plant, the *Lagenaria*, had been considered by the famous Swedish ethnologist Erland Nordenskiöld as "the principal proof of pre-Columbian communication between Oceania and America."[11] And recent excavations in the desert tombs along the Pacific coast of Peru had already shown that gourds, fire-baked and used for precisely the same purposes as on the Polynesian islands, were placed as grave goods with the oldest pre-Inca mummies. In the oldest Peruvian tombs at Paracas, and at Arica, on the Pacific coast below Tiahuanaco, gourd containers had been found interred together with the center boards, paddles, and raft models of the ocean-minded local merchants and fishermen.

And in the gourd containers, pre-Inca families had sometimes left dried sweet potatoes as provisions for their deceased in their journey after life. I knew that nothing had created so much controversy between botanists and anthropologists as the fact that the sweet potato, *Ipomoea batatas,* was cultivated throughout Polynesia when the Europeans arrived, although it was a strictly American plant and needed thorough human care to be carried as a viable tuber across an ocean. No other plant had puzzled, and actually irritated, many anthropologists to the same extent, for the simple reason that it was known to all Polynesian tribes by the same name as in the Quechua dialects of ancient Peru and Ecuador: *kumara.* Those who had the wildest imagination had proposed that a sweet potato might have been caught between the roots of a tree that fell into the ocean and drifted to Polynesia. The name, however, could hardly have drifted with it. Others, therefore, argued that the plant, with its name, could have been brought across by the Mendaña

[11] E. Nordenskiöld, *Origin of the Indian Civilizations in South America,* Comparative Ethnographic Studies, Vol. 9, p. 269 (Gothenburg, 1931).

expedition. The pilot of the Mendaña expedition, however, recorded that they had tried to plant only maize. Besides, when the Europeans arrived, they found that the *kumara* was already the principal Polynesian food plant, from lonely Easter Island in the east up to Hawaii in the north and down to New Zealand in the south. The noted American ethnologist R. B. Dixon had therefore re-examined the whole problem shortly before I left for Polynesia, and concluded: "We are brought face to face with the problem of pre-Columbian contacts between South America and Polynesia, and must explain the presence of the sweet potato in the Pacific as due either to Polynesian voyagers who, reaching American shores, brought back the plant with them on their return to their homeland, or to Peruvian or other American Indians who sailed westward and carried the sweet potato with them to Polynesia thousands of miles away."[12]

I knew, however, that Dr. Dixon had quickly come back and modified his statement, for, the same year as his publication on the sweet potato, the South American balsa log raft had been deemed not seaworthy by maritime experts. A leading American archaeologist and expert on early American Indian watercraft, Dr. S. K. Lothrop, had come to the conclusion that a balsa raft could be used only in coastal voyaging, as it would sink within a fortnight or so due to water absorption. Since the aboriginal Peruvians had no better ships than balsa log rafts and *totora* reed boats, and since a boat of reeds was assumed to be too flimsy even to be taken into consideration, the ancient mariners of Peru had no possible means of reaching Polynesia. Ergo, Dixon came back to the sweet potato two years later and affirmed: "The plant could only have reached Polynesia from America by the aid of human hands, and since we have no evidence that at any time the Indians of the Pacific coast of South America, where the sweet potato was grown, had either the craft or the skill for making long sea journeys, we are forced to conclude that the transference of the plant was carried out by Polynesians."[13]

While I was on Fatu-Hiva, the famous Maori scholar Sir Peter Buck published his best seller on Polynesia, in which he accepted

[12] R. B. Dixon, "The Problem of the Sweet Potato in Polynesia," *American Anthropologist*, Vol. 34, p. 59 (Menasha, Wis., 1932).

[13] S. K. Lothrop, "Aboriginal Navigation off the West Coast of South America," *Royal Anthropological Institute*, Vol. 62, p. 238 (London, 1932); R. B. Dixon, "The Long Voyages of the Polynesians," *Proceedings American Philosophical Society*, Vol. 74, No. 3, p. 173, 1934.

the unsuitability of the balsa raft as an axiom and ended his book
with the following words: "The unknown Polynesian voyager who
brought back the sweet potato from South America, made the
greatest individual contribution to the records of the Polynesians.
He completed the series of voyages across the widest part of the
great Pacific Ocean between Asia and South America. Tradition is
strangely silent. We know not his name or the name of his ship, but
the unknown hero ranks among the greatest of the Polynesian
navigators for he it was who completed the great adventure."

Buck was to repeat the same doctrine in his textbook for students
of Polynesian anthropology. Thus, the claim that Peruvian watercraft were not seaworthy, which meant that the gourd and the sweet
potato must have been carried across the waters between South
America and Polynesia on a two-way trip by Polynesians, became
generally accepted.[14] No one gave any thought to the strange fact
that precisely the gourd and the sweet potato were the two plants
that grew in the ancestral fatherland, according to numerous Polynesian traditions. Indeed, they were brought along by the earliest
god-men, as opposed to breadfruit and certain other food plants
that were said to have been introduced later.[15]

I was not a sailor. I had no experience of the ocean, apart from
my passage from Europe, which seemed to pertain to another life,
and my more recent experiences in a dugout canoe and a lifeboat off
Fatu-Hiva, which I recalled almost as nightmares. But I had begun
to look at the Pacific Ocean and so-called primitive peoples with
other eyes. This ocean was not a barrier but a conveyor. These islands lay in the flow of South America's mightiest river. Ancient
people were just like us, even though they had no typewriters or
steam engines. Why would the great, truly great, civilizations of
Peru continue for centuries and millenniums to navigate their unprotected Pacific shore in balsa log rafts and totora reed boats if
these peculiar kinds of watercraft were not seaworthy?

That evening, at the campfire, I brought up the question of
whether a raft would be less safe than a dugout canoe on a sea
voyage. Liv agreed that we ourselves had seen how a small vessel
can be perfectly safe in a truly rough ocean, provided it is small
enough to have sufficient room between the seas. Big waves are not

[14] P. H. Buck, *Vikings of the Sunrise*, pp. 313–16 (New York, 1938); P. H.
Buck, *An Introduction to Polynesian Anthropology*, B. P. Bishop Mus. Bull.,
No. 187, p. 11 (Honolulu, 1945).

[15] T. Heyerdahl, *American Indians in the Pacific*, pp. 428–45 (Chicago,
Rand-McNally & Co., 1968).

harmful to small craft, unless they are able to fill a hull and thus make the vessel sink.

Tei Tetua was not a sailor, but he knew that rafts were looked upon in former times as safer than canoes. Canoes, however, were faster and easier to handle. Then Tei began to tell us a story: During one of the last wars on Fatu-Hiva, the Manuoo tribe was defeated and threatened with being killed and eaten by victorious enemies who climbed like rats across the mountains to invade their valley. To save their lives, the entire Manuoo tribe, men, women, and children, had embarked upon a number of large rafts made from thick bamboo lashed together with bark rope. They stored plenty of coconuts, *poipoi*, and other provisions on board. They brought fishing gear as well, and carried a fresh-water supply in very thick bamboo canes with pierced joints. All the rafts left Fatu-Hiva in one great flotilla and disappeared over the sea. Years later, one of the Manuoo refugees turned up on the island of Uapou, in the heart of the Marquesas group. From him, people got the news that all the rafts had landed safely on a coral atoll in the Tuamotu group, where the refugees had a friendly reception and decided to settle.

I remembered that Handy had recorded a tradition of how some natives on Hivaoa had visited the Hawaiian Islands. The tribe of the Hanaupe Valley, on the south coast, had been defeated in war. To save their lives, they, too, had resorted to the open ocean. With their chief, Hepea-Taipi, they had built a raft from thick bamboo in five levels. With this raft, they had made a voyage to Hawaii and back. It was as a result of this raft voyage that the people of Hivaoa knew of Hawaii, according to Handy's informants.[16]

"What kind of boats did Tiki have?" I asked.

Tei did not know. He knew nothing except that Tiki had come sailing "down." From Te-Fiti. From the East.

We sat there staring at the drifting clouds and the heaving, moonlit sea. Tei took a stick and stirred the dying embers of his little fire. He picked up his bamboo nose flute, pressed it against one nostril, and began to play. Wide awake and full of the romantic atmosphere around us, we allowed no impression to escape us. Our own nostrils were filled with the scent of luxuriant foliage and salty air, and we listened to the delicate tones from the island's past: the nose flute, the wind rustling in the coconut palms, and the cannonade which drowned out all other sounds each time a mighty

[16] E. S. C. Handy, *Marquesan Legends*, B. P. Bishop Mus. Bull., No. 69, p. 137 (Honolulu, 1930).

roller broke against the boulder barricade we sat on. I sat and marveled at this sea which never stopped proclaiming that it came this way, rolling in from the east, from the east, from the east . . .

Tei Tetua finished his tune. With Momo at his heels, he headed for his cabin, straight across the stream. We crawled to bed on the heap of palm leaves in our own pole hut. But my brain was still haunted by old Tei Tetua's stories. I thought of rafts and skull operations. Of pineapples and sweet potatoes.

"Liv," I said, just as she was falling asleep, "do you remember how the big stone statues of Tiki resemble those of South America?" I could not refrain from bringing this theme up again. Liv merely grunted. Only the rumbling surf seemed to reply in approval. I could not sleep. It felt as if time no longer existed, and Tiki and his mariners were standing in the bay with full sails. Red- and black-haired men and women jumped ashore on the boulder barricade. They unloaded baskets full of roots and fruits to be planted.

I felt for my own pile of pineapples. It was there. It was real.

I turned over onto my side and slept.

10. CAVE DWELLERS

We were back to nature on Fatu-Hiva. Civilization was incredibly far away. When we thought of it, it sometimes gave us an eerie feeling. When we spoke of it to Tei and Momo, neither they nor we seemed quite to believe our words.

One day, after a bath in the river, we lay on the grass gazing at the black frigate birds with scissor-shaped tails cutting through the air against a background of white clouds and blue sky.

"Tei," I said, "in my country men can fly above the treetops like cuckoos and frigate birds."

Tei grinned. Momo laughed. I started to wonder whether what I had said was true. Or had I dreamed it?

"It is true, Tei," I insisted. "We just crawl into a sort of hut built like a bird with open wings. The whole thing lifts into the air, with us inside. I once flew together with my mother. Four people inside. The hut had one pair of wings above the other and was pulled along by a thing that went round and around."

I looked about me to see if there was something to illustrate what I meant, but there was nothing that went around on Fatu-Hiva. Neither windmills nor wheels.

Tei looked at me with a twinkle in his eye and wound his hand understandingly around and around, just like me. Of course, I realized, he neither understood nor believed.

"When I flew in the air with my mother," I went on hesitantly, "she asked the man who made the thing go around and around if he would fly over our own house. In our village lived more people than in the whole Marquesas group together, and they all watched us as we circled above the roofs and the treetops, even high above the boats in the bay."

I was going to add that one man had already flown alone all the way from America to Europe, but realized that Tei's and Momo's geography did not extend far beyond the Tauaouoho Mountain Range.

I ran instead to our pole cabin and fetched some crumpled pages of an old magazine that Mister Bob had used for wrapping up our marmalade jars. No pictures of airplanes. Never mind. Here was a picture of a New York skyline anyhow. Manhattan. The Empire State Building. Triumphantly, I unfolded the picture for our two friends.

Tei and Momo looked carefully at the picture, then at me. Not a bit impressed.

"See the size of the houses," I explained, flabbergasted at their phlegm.

They looked again.

"E. Yes."

Tei finally grabbed the paper, turned it upside down, around, and viewed it from all directions. Suddenly he shouted: "Look!"

We all looked. There was a picture of a man and woman in the door of a two-story suburban house. Tei and Momo were equally excited. A house with another house on top. Never had they dreamed that a house as big as that existed. They had not even realized that the Manhattan skyscrapers were houses. They were too big, and made man look too small. To their imagination, a little dot, tinier than an ant's egg, could not be a man. But Tei and Momo were entertained for the rest of the afternoon by the picture of the white-washed suburban residence. I took a second look at the familiar picture of Manhattan. Was this true? I had an eerie feeling that my own world was unreal: I remembered it as if it were a vision into the future.

There were days when I roamed alone in the forest. Tei might be pounding *poipoi* or preparing some rather time-consuming dish. Or he could be out trying to catch a hog with his dogs. I realized I was a hypocrite not to join him, for I enjoyed eating the baked boar, but I hated seeing it slaughtered. The girls were always somewhere near the cabins and the sea. Sometimes, if I got warm or tired of roaming about, I would sit down in the shade on a fallen tree or perhaps on the moss-covered stones of an old *paepae*. I would sit and meditate about just anything. I felt so mentally relaxed. Here, unlike at home, I thought, we toil with our bodies and use our rested minds to enjoy all kinds of thoughts and emotions. This is a fine way of providing for ourselves and for our women. Tei and I hunt and fish, we pick berries, we stroll in the woods, we climb the hills, we swim: all for a living. We do as work what other people do in their holidays. They sit at typewriters, stand in shops, or work with screwdrivers eleven and a half months out of twelve to get two weeks for personal pleasure. They then rush from their big houses to cabins or tents. To any place in the sun. To a place where they can hunt or fish, pick berries, stroll in the woods, climb the hills, or swim. Primitive man's work has become modern man's leisure. Even fresh air and sunshine is luxury to modern man, I thought. He locks himself up with his vacuum cleaner and electric bulbs and toils indoors to earn enough to pay his electricity bill and his two weeks in the sun.

I will never tell this to Tei, I thought. I have tried to tell him about airplanes. But I will never tell him that people at home do their work seated in chairs and get up to relax by lifting heavy iron dumbbells or by rowing bottomless boats that never get out the door. Tei would perhaps not understand.

I heard Tei shouting somewhere far away. His dogs were barking. For some reason, he needed help. I ran as fast as my lungs permitted across the valley to the mountainside, from where the angry barking came without a pause. I found Tei waving, unhurt at the foot of the cliff, his two dogs dancing ferociously on their hind legs, trying to get up on a rock shelf. A beautiful, shaggy goat, white as snow, stood on it with head and horns lowered, ready for brave self-defense. When I joined him, Tei sneaked up from behind and grabbed the goat by its hind hoofs, holding it firm until I succeeded in getting a good grip on the horns. The goat was ours.

It was a hard fight to keep the dogs away and get our struggling booty down to the coast, where Liv and Momo helped us to tether the pretty animal to a pole beneath our cabin.

"Now we can get milk!" Liv exclaimed enthusiastically. Momo bent down and shook her head. There was no milk to be had from a billy goat. Liv offered the goat a banana, and it ate. Before evening, the wild creature was relaxed and unafraid, with its belly taut from fruits and *taro* leaves. We had our first domesticated animal friend, and called him Maita, meaning "white."

Weeks passed. Weeks so full and rich that each month felt like a happy life span. There was no shop, no market, no middleman, and no expense. It took time to search for and to harvest our daily bread, but animals and artifacts were collected on the same trips, and still there was time for rest and entertainment. The land snails and insects were different in many respects from the fauna on the other side of the mountains, but the archaeological remains were all the same. Stone adzes and pounders, grooved sinkers and octopus lures, shell scrapers and worm-eaten bits of wood carving. A strange object Tei dug up, and which had been exceedingly common both in the Omoa Valley and on Hivaoa, was a flat stone disk as big as the bottom of a bottle, perforated in the center like a wheel. This local kind of relic was inexplicable even to the natives. Some had suggested that these stone disks might have been rolled along the ground in a game in which spear throwers aimed at the hole. Others thought they had served as rotating weights on a wooden shaft twisted for drilling.

These objects were indistinguishable from certain types of South American spinning wheels. But the Polynesians knew neither spinning nor weaving when the Europeans found them. Strangely enough, however, they did have cotton. Large quantities of cotton grew wild on several Polynesian islands, notably in the Marquesas group, Hawaii, and the Society Islands, although no cotton grew in Australia or Melanesia until the Europeans planted it there. In Tahiti, the missionaries, surprised to find spinnable cotton, tried to encourage the natives to start to harvest it for export. But the islanders did not bother. It was enough for them in their warm climate to dress themselves in a light loincloth and poncho of *tapa,* so much more easily beaten from the bark of mulberry, hibiscus, and breadfruit trees.

It was a real puzzle how the spinnable cotton had reached ancient Polynesia, as it could not have come from Austro-Melanesia like the breadfruit and the sugar cane. Sea birds do not eat cotton seeds and could not have spread the plant to these distant islands. On the other hand, fish do eat cotton seeds and would have prevented any from drifting with the current from South America, where, indeed, both wild and cultivated cotton were very common in pre-European times.

As I strolled about on Fatu-Hiva, thinking about the forgotten sailors who must have come here from South America with primitive craft stocked with *kumara* tubers, gourds, pineapple seedlings, coconuts, and the seeds of papaya and husk tomatoes, I never thought for a moment that cotton had to be added to the list. It was not until several years later, the very year in which I sailed a raft from Peru to Polynesia, that three American cotton experts dissected and anatomized all the world's cotton species. They found that all wild cottons had thirteen chromosomes and so did all cultivated cottons, with one, singular exception. The ingenious cultures of ancient

Mexico and Peru had managed to produce, through skillful hybridization, long-linted cottons with twenty-six chromosomes. It was now easy to trace and determine the route of cotton into Polynesia, for all Polynesian cottons were found to have twenty-six chromosomes. That is, they were not wild cottons at all but a product of an American culture that came into existence only in the agricultural fields of Mexico and Peru, together with the sweet potato, after pre-Columbian civilization had been fully developed.[1]

This I did not know, but there was already enough concrete biological evidence for me to be convinced that these islands had been settled, at least in part, from South America. After all, Sullivan had shown that a clear amalgamation of people had formed the island tribes we call Polynesian, and that they did not resemble the peoples of East Asia in the least. I was on the lookout everywhere for more evidence of contact with America. It dawned upon me that the local linden hibiscus, which Brown had termed "one of the most useful of all the trees cultivated by the early Polynesians," had created a wild scientific controversy. Not that anybody denied its great importance to the islanders. Its young shoots were eaten, and we had seen how its flowers were used as medicine, its bark for rope making, and the wood for fire rubbing and countless other everyday services. The two American botanists O. F. and R. C. Cook had long since shown that the tree served the same uses and was known by variants of the same name in both Polynesia and ancient America, *maho* in aboriginal America, *mao* and *hau* in Polynesia. Although it was widespread in the tropics, the plant was considered a native of America, and the two botanists had therefore concluded that, even though the seeds were water-resistant and could have drifted across alone before man arrived, the name could not have come alone. They recommended to anthropologists that they bear in mind that here was an important plant, not to be overlooked in studies of possible contact between inhabitants of tropical America and the Pacific islands in pre-European times. This view had barely been presented before it was vigorously opposed by one of their colleagues, E. D. Merrill, the most passionate defender of the dogma that none could have left or reached America by sea before the Europeans came. The local hibiscus, in his opinion, should be ignored, as long as it could have been disseminated in ages past by ocean currents alone. It was not until years after my own stay on Fatu-Hiva that the prominent

[1] J. B. Hutchinson, R. A. Silow, and S. G. Stephens, *The Evolution of Gossypium and the Differentiation of the Cultivated Cottons* (London, New York, Toronto, 1974).

American plant geographer G. F. Carter came back to the same
puzzle and wrote: "Clearer proof for contact between peoples from
the Pacific with the peoples of Middle America could hardly be
asked than that supplied by the sweet potato and by the hibiscus
known as maho."[2]

I racked my brain to remember all I had read before I came to
this island, for on Fatu-Hiva the only books available, if any at all,
were the Scriptures in the two competing churches of Omoa. Catholics and Protestants go by the same Bible. Yet from it they derive
different faiths. No wonder, then, that biologists and anthropologists, who do not read the same books, can collide in their views.
Even two anthropologists may get different replies to the same
riddle if one studies skulls only and the other merely the spoken
word. Before I had left for Fatu-Hiva, I had noticed that, where
America before Columbus was concerned, scientists, just like lay-
men, had split into two almost religious faiths: Diffusionists and
Isolationists. The former were quite convinced that the early Spaniards were not the first to have crossed the ocean between the Old
and the New Worlds. The latter were equally passionate in their
conviction that until 1492 the world oceans had been complete
barriers for man. I had the impression that it would have been
easier for Pakeekee and Father Victorin to baptize an atheist than
for a diffusionist to convert an isolationist, or vice versa.

Sitting meditating in my pole cabin, I began to think of myself as
a diffusionist, for I was getting more and more convinced that
America had not been isolated from Polynesia in pre-Columbian
times. But no, I could not be a diffusionist. How could I be? I was
becoming more critical about aboriginal ocean travel than all the
isolationists. Since they struggled to keep America apart, they all
took it for granted that the Polynesians had come in canoes from
Indonesia, twice as far away, and against all prevailing winds and
currents. Thus, anyone who defends isolationism when it comes to
America yields automatically to marked diffusionism when it comes
to Polynesia. No, indeed, I was not a diffusionist. I could not believe that the Pacific, which fills half the surface of the earth,

[2] O. F. and R. C. Cook, "The Maho, or Mahagua, as a Trans-Pacific Plant,"
Jnl. Washington Acad. of Sciences, Vol. 8, p. 169 (Washington, D.C., 1918);
E. D. Merrill, "Comments on Cook's Theory as to the American Origin and
Prehistoric Polynesian Distribution of Certain Economic Plants, Especially *Hi-
biscus Tiliaceus Linnaeus,*" *Philippine Jnl. Science,* Vol. 17, p. 195 (Manila,
1920); G. F. Carter, "Plant Evidence for Early Contacts with America,"
Southwestern Jnl. Anthropology, Vol. 6, No. 2, p. 181 (Albuquerque, N.M.,
1950).

could be crisscrossed by stone-age voyagers in canoes as easily as island-hopping with a pencil on an already plotted map. People on Fatu-Hiva were even worried about passing the shelter of the north cape for fear that their canoes might be carried away with the waves and clouds toward the west. This ocean had an "upper" and a "lower" side, which did not show up on a map. If I was anything at all, perhaps I could call myself a directionist, for here it was up and down that counted. If the isolationists could argue that an American *kumara* potato could have drifted here all alone on a tree, and a *maho* seed by itself in the current, then nothing could have stopped a floating craft from drifting with them on the same mighty escalator.

Back in the cabin late one afternoon, I lay musing about these problems that had gradually come to fill my brain. A conflict was brewing between a bearded aspirant to primitive man's life and a former university student tantalized by an academic riddle. I was concerned by the thought that my own subjects, biology and geography, were taken too lightly by anthropologists; they did not even include them in their scholastic training. Then I was brought abruptly back to myself on the palm-leaf mattress in the pole cabin. Dogs! I heard them again clearly, barking far away up the valley.

Tei was just wading across the shallow river with a huge leaf topped with a steaming-hot evening meal. His two dogs at his heels immediately stopped following him and bent back their necks to reply to their distant relatives with wild barking.

Somebody was coming, for we had never seen or heard wild dogs down in the Ouia Valley. I had thought I heard voices high up in the cliffs earlier in the afternoon, when I was in the valley cutting firewood. But then I had thought it was only imagination.

The barking of the dogs increased to a deafening crescendo as a whole pack of white and spotted mongrels of pointer type came out of the thickets and down through the open palm grove with a group of men, women, and children in their wake. They shouted, waved, and saluted. They were our fine friends Veo and Tahia-pitiani, from Omoa, together with another couple and a lot of children, among whom we recognized the little rascal Paho. The calm valley became noisy with shouting and laughter. Paho's first question to Momo was whether we had finished all the jam and corned beef. Tei had not opened a thing. Nor had we disposed of all Mister Bob's sweets for fear of ruining Tei's and Momo's perfect teeth.

Obviously, it was not the good wind of Ouia that had lured these unexpected guests over the mountains. Either it was rumors of our supplies from Mister Bob, or it was because people on the other side wanted a report on what we were doing. We should have preferred that they had forgotten about us. We therefore wholeheartedly joined old Tei when he begged the visitors to stay: The wind was good in Ouia, and there was plenty of pork. Breadfruit in the valley and *faa hoka* up on the hills. Why go back to all the sick people in Omoa?

A new piglet had just come out of Tei's underground oven and the *poipoi* was ready, so there was food for all. The newcomers needed no further persuasion. With all their children and the pack of dogs, they entered the stone enclosure around Tei's residence, and when the piglet had been devoured to the last bone, we saw through the gaping bars of our hut that they all crawled into Tei's empty guest house.

The newcomers decided to remain. They built no new homes, but settled with Tei and ate with him. They were the finest colonists we could possibly have received from the other side. Friendly, energetic, healthy, and remarkably good-looking. Veo was the best hunter on the island, and although Tei's half-domesticated supply of boars was exhausted, there were still plenty in the valley. Veo's hunting equipment was his pack of dogs and a strong loop of hibiscus rope. The others were experts in climbing trees too difficult even for Tei to tackle, and they were incredibly skillful in supplying our joint household with fresh fish and other sea food. It was as if the old era had returned to the valley. There were people in the hills and along the seashore. Children were shouting and women were laughing. Tei was happy. We were all happy. We worked together and shared everything.

Some days, to our surprise, the sea became so calm that we could dive into the surf and swim. The clouds drifted sideways for a change. But only for a couple of days, and then they were back on their normal course.

Paho and the other children were masters in catching octopus. They ate them raw. Admittedly, they were a delicacy if cut into cubes that were soaked overnight in lemon juice, but to tease us, they even ate them alive. They chewed on the body of large octopuses, which twisted long tentacles around their necks. If we shuddered at the sight, they would laugh until they rolled over on the beach. Momo enjoyed touching Liv with a feather or straw on the soles of her feet, and as Liv was ticklish Momo doubled up with amusement. She would take a sharp flake of lava and cut off a thick piece of skin from under her own foot, which was just like the sole of a shoe. When Liv shrieked at this sight, all the island children would roll about laughing.

At night, around the campfire, we all joined Tei Tetua in singing the old melodies he taught us. Or we listened silently to his tales from his childhood in this valley. There were schools on the island in those days. Regular schools, where the main activity was, under threat of punishment, to learn verbally and word by word myths and traditions of former times. In those days, kings married their sisters and men were closer to the gods. There were plenty of turtles all along the coast, and people lived right to the top of the Natahu Peak. Today, up there, one could find nothing but some strange vertical shafts leading down to empty underground chambers. Times had changed on Fatu-Hiva. It seemed as if Tei had a silent hope that all of us together might now turn it back to what it once was. The old man was more vigorous and active than ever.

A few weeks later, other people began streaming down into our valley. Since Veo and his company had not returned, a large number of men and women from Omoa had made the trip across the mountains, led by our own guide, to find out what was really going on.

These newcomers included some of the worst troublemakers. They all accepted Tei's invitation and crawled into his two huts. Tei alone struggled in the kitchen. His latest guests did not even bother to help in providing food. Instead they started to brew a kind of beer from our supply of oranges. They sat all day squatting along Tei's walls, or lay stretched out dozing, insisting on being fed by Tei and Momo while waiting for their brew to ferment. Alcoholic beverages of any sort were unknown in Polynesia when the Europeans arrived. The Indonesians, indeed, brewed palm wine. And the Asiatic custom of chewing betel with lime had spread as far east as the border between the Melanesian and Polynesian islands, but no farther. There it met the *kava*-drinking custom, a ceremonial drinking habit characteristic of Polynesia. The great importance of *kava*-drinking on almost every island in Polynesia shows that the custom has deep and ancient roots, and must have come down from some common parental culture. An analogous custom is found only in the ancient *kasava*-drinking ceremonies among American tribes from Mexico to Peru. Along the Pacific coast of South

America, this brew is termed *chicha, aqha* or *kawau,* and it is made exactly as the *kava* of Polynesia. Throughout this American-Polynesian area, this ceremonial drink is produced by chewing a root, in America sometimes even maize. The vegetable mash thus made is spat into a bowl of warm water. When sufficiently fermented, the fibers are strained and sifted, and the resultant non-alcoholic but salivary ferment is ready to be drunk in honor of the divine ancestors. The American Indians and Polynesian tribes had no other intoxicating beverage until the Europeans arrived. The *kasava, kawau,* or *kava* does not provoke noisy behavior and gaiety, as does alcohol; on the contrary, the participants in the drinking ceremony get morose, quiet, and drowsy.

But when alcohol reached these islands with the Europeans, *kava* disappeared. Over at Tei's crowded place, men and women were now just sitting waiting for their orange beer to get ready for a real orgy. We, on our side of the river, were worried. We knew that a drunken Polynesian could be up to just anything, since he usually lost control of himself completely. Some of the most horrible slaughters, with people even eating other people's heads, had taken place in the Marquesas when these islanders first got to taste alcohol, a very few decades ago.

Then the drinking began in the crowded courtyard across the river. Tei struggled alone in the kitchen, but was pulled away to join the party. He was made to drink with the rest, and even the small children were plied with the brew till they were completely intoxicated. Little Momo, too. A big islander of mixed blood, named Napoleon, was worse than the rest. He became completely insane whenever he tasted alcohol. He had whipped two wives to death when drunk. Now he was making up to Hakaeva, a widow who had come across the mountains with the others since her husband had died. Father Victorin had been duly paid before he left, to see to it that the husband got to Heaven, so now she was back on the market, with a flower behind her right ear.

That night, we had several visitors who tried to climb up our ladder, but they were too drunk to succeed and we pushed them down. Yet, some of the gifts declined by Tei disappeared when for a moment we fell asleep. The noise from across the river was incredible. If this company was to continue, we could not remain.

There was no sign that the party from Omoa had any intention of returning to their own homes. On the contrary, those who were not too hopelessly drunk next morning staggered into the woods to look for more oranges to start the next brew. To our dismay, old

Tei Tetua came slouching across to our cabin and called me down from the ladder in a thick, hostile voice.

Red-eyed and reeling, all he could say when I climbed down to him was: *"Etoutemonieuatevasodiso."*

He had to repeat it twice before I got the point. It meant 17.5 francs, the daily pay in Tahiti requested by Ioane when he and his friends helped us put up the bamboo cabin. Obviously, Napoleon and his friends had sent old Tei over to demand daily wages.

"But, Tei," I said, "you cannot use money, and you would not even accept most of the things I wanted to give you. Can I give them to you now?"

Tei hardly heard what I said. He just turned around and staggered across the river, mumbling once more, *"Etoutemonieuatevasodiso,"* as he left.

Liv was worried, and with good reason. As for me, I stopped troubling my head about where Tei Tetua's first ancestors had come from, and had no other question in my mind but where we ourselves could go. For we could not remain here.

A couple of days later, I was sitting on the ladder of our pole cabin, looking out to the open sea. Over at Tei's place, people were sleeping or sitting along the walls, waiting for the next lot of booze to brew. A couple of women sat naked in the river and splashed water over their shoulders. Then I noticed a fine column of smoke far out in the ocean. A steamship! This was the first we had seen from Fatu-Hiva.

I had never before been able to understand why shipwrecked people sat ashore scanning the horizon for a ship that might pick them up, once they had been lucky enough to end up like Robinson Crusoe on a beautiful South Sea island. Now I was sitting that way myself, bearded and long-haired, on the ladder of my Robinson Crusoe home in a mountain-girt palm valley. I followed the column of smoke with intense excitement. The masts came indistinctly into view above the horizon, then the smokestack and part of the high bow.

The ship was approaching the island!

Liv was now at my side. Soon we saw the whole ship, heading obliquely toward Fatu-Hiva. Out there, on board that black hull, were people from our own world. They were surely lined up at the railings, watching the beautiful South Sea island. Just as we had once done ourselves, when we came steaming toward Tahiti, seemingly a lifetime ago.

Now, through their binoculars, they were undoubtedly staring at the pole cabin on the beach. They surely took it for a native hut. For the steamer slid slowly by, far out at sea, probably bound for Tahiti.

Then we were left alone, without anyone we could trust.

Next day, a young man took off from Ouia to return across the mountains. We asked him to take a letter to Pakeekee, but he refused. We offered to pay for this service, but he still declined.

Shortly after this, Liv woke up one night with a terrible sting in one thigh. She grabbed at the spot and told me the bed was full of insects. I realized at once what it must have been. She had not been attacked by a train of insects, but by one long and jointed giant centipede.

In the sparse moonlight, we searched everywhere among the crumbling palm leaves beneath us, but the poisonous intruder was gone.

We squeezed lemon juice into the tiny double mark pierced by the pincerlike jaws. This both soothed and cured. Next day, she was only stiff in the leg. As the first rays of the sun began to play through the sticks of the wall, we got up and checked every leaf in our bedding. Then we found the yellow centipede rolled up alive like a tiny serpent beneath us. I severed its head with the machete. We went on searching and found one more, which I also killed, whereas still another big one wriggled down through the cracks in the floor and dropped away.

That day, we learned from a red-eyed and confused Momo that several big *poe* bowls with orange brew were ready for a much greater treat than the last one. Why did we not join in? I managed later to get hold of a young man who came alone to the river, and as he confessed that he knew the trail back across the mountains, I bribed him to stay away from the party and follow us into the highlands that night before dawn. He consented against advance payment.

A happy event had just taken place in the valley. A wild sow had just produced a sextet of piglets, and in the confusion, as the piglets ran in all directions when the dogs chased the mother, Momo had grabbed one and made a present of it to Liv. It was the cutest little creature, with laughing eyes and a happy grin on its long, thin snout. It had a coquettish curl on its minute pig's tail, pink hoofs like a toy cow, soft fur like a red-haired boy with a crew cut, and was beautifully speckled with black dots. Liv was completely lost with tenderness, and tucked it safely away in the cabin. The piglet was adopted in the midst of all this tragedy and confusion, and given the name of Mai-mai, Momo's pet name for a baby pig.

That night we hardly got a wink of sleep for the racket that went on across the river. Napoleon's voice screamed and shouted above all the rest. But the young man with whom we had an appointment kept his promise and was even reasonably sober when he arrived. Liv had no objection to my letting the billy goat, Maita, loose to escape into the mountains where it belonged. But when she came down the ladder with her snuffling piglet under her arm, she placed it carefully on the ground like a lap dog, tied with a leash of hibiscus bark. She insisted on taking Mai-mai along, even to Norway.

"You're crazy," I whispered. "Before we get away from this island, Mai-mai will be big and fat and cause havoc among other passengers on the ship."

But Liv was not to be persuaded. And as we took off for the dark forest, she gave the stubborn piglet to our guide, as it bluntly refused to follow her on the leash. The guide, on the other hand, indignantly refused to carry the pig, so I carried it myself, together with the camera, in a rug. The guide willingly grabbed everything else we decided to bring along, and was particularly pleased to be entrusted with the burden of tobacco and similar luxuries from Bob's store that Tei had declined to accept.

We bade farewell to nobody. They were all drunk, and, with the centipedes fresh in our minds, we knew we should be in grave trouble if Napoleon and his army realized we were about to escape from their clutches.

We had not gone very far before we decided to wait for daylight, as there was no trail through the boulder-strewn hibiscus forest in the inner part of the valley. But at least we had escaped, and when the drunkards came across the river they were destined to find our pole cabin empty.

As soon as day broke, we continued inland along the valley bottom. Mai-mai screamed and shrieked, and wriggled like a freshly caught salmon. I carried her in my arms, on my shoulder, against my chest, and inside my khaki shirt, but the piglet screamed no matter what I did. And now the sun began to bake us. She had to be taken out of the rug, although it made me hot carrying her in my arms.

When we finally crossed the stream, I dipped Mai-mai into the water with the intention of cooling her off a bit, but then she shrieked worse than ever. It was just not bearable. Our guide, who had walked in front, increased his pace and, with the pack, disappeared completely. And when we reached the foot of the Tauaou-oho Mountains and entered *teita* grass almost as tall as we were, he was gone. Lost, as if he had sunk into the earth. We had to begin searching for the overgrown entrance to the mountain trail all on our own.

The Ouia Valley ended here, and we were to begin our ascent in serpentines up the burning rock wall. There was not so much as a tiny tree to give shade, and the sun was baking hot on this low part of the mountainside without a breath of wind. The dry *teita* grass let the stinging rays pass through everywhere. Mai-mai's piercing shrieks seemed to augment the sting of the heat, and I suggested meekly that we set the piglet free. But Liv protested vigorously.

"The poor creature will just fry to a crisp on the hot rock," she explained.

And we advanced slowly, higher and higher, walking and crawling. The steep trail we were following was indistinct and grew even worse, until we followed nothing but some barely visible tracks in the sand between the stems of the tall *teita* grass. At last we came to some overhanging cliffs and sheer drops, and here we were completely stuck. I knelt down and examined carefully the tracks we had followed. They were those of a wild boar. We were lost.

To advance into the *teita* had not been so easy. But to return along our own tracks was worse. Now the long, sharp blades were bent, and turned like bayonets against us, cutting our skin like the edges of opened cans. By now, we began to fear that we had been led into a trap. The fellow who had disappeared with all our worldly property might now be back on our heels with a posse of drunken natives. We had to hurry up. Hurry back to where we must have passed the right entrance to the mountain trail. Hurry to the plateau, where we could escape to anywhere. In this spot we were really cornered.

When we finally discovered the right track, we were just about exhausted. The air stood around us like the mountain walls, hot and motionless, like the inside of a baker's oven. The sun scorched the countless cuts and scratches, and all our pores were sealed with dusty sand and perspiration.

The piglet was hot and damp in its short, thick fur, and gave us not a moment's peace. The piercing pig screams cut through our bones and marrow in this heat, and at times I felt a desperate desire to throw the wriggling thing over the cliff.

The wall rose high above us; we were not yet halfway up. We should never get all the way up without a rest, and to rest was impossible in the baking sun. The sand and the rock itself were burning hot; only the wide hats plaited by Liv and Momo from pandanus leaves saved us from sunstroke in the equatorial heat. It felt as if we were breathing in and out the very same, sultry air. We had to climb even higher, for up there somewhere we should get into the breeze. Our fixed idea was to reach a strange rock formation high up in the cliff face. We remembered the place from our descent into Ouia. Somewhere up above us were two pinnacles shaped like twin trolls in a Norwegian fairy tale. Two big petrified sentinels overlooking the valley and the sea. They straddled to leave space for a short tunnel between their legs. And this was the only place in the entire mountain wall with any shade at all. We had been told during our descent that even when the air hung dead calm and quivered with heat everywhere else, a gust of air moved up through the tube straddled by the two stone giants.

It felt as if an eternity passed from the moment we sighted these twin trolls above us until they seemed to grow and move nearer. The last stretch became too much for Liv. She stumbled continually and had to be fanned with the big hat. During this procedure, even Mai-mai grunted contentedly, but then the little devil shrieked twice as hard, when the fanning stopped.

It was an indescribable treat, a superb physical pleasure, when the trolls stood above us and we dived into the dark, airy tunnel. The main rock face continued above us, but up here we could see that nobody was on our heels. We could stay until night fell upon the island, even though our guide had escaped with all our provisions: the coconut milk as well as the baked taro roots Liv had prepared for the crossing.

When our eyes grew used to the shade, the tropical valley below us seemed blinding white in the intense light of the midday sun. Mai-mai grunted peacefully and fell asleep in Liv's arms. The shade and breeze cooled and dried our skins, and, a few hours later, we felt an itching desire to continue our escape into the highlands. We crawled back into the afternoon sun and resumed our ascent.

In a difficult spot, I had to put the wriggling, screaming pig with the camera into a sack formed by the rug on my back. Thus I had my arms free. After a while, the noisy animal calmed down.

"It thrives in the dark sack," I said, happy at having found a solution. But Liv insisted on peeping down into the plaid, and there the piglet lay as motionless as on a Christmas table. She quickly fished him out, and, restored to a pig's full senses, he began to scream as before.

In this way, we reached the edge of the precipice. The inland mountain plains lay before us. The strong breeze had caught up with us during the last part of the climb, and now we had only one thing in mind: to head for the nearest mountain spring.

We drank from every spring and rivulet we passed. The first pool tasted better than iced champagne. Mai-mai shared our pleasures. We were hungry, but we did not want to descend into Omoa. We did not want anybody to know our whereabouts any more.

As night fell, we found ourselves in a gorge between the hills. Now it felt terribly cold. We shivered and longed for a fire. While Liv used the last daylight to collect ferns for our bed, I struggled until I was exhausted with two dry rubbing-sticks. The wood grew black and smelled like sweet incense, but that was all. With numb arms I gave up, but cold and despair made me start again. Smoke. Immediately, Liv was at my side ready with tinder, but I could hardly hold out any longer. We should just have to freeze under the open mountain sky. I was longing for a match. Just one match. Or at least Tei's flint. This wood was not right. Then a spark was born in the tinder, a little star. Liv blew with the utmost care. As living fire came out of my sticks and flamed up from the tinder, I felt as proud as the owner of Aladdin's lamp, able to light up the invisible surroundings and create a pleasant temperature in the chilly mountain air. To give us a feeling of security against centipedes and wild dogs, I lit a ring of small fires around us. Liv had made a soft, green berth in the middle of the trail, the only place where we could find smooth, open ground.

Then we lay down in the gorge, covered by our rug, enjoying the free view of a million tropical stars and constellations rotating slowly above us. A global compass framed by rugged mountain silhouettes.

But Mai-mai screamed so angrily in Liv's arms that neither of us could sleep. We had discovered that the piglet was not a he at all but a she, and I took the opportunity of renaming her Siren, which seemed the most fitting name.

After a while, even Liv recognized that Siren's company was unbearable. I happily suggested tying her somewhere out of audible range, and Liv consented, on condition that the innocent little Satan should get our only rug. I walked far down the trail and tied the rug, like a sack with Siren inside, to a stone. From now on, we heard only the night wind in the trees, and we fell asleep with flickering fire on all sides.

In the middle of the night, we awoke to hear and feel the drumming of heavy hoofs. I was stiff from cold; all the fires had long since burned down. But what woke me up in less than a second

was the sight of two wild horses coming straight toward us. Silhouetted in the moonlight, with long, flowing manes and tails, they
came chasing through the gorge at a mad pace.

I sat up with a terrible yell to scare the horses, but too late. The
one in front did not manage to stop and, panicky from fear, it made
a terrific leap over both of us, while the second horse managed to
skid to a halt at the edge of our rug, then it reared and galloped off
in the opposite direction.

Both of us leaped to our feet and poked life into the fires, whereupon we threw on more branches to see and be seen, and to get our
blood back into circulation.

"Siren," was Liv's laconic comment.

No doubt whatsoever. The little piglet had been disturbed in its
sleep by the sound of big animals coming along the trail. Starting to
scream and dance about inside the rug, like a ghost in the moonlight,
she had scared the two wild horses out of their wits. The little
scoundrel had unwittingly given us a narrow escape.

Empty stomachs made us surrender next day. We descended into
the Omoa Valley to look for food. The mountain trail ended by the
water's edge, and down there, to our surprise, we found Willy sitting on the beach as if he were waiting for our arrival. With his
usual calm smile, he told us that our other rug, with all the stuff our
guide had carried across the mountains, was safe in Willy's own
house. He had seen the man coming down the trail and had made
sure that everything was taken proper care of until our arrival.

We had almost forgotten that we had a friend in Willy. He was
like a European, different from all the others. He had never sided
with those in the village who had caused us trouble. Yet, while he
kept aloof from them he was at the same time so introverted and
shy that we ourselves had never had any close contact with him.

Grateful to Willy, and restored by a sturdy corned-beef meal in his
bungalow on the beach, we left our gentle host with all our recov-
ered property. We had only vague ideas about what to do. First
we headed for our old friends Pakeekee and Tioti.

On the road, we were stopped by a man in a straw hat and a loincloth, who offered me a bargain. If I let him have Liv, he would
give me his wife and four children in exchange. He opened his arms
as if he were measuring a barrel to make me understand that in
size I was getting the better part of the deal. He seemed surprised
when Liv and I jointly turned the offer down.

We hurried on and found Tioti. He was pleased to see us and even pleased to be presented with Siren, who was hoarse from screaming but calmed down and started grunting like other pigs when she was left to run loose among Tioti's chickens. Tioti had a solution, as always. When the village was asleep, we should proceed to Tahaoa, the beach with the white coral sand. Here he would come and bring us food from time to time, and when the schooner arrived he would hurry over and let us know.

When the village slept and darkness reigned in the forested valley, we sneaked down to the open, starlit coast and began to fumble our way with our few possessions over and along the boulder-strewn foot of the seaward cliff. We headed for Tahaoa. We knew the way.

At night, the hidden beach of Tahaoa seemed emptier, and the white corals whiter, than in the daytime. With the open sea in front and the skyscraping precipice at its back, the place seemed the symbol of loneliness. Nobody but birds and cold-blooded creatures from the reef belonged to this area. The narrow strip of grass-covered land between the beach and the vertical rock face had hardly ever been inhabited by man, not even in the days when the island was crowded with people. There was danger of rockfalls everywhere. No remains of *paepae*. Only a couple of tall coconut palm and a very few small trees, among them a bouquet of slender poles with huge palmate leaves encircling a cluster of heavy fruits as large as melons: papaya.

Tahaoa was a world of its own; and more so at night. Lonely and empty. Even the birds slept. We stood as if petrified, looking at the starlit sea, introducing ourselves silently to the new surroundings. We came as the new lodgers, luggage on our backs. All we owned was carried bundled up in two rugs. A tent, which we could not use here for fear of rockfalls, our long knife, and two palm-leaf baskets filled with fruits and baked tubers donated by our friends in Omoa. At last we had left behind the stupid tobacco and sweets, which had led to so much trouble along our path. We ourselves did not smoke, and the toothless Tioti was speechless with delight. I had not even bothered to bring tubes and jars for collecting animals. Where the brain was filled to the brim with thoughts of survival, there was no room for science.

Friendly little waves, washing gently in across the starlit platform reef, were the only signs of life to welcome us. The barely surfacing barrier denied access to the angry billows of the ocean, thundering at Tahaoa's frontiers, far out at the end of the reef. We, however, came in at the back door—there was nothing to stop us—

and we jumped down onto the white sand, looking for a place to sleep.

When we had last come here, with Tioti and his *vahine*, we had observed a little rock shelter that would be a secure retreat should stones start to fall down from above. We made straight for that place with our bundles. On this beach, the canvas tent we had carried along was even less safe than under a coconut palm. The cave was the obvious place to pick for our new home. The ceiling was of hard, black lava. No insect would eat these walls and no boar would make them sway.

The floor of the cave was covered with a jumble of large and small boulders as smooth as eggs. I rolled the biggest boulders out in front to form a sort of barricade against the sea, and removed even the pebbles to make a smooth place for a bed. There was white sand beneath. As I rolled a large boulder over to reinforce the rampart from the outside, a giant, glittering moray eel twisted angrily about like a fat, green-and-black spotted serpent. It finally made up its mind and slid away between my legs and into the interlocking pools of the reef.

I had no idea that these nasty marine beasts would move up onto the land. Surely at high tide the mouth of the cave must be awash. The boulders outside our rampart were glittering wet underneath, and sea water seeped into the deeper depressions. Nevertheless, the moray had wriggled seaward over perfectly dry stones, like a short and stubby boa constrictor.

We had learned to fear these snake-like beasts more than any shark. When fishing with the natives, we had seen how the men pulled sharks right onto the rim of the canoe and then just hit them on the head with a heavy club. But if the hook was swallowed by an evil-eyed moray eel, and it came up gaping with its awl-like teeth, then they would yell excitedly and never pull it in until they had pierced its head repeatedly with their three-pronged spears. The thin teeth of the moray had a poisonous effect, and according to our island friends, big specimens could tear off a man's arm. They were often thicker than a human leg, and once, in Ouia, I had stared into the snake-like eyes of a colossus waving its fore part outside an underwater grotto, its body as thick as my thigh. Several islanders claimed to have seen a moray with a body as stout as the trunk of a normal coconut palm. Allowing for a fair amount of exaggeration, they were undoubtedly referring to the existence of truly giant specimens, which might have passed for veritable sea serpents but for the fact that the morays are always remarkably short in proportion to their cross section.

I was more careful about where I put my fingers and feet when I resumed rolling over the boulders. There could be other morays under just any of these stones. In the dim light from the night sky, we completed the fitting up of our new residence. Liv had gathered as much grass as she could find, and with it she covered the floor of the cave. We crawled to bed, rolled up in our two rugs, and slept until the intense reflections of bright sunlight on the reef woke us up, in the late morning.

Drowsily I sat up and looked around me. Rocks and water. Liv lay wide awake, her hand under her chin, and gazed out over the sea with no expression that revealed her thoughts. She had by now taken a lot of beating, and had never complained. She had never said that this was all my idea, or asked why all this had happened to her. Never said that she wanted to go home. Her home had been Fatu-Hiva. Wherever we lighted our campfire, she had adjusted herself to the conditions.

As for myself, I did not quite know what to think any more. We had been defeated, and yet not quite. We were refugees, but were still as free as the frigate birds sailing about over the reef. We had come to live close to nature, and we admired nature more now than ever. Yet things had not worked out the way we had expected them to. We had tried to live deep in the jungle, in the open hills, and under the palms by the sea. We had succeeded for a certain length of time, but something had always turned up to put a spoke in the wheel. Now we were to start as cave dwellers. Cave dwellers on a beach. We were squeezed in between the black toes of a hanging rock wall and the licking tongue of the sea. Fresh water came dribbling down the rock face, and there was enough food to pick and to catch in salty pools to keep us alive. Yet this was not exactly what we had dreamed about when we packed our suitcases for the long journey back to nature.

I crept out and warmed up in the sun. What an enormous ocean! And there was such a narrow strip of land at our disposal. I looked up. I hoped that goats and booby birds would mind their steps up there, otherwise eroded rock would tumble down upon us.

This was not a place to remain in for life. Not a place to raise a family in. Liv could be blessed with a baby at any time. Nature alone decided. Her motherly instinct had been revealed in the way she had fondled Siren.

Liv and I did not have much to say as we set to work to organize our new life. There was not much to say about a future on the Tahaoa beach. There was little to organize, but we had to construct a sheltered fireplace and pull in under the overhanging cliff as much driftwood as we needed to keep our hearth going. No table, no bed, no bench were required here. We still had our coconut cups, our bamboo spoons and beakers. We needed no door to keep boars or mosquitoes out. If rain came from the direction of the sea, we could hang our tent down over the cave opening.

I tried to climb to the top of the shortest coconut palm. It was too high. We had to wait till Tioti came, and be satisfied with the few nuts that had fallen to the ground. A mediocre climber could easily crack his skull, and there was no *taoa* here.

Liv was wading with her *pareu* held up to make a pocket, which she was filling with edible mollusks. I joined her. We agreed that the reef was the most beautiful aquarium we had ever seen. Otherwise, we did not say much. I warned her to be on guard against octopuses and moray eels, and not to step on sea urchins. She said yes. That was all.

As we sat on the boulders eating our sea food with coconut milk, I proposed that perhaps we could fine some sea bird's eggs. She agreed. Perhaps we could. Then we finished our meal in silence.

I tried to read Liv's mind, and came to the conclusion that, if she was thinking at all, both of us had to be thinking along the same lines. We had started this experiment with the same ideals, the same dreams. We had lived through exactly the same experiences, seen the same wonders, suffered the same disappointments. We were not as green as we had been when we came. Both of us had hardened a bit. Both of us had come to realize that we had been too egocentric and had almost ignored the fact that there were other people in this world. We were not so stubbornly sure of all our own visions and calculations. Things had worked out differently from what we had expected. Unpredictable obstacles had thrown us off what we had thought to be an open road. Now, in fact, we were not on any road. We had to digest all our unexpected experiences to set ourselves on firm ground again.

In our cave, there was ample time for thought. For rethinking. For examining our own present feelings toward the civilization from which we had sought to escape. To crystallize our various notions as to what had come out of our experiment of turning back to nature. What now? What next? This beach was clearly a blind alley.

For several days, neither of us spoke out. Perhaps we felt uncertain of each other; perhaps we felt uncertain of ourselves. We spent much of our time bathing in the clear pools or wading on the reef, catching fish, crabs, and other crustaceans with our bare hands. At low tide, it was difficult for them to escape from the landlocked channels and pools. And there were delicious sea snails and other edible mollusks that did not even attempt to escape. We picked them as a farmer picks tomatoes.

Only once did Tioti and his wife visit us. When they came, however, they brought with them a huge load of fruits, nuts, tubers, and even poultry. We hoarded everything in the cool, innermost nook of our cave. Our visitors left, and one day followed the next. We rose with the sun and crawled into our cave when it set. And we made sure that the embers of our fire never died out.

But, most of the time, we just sat in the shade of our rock shelter, scanning the horizon with eager eyes. We sat once more as if shipwrecked on a reef, with one, ever-growing desire: to see masts, a column of smoke, or a white sail on the fine line dividing the blue of the sea from the blue of the sky. Our hope was suddenly to see a white spot that would grow bigger and bigger and not one that would just come and go like the thousands of white wave crests that filled the sea wherever we looked. But no such spot took shape on the horizon; off the reef there were only whitecaps and a blue emptiness.

"What do we do if we see a schooner?" Liv asked one day, after we had been sitting all morning doing nothing but watching the waves on the horizon.

"We hurry to Omoa," I replied. "And if it arrives at night, Tioti will come and fetch us."

"Why?" asked Liv. Her voice was gently challenging.

Why? I thought. I sat for a moment looking out to sea, not knowing how to answer. So far, I had not quite allowed the idea to enter my own mind that our venture had reached a dead end. I felt Liv watching me, trying to read my mind.

"I know," she said. "We are just running away from everything here. This is not what we came to do."

She had taken the words out of my mouth.

"We are just killing time now," I admitted. "Like the village people, sitting waiting for their coconuts to fall."

We had confessed openly what both of us had felt at the bottom of our hearts since we had come to settle in Tahaoa. It felt as if a coat of ice had melted. The intensive play of sunlight on the water and the warm colors of the reef were suddenly as beautiful and pleasant again as when we had first seen this place. We were not prisoners here at all. We were not wedded to Tahaoa. The crowded world we once knew, and which for so long had been far from our thoughts, was still there. Our parents too.

For the first time since we had come, we were lost in reveries about how it would be to see our parents once more. When we boarded the train that cold Christmas day and took a seemingly joyous farewell, inside ourselves we had bade them a sad good-by. We had not been at all sure that we would ever have come back to civilization again. In fact, when the French island administration had demanded prepaid return tickets to let us disembark in Tahiti, I had been obliged to comply with the regulations but found it a silly waste of money. We could use those tickets now.

Yet Liv stressed that she would not have missed our experiences on this island for all the treasures in the world. That went for me too. I would not have missed a day of what we had behind us.

"But do you realize something?" I said to Liv. "If things had worked out differently, we should still have left Fatu-Hiva. If we had found that man could rid himself of all modern problems by going straight back to nature, we should have been pestered by guilty consciences until we went home and told others."

Something of the insect is within us. An ant has invisible ties to the anthill. A bee finds no satisfaction in hiding from the hive and licking its harvest in solitude.

"But do you know something?" interrupted Liv. "If things had worked out the way we had expected, we still couldn't go home and recommend a mass migration back to nature. Think of our map."

She was referring to the way we had been forced to cross out continents and islands bit by bit and one by one before we encircled Fatu-Hiva as the only place that seemed possible for our back-to-nature experiment. Not even Tahiti would have done. And not one of the other islands we had seen. The kind of food modern man is able to digest no longer hangs on trees in no man's land. The world itself has changed as much as man since the early day when he started his long trek away from nature. There was no road back all the way to the abraded point of departure.

"There is nothing for modern man to return to," I admitted. I said it most reluctantly, for our wonderful time in the wilderness had given us a taste of what mankind had abandoned and what mankind was still trying to get ever farther away from.

"We are in the middle of a long road. There is no way back, but don't let that ever make us believe that just any road ahead is progress," I added. On this, we both agreed.

And here we came to the lesson we had learned from our long year on Fatu-Hiva. The longest and most timeless year in our lives.

Man has conceived a bedeviled word. We first let it out of our own mouths and next permitted it to grab us by the nose and lead us astray. The word is "progress." When first conceived, this term was meant to describe a forward motion, a change from something bad or good to something better. Never to something worse. Then we took one step further.

With superb self-confidence, we assumed that we ourselves would never change anything for the worse, so we were quick to adopt the same word to describe man's move away from nature. Any invention, just any artificial product or device, was progress. Each step away from the world of yesterday was progress. Progress became something determined by the clock and not by quality. Still tied to its original meaning, progress can never run backward, irrespective of whether we judge it with a compass or with a watch.

No architecture left by the early Egyptians can therefore ever be said to represent progress from what Europeans built in medieval times, even if everyone agreed that the Egyptian buildings were superior. An ancient Greek sculpture of Venus of Milo can never represent progress from a modern composition of a corkscrew and a cogwheel hanging from the spokes of an umbrella. The term progress is always in favor of the living generation, will therefore never go out of fashion, and the dead can never turn it to run counterclockwise, in their favor.

We like to think of progress as modern man's struggle to secure better food for more people, warmer clothing and finer dwellings for the poor, more medicine and hospitals for the sick, increased security against war, less corruption and crime, a happier life for young and old. But, as it has turned out, progress involves much more. It is progress when weapons are improved to kill more people at a longer range. It is progress when a little man becomes a giant because he can push a button and blow up the world. It is progress when the man in the street can stop thinking and creating because all his problems are solved by others who show him what happens if he turns on a switch. It is progress when people become so specialized that they know almost everything about almost nothing. It is also progress when reality gets so damned dull that we all survive by sitting staring at entertainment radiating from a box, or when one pill is invented to cure the harm done by another, or when hospitals grow up like mushrooms because our heads are overworked and our bodies underdeveloped, because our hearts are empty and our intestines filled with anything cleverly advertised. It is progress when a farmer leaves his hoe and a fisherman his net to step onto an assembly line the day the cornfield is leased to industry, which needs the salmon river as its sewer. It is progress when cities grow bigger and fields and forests smaller, until ever more men spend ever more time in subways and bumper-to-bumper car queues, until neon lights are needed in daytime because buildings grope for the sky and dwarf men and women in canyons where they roll along with klaxons screaming and blow exhaust all over their babies. When children get a sidewalk in exchange for a meadow, when the fragrance of flowers and the view of hills and forests are replaced by air conditioning and a view across the street. It is progress when a centuries-old oak is cut down to give space for a road sign.

We had come to Fatu-Hiva full of contempt for twentieth-century civilization, convinced that man had to start all over again from scratch. We had come to take a critical look at the modern world from the outside. Now we were sitting in our cave with a rock wall behind us, staring into the empty blue, waiting for means to turn back, not to nature, but to civilization. We were milder in our judgment. We had seen that without Willy's mosquito netting we would have been driven out of our minds in Fatu-Hiva's jungle and ended up with elephant legs; or, rather, without Terai's ointment on Hivaoa, we would have ended up with no legs at all.

Yet, we had not gained full confidence in modern civilization. We had seen how simple life could be, how perfectly relaxed and intensely happy a person could be, deprived of the countless items we struggle to get access to when we want to live like others in a city block.

We felt an urge, an inconvenient need, to return to civilization. But we did not want to be a single step farther from nature than life in our part of the world made necessary. Primitive life in the wilderness had filled us with a well-being, given us more than the city life as we knew it had ever been able to give us. Never had we seen people at home, not even our own relatives, laughing so readily and reflecting such a free and healthy spirit as Tahia-Momo and Tei Tetua, who were poorer in property than any other people we had ever met.

I had no sooner reminded Liv of this than she corrected me.

"The old Frenchman in the funny shack on Hivaoa," she said. "He was indeed a civilized man. His home was full of inventions. He had read all sorts of books."

I was left bewildered. That happy old man was neither a child of nature nor an illiterate. His recipe for happiness was to be found at its very source: within himself. If the environment had facilitated his search, it could be crystallized in one word: simplicity. Simplicity had given him what millions of others searched for through complexity and progress. The old man's requirement, his world, was a tiny shack in a vegetable plot. Neither a cave in the wilderness nor a castle in a park.

Simplicity is indeed another magic word, denoting something so modest that it is easy to step over in all its unpretentious greatness.

Progress can today also be defined as man's ability to complicate simplicity. Nothing in all the procedure that modern man, helped by all his modern middlemen, goes through before he earns money to buy a fish or a potato will ever be as simple as pulling it out of the water or the soil. Without the farmer and the fisherman, modern society would collapse, with all its shops and all its pipes and wires. The farmers and the fishermen represent the nobility of modern society; they share their crumbs with the rest of us, who run about with papers and screwdrivers, attempting to build a better world without a blueprint.

Once we had admitted to ourselves and to each other that we wanted to leave our cave and return to our own world, we sat until dusk, eating clams and discussing civilization the way we saw it from a distance, with all its blessings and all its adversities. When the western sky turned as red as a royal carpet in the wake of the retiring sun, and a violet veil was slowly drawn up across the other half of the sky, Liv scraped away the thick cushion of ashes from our precious embers and blew new life into the dormant fire. For the first time since we came to the beach, we sat on the boulders talking until the same red and the same violet came back upon the heavens, now with their positions interchanged on a sky where the stars were fading away.

There was no schooner the next day, nor the next. We strolled on the beach among dead shells and rattling hermit crabs, talking, always on the lookout seaward. A distant wave breaking white against the blue sky, a killer whale leaping as from a springboard, a white bird on the horizon; nothing more was needed to put us on the alert. Often, we would climb up on large blocks of lava to scan the distant blue. The schooner must not pass unnoticed. We had a wide view, which embraced the entire western horizon, and should be able to detect anything heading for Omoa in the daytime.

The ocean seemed to overflow and enter into my very soul during those days in Tahaoa. The salty air filled every breath, and at high tide the smallest ripples across the reef ran right up to the mouth of our cave. Hermit crabs crawled across our barricade and stole our food like rats. Fish were begging like dogs at the foot of our table. All we chewed and swallowed tasted of seaweed or the salty ocean.

Sitting staring out into the blue Pacific, which ran without a clear transition into blue space, I felt that the ocean was immense, endless, bottomless. There was something beyond human comprehension about its immeasurable size, since the Amazon, the Nile, the Danube, the Mississippi, the Ganges, all the rivers, floods, and sewers in the world could enter into it ceaselessly without the surface level ever changing an inch. All the running water in the world heads for the ocean, yet it only churns its currents around as in a witch's caldron, its surface calmly rising and sinking with the tides, ignoring the fact that it ought to overflow, that it ought to run slowly into our cave and start rising up the cliff wall behind us. All the rain and all the rivers have no effect on its level. All the mud, the silt, the rotting vegetation, the carcasses and excrement of animals from sea, air, and land that have washed into it since the days of the dinosaurs and the first life on earth have failed to pollute it and have left it perfectly clean. For man, the sea and the sky have been the two symbols of endless dimensions and permanence.

This was my subconscious feeling about the boundless masses of water in front of me as we sat in the cave and saw how it merged into the vault of heaven as part of blue space. Although my textbooks had told me its width in miles and its depth in feet, and although I knew the secrets of its permanence, I was still sitting there like illiterate Polynesians before me, and Europeans in medieval times, feeling that the land was man's domain but that the ocean was part of space.

How wrong I was. And how much I had to wrestle with the world ocean before I changed my view completely, before I saw it as the pulsating heart of our own living biosphere. As a nonstop mechanism, running like a pump and filter to our own world, although innocently camouflaged as an immense watery waste with no beginning and no end, I still had to discover that the biggest ocean can be crossed by landlubbers in the smallest craft, before I realized the true dimensions of the ocean. The buildings of downtown New York would rise high above sea level if placed on the bed of the North Sea, and the average depth of all oceans amounts to about five thousand feet, the distance covered by a runner in less than four minutes. If the ocean were to be represented in its true proportions on a normal globe, no blue paint could be smeared on in a coat thin enough to give the proper dimensions. In this water, nearly all life is concentrated near the very upper layer, which is penetrated by the life-giving rays of the sun.

Days were to come when I should be drawn to the ocean, be fascinated by it, and learn to adjust myself to its laws. But not while I lived dry in a coastal cave. I still feared the ocean in those days. I had barely learned to swim, and neither of us dared to venture too close to the edge of the reef, where the violent surf sent mad cascades of water into the air. We heard it as a cannonade when we lay in the cave at night, leaning against the rock, trying to read the stars. We had plenty of time to dream and to plan the future. The sun, the moon, and the tropical constellations rotated above us, and the tide rose and sank at our feet.

How obvious it seemed that ancient desert people and seafarers with an open view of the glittering night sky should get to know the ever-repeated itineraries of the astral bodies so well that they needed nothing else for finding their bearings and latitudes. But how strange, with this endless myriad of stars to choose from, that the Polynesians, on all their far-flung islands in both hemispheres, should start their new year the first day the insignificant Pleiades appear above the horizon. Just as people did on the coast of Peru and among some ancient Mediterranean civilizations.

Indeed, when we returned home, we were to move far away from the ocean and live in a log cabin high up in the mountains, but we were to travel far and wide in an attempt to solve the Polynesian riddle. Only the threat of war hovered like a ghost somewhere over the horizon. I was thoroughly convinced that a second world war was somewhere around the corner. We had come to Polynesia to escape from it and to avoid participating in what I was convinced would be the collapse of modern civilization, and in spite of this we were now determined to go back and face whatever was coming, as if it were an inevitable punishment we had to live through together with everybody else.

The stars told us nothing of the future; they were millions of years behind and had so far not even seen the Polynesians reaching these islands. We dreamed about the future, but we knew nothing. We did not know that a year later we were to live among the Bella Coola Indians, on the Pacific coast of British Columbia. We were to look for the missing steppingstones of the early seafarers from Asia to Polynesia. To try to track down a feasible route explaining the mixture in Polynesian race and culture. South America alone could not explain everything, and up in the North Pacific, among the maritime Northwest Coast Indians, travelers and scientists since the time of Captain Cook and Vancouver had pointed out numerous striking similarities to Polynesia. The coastal archipelago of northwestern America was warmed by the strong Japan Current, which came straight from the Philippine Sea, and if the huge, seafaring double canoes of the Northwest Coast Indians were trapped by coastal fog, the same Philippine current made a sweeping curve along their coast and carried everything, even local driftwood, straight down upon Hawaii, in Polynesia.

Rafts from Peru and canoes from the Philippine Sea by way of the Northwest American archipelago: that was the recipe for the mixed population in Polynesia. Airplanes and tanks droned across continental Europe and battleships conquered Norway before I was to leave these peaceful Indians. Before I wrote a summary of my findings,[3] and was parted from Liv and the rest of my world. Lost for four years in the smoke of burning cities and in the total darkness of Arctic minefields between Russian and German lines in northern Norway.

With Fatu-Hiva's palm valleys just around the corner, we sat waiting for a schooner which we were convinced would take us to a crumbling world. Who would fight whom? I had not the faintest idea. I had no enemies. But older men in government would certainly help me to get some and tell me who they were. My father feared Stalin and the Red Army. My mother feared Hitler and his Nazi troops. I feared a nameless robot that would pull all of us along by the nose.

But how differently it all worked out from my visions in the waves and the stars. Civilization was not doomed to collapse. When millions were dead, it rose and grew on, unwounded. Only people of flesh and blood were wounded. Some young people who survived,

[3] T. Heyerdahl, "Did Polynesian Culture Originate in America?" *International Science*, Vol. 1 (New York, 1941).

such as Liv and I, were mentally severed from each other forever after years of separation in different worlds. But a million machines mended the loss of tanks and airplanes, and with the invention of more modern weapons, civilization was better protected than ever before.

The ocean? How could I know that the endless Pacific before our beach would shrivel to quite comprehensible dimensions in my mind as soon as the war had ended and I no longer saw it from the decks of big aircraft carriers and destroyers, hostile to the waves? It was to shrivel in size and fury as soon as I saw it from a little wash-through balsa raft dancing obediently in the arms of the sea, between its waves. I had not the faintest idea that I was to come back to Polynesia with five friends sailing with me from Peru on an Inca-type balsa raft.

How could I know that I should feel so perfectly safe on a little wash-through craft of the type used by the people of ancient Peru that I should decide to test their other variety also, the reed-bundle boat? This was the second type of vessel of great importance in ancient South America. Indeed, it was also reported from all corners of the Polynesian triangle: Easter Island, Hawaii, and New Zealand. The reed boat, moreover, was the earliest watercraft also where the cradle of civilization had stood: in Mesopotamia and Egypt.

It was on the day I stepped on board man's oldest type of ship-shaped watercraft that I learned to see the true size of the ocean and realized the most apparent threat to mankind. The ocean is so very much smaller than we feel it to be, so small that some four billion people, busy flushing all their modern, non-transformable waste into it through all the sewers of the world, are able to destroy our planet's marine heart by pumping venom through its veins.

It is enough to step on board a few floating logs or onto a couple of reed bundles in one continent and step off them in another a few weeks later to see what the astronauts marveled at from space: The ocean is just another lake. It has no beginning and no end, but neither has an apple. Its surface just curves and meets itself. It does not overflow, because the rain and the rivers that run into it amount, to the ounce, to the quantity that evaporates from its surface and returns once more by way of the clouds. It has never turned filthy, because nature, unlike modern man, has carefully avoided putting its own atoms together to form molecules that bacteria and plankton could not transform into useful new life. Nature, with all its mud, carcasses, and excrement, could go on using its rivers as sewers forever.

The ocean was there with its millions of inhabitants to filter all the water that reached it and transform the waste into new organisms ready to continue the filtration, sending only purified, clean water back to land by way of the clouds. Man has started to throw loose bolts and nuts into an already functioning and perfect *perpetuum mobile*. Plastics, insecticides, detergents, and other combinations of molecules that nature wisely ignored so as not to plug up the machinery, now arrive and remain. We were to see visible pollution floating past our reed bundles every day when the papyrus boat *Ra II* crossed the Atlantic in 1970. We sailed past tarlike clots of oil forty-three days out of the fifty-seven the crossing lasted. Earlier, in 1947, we had sailed in perfectly pure water from Peru to Polynesia on the *Kon-Tiki* raft. We found no pollution then, although we sifted the sea water by towing behind us a fine-meshed plankton net.

But all this was much later. Now I was sitting watching the ocean as something with no beginning and no end, that man could never threaten. Suddenly I was torn out of my reveries as I focused my eyes on one point on the horizon.

"Liv," I shouted. "A sail!"

"Where? Yes! I can see it!"

We both climbed onto a lava outcrop and gazed at the majestic white sail of a schooner fixed in one spot among the changing whitecaps on the horizon. It grew bigger. It was coming from Tahiti and was heading for Fatu-Hiva.

We jumped down onto the sand and ran for the cave to get the camera and the machete. We lost no time over anything else, and then ran as fast as we could along the white beach, up on the black lava boulders, and leaped and climbed from stone to stone along the foot of the cliff toward Omoa.

The schooner was just rattling its anchor chain to the bottom as we jumped down onto the grass of the sunny bay. Everybody was there: Tioti, Willy, Pakeekee, Ioane. Everybody was smiling sadly because we were about to leave. We liked them all. They helped us to carry all our heavy boxes of stones and bottles down from our jungle hideout and dragged them into the lifeboat. The solid lifeboat from the schooner.

We hated leaving. We hated going back to civilization. But it was something we could not resist. We had to do it. We were sure then, and I still am, that the only place where it is possible to find nature as it always was is within man himself. There it is, unchanged, now as always. Man has succeeded in changing his environment and his own attire. Some peoples have resorted to tattooing and body paint, head-flattening, ear extension, filing their teeth, and stunting the growth of their feet. Men shave and cut their hair, and women dye and curl their hair, paint their faces, and put on false eyelashes, but below the skin nothing is ever altered. We cannot get away from ourselves. We have nowhere to retreat to, no choice but to help one another to build a durable civilization in harmony with whatever natural environment we have left. What we can no longer find wild, we can cultivate. Nature itself is like a hearth: We can revive the fire whenever there are embers.

Young people will have a future, not through escape, and still less by sitting on the floor and leaving it to others to blunder, but by getting up to hack off the tentacles that are dragging us away from a sensible path. By confronting the mighty octopus that we ourselves have created. By subduing it. By loosening the grip of any of its stupid, harmful, and superfluous tentacles, and making it follow us once more as a useful creature, instead of letting it entangle us and drag us along helplessly.

From all parts of the world, we suddenly begin to hear the desperate voices of doom prophets, who tell us with computer curves and convincing statistics that mankind is heading for a total catastrophe. Their opponents—we could call them lullabymen—are equally busy telling the masses to sleep on in peace: Science can take care of everything. The common man can go on watching television.

More and more young people are getting confused. They protest and try to get away. They run away from comfort by living like tramps. They hide away from elegance behind hair and rags. They show their contempt for the modern world around them and emigrate by going on "trips."

We reproach them, and they reproach us. But we are the parents of the past, and they are the parents of the future. With young minds and fresh eyes, they are trying to tell us something. They are trying to tell us that we complicate a life that can be so simple.

Since we believe in progress, that every generation is smarter than the one before, let us listen to them. Let us try to get the message and get on speaking terms with those who inevitably will take over. Those who want to simplify what we have made so complicated. We, who can even judge from our own experience, ought to see, with them, that real treasures cannot be brought home with armies, or conquered with arrows and slings that can zoom fifteen times around the earth and hit ourselves together with our enemies. Real treasures are not to be looted in enemy territory or robbed from a bank. They are weightless and on the wrong side of our eyes, so we do not see them.

Nobody can take away what you want to preserve inside you. Nobody can take Fatu-Hiva away from me. When I returned home, I published a little book in Norwegian which ended with the words I will repeat as an end to this extended version.

When we sat on the thwarts of the lifeboat and our Polynesian friends rowed us out to the anchored schooner, I fumbled in a moldy suitcase for our return vouchers.

"Liv," I said, "one can't buy a ticket to Paradise."

INDEX

Aboriginal peoples, 229–30
Alcoholic beverages, 245–46
Allaux (artist), 87–88
American Anthropologist, 233
American Indians, 171, 233, 246
American Indians in the Pacific (Heyerdahl), 70, 219, 226, 234
Amundsen, Roald, 3
Ananas sativus (pineapple), 229
Ancestor worship, 167–68
Animal birth control, 64–66
Archaeology of the Marquesas Islands (Linton), 174
Artifacts, archaeological, 69–71
Atanoa (god), 216
Atea (god), 216, 221
Atuona Valley, 103, 147–48, 185
Atuona village, 151–60, 181–83
Aymara Indians, 170, 219
Aztec Indians, 168

Balsa rafts, 233–34, 266
Bananas, kinds of, 47–48
Bella Coola Indians, 265
Belvas (wireless operator), 152, 181, 182
Biarne (grandson of Teriieroo), 19
Black sea urchins, 65, 66
Blue sharks, 119
Bonnevie, Kristine, 10

Borao trees, 208
Brander, Captain, 26–31, 87, 89, 98, 105, 132, 152, 153, 157
Broch, Dr. Hjalmar, 10, 205
Brown, F. B. H., 229, 230, 241
Buck, Sir Peter, 175, 233–34
Burial caves, 83–84
Burial customs, 74, 222–23

Cannibalism (*kaikai enata*), 36–37, 105, 110, 166, 172, 204–5, 222; last recorded instance of, 199–200; as a religious ceremony, 223
Cannibal valley, the, 193–236
Carter, G. F., 242
Chicha (aqha or *kawau*), 246
Child-bed fever, 73, 78
Chin Loy, 157, 160
Christian, F. W., 162
Club and sling (weapons), 224
Coconut palm, origin of, 231–32
Columbus, Christopher, 3, 53, 54, 242
Con-Tici-Viracocha (god-king), 220
Cook, Captain James, 21, 22–23, 53, 168, 188, 221, 265
Cook, O. F. and R. C., 241, 242
Cortez, Hernando, 3, 168
Cotton species, 240–41

Darwin, Charles, 4, 5, 98, 120
"Did Polynesian Culture Originate
    in America?" (Heyerdahl), 265
Diffusionism, 242–43
Diogenes, 212
Dixon, R. B., 233
Dromia crabs, 115

Easter Island, 162, 171, 175, 176,
    191, 192, 220, 230–31, 233, 266
Ecuador, 218, 232
Egypt (ancient), 79, 266
Einstein, Albert, 5
Elephantiasis, 30, 34, 73, 89, 99,
    177, 199
Equilibrium, law of, 64–66, 77
Ethnology of Easter Island
    (Métraux), 175
Eute trees, 110
*Evolution of Gossypium and the
    Differentiation of the Cultivated
    Cottons* (Hutchinson, Silow, and
    Stephens), 241

Faa-hoka (ancient fruit), 228–29
Fai (guide), 105–7, 109–13, 117,
    118–19
Fatu-Hiva: barren rock of, 195;
    Cannibal valley of, 193–236; cave
    home on, 255–69; decision for,
    13; departure for, 13–24, 25–30;
    exodus to the highlands, 85–99;
    first life on, 195; first petroglyph
    discovered on, 69; food and
    drinks, 47–49; influenza epi-
    demic, 71–74; jungle conditions,
    46, 51–52, 54–55; landing on,
    30–34; living in nature on, 25–58;
    location of, 12–13; Omoa Valley
    home on, 40–59; plant species of,
    228; Polynesian dialect spoken
    on, 33–34; property ownership,
    35; Spanish discovery of, 220–21;
    taboo land exploration, 101–21;

    tribal wars, 235; white men and,
    59–84
Faufau Taahitue, Chieftainess, 16,
    17, 23, 53
Fawcett, Colonel, 3
Fe-fe (disease), 126–27, 128, 132,
    138, 199
Fei (mountain banana), 16–17, 36,
    47, 56, 58, 76, 85, 87, 97, 152
Fernández de Quiros, Pedro, 220
Flora and fauna, 50–51
Flora of Southeastern Polynesia
    (Brown), 229
Flying fish, 124–26
Food plants, 48–49, 240
Fram (ship), 3
Garibaldus (lizard), 129, 135, 180
Gauguin, Paul, 14, 22, 29, 32, 138–
    39, 140, 147, 159–60, 165, 183,
    185
Gauguin, Pola, 139
Gourds (pre-Inca), 232, 240
Grelet, Willy, 32–35, 37, 39, 41, 52,
    72, 106, 135–41, 143, 146–48,
    152–54, 157–58, 165, 197, 253,
    261, 267
Günther, Professor, 79

Haii (voyager), 89, 94, 135
Hakaeva (widow), 246
Halligan, Charley, 20–21
Hamon, Renée, 156, 185
Hanaiapa Valley, 178–81
Hanativa Valley, 208
Hanaupe Valley, 235
Hanavave, island of, 29–30
Hanavave Valley, 71, 93, 118, 123;
    animal society, 94–95; archaeo-
    logical sites, 123–24; taboo
    ground in, 104–11
Handy, E. S. C., 52, 216–18, 226,
    235
Handy, Mrs. E. S. C., 52
Hansen, Armauer, 74

Hawaiian Islands, 233, 235, 240, 266

Hepea-Taipi, Chief, 235

Hermit crabs, 114–16

Heyerdahl, Thor: arrival in Tahiti, 13–24; background of, 1–13; education of, 4–7, 9–11; Polynesian name for, 24; return to civilization, 264–69

Heyerdahl, Mrs. Thor (Liv), 8–11, 20, 23, 29, 32, 36, 37, 40, 42, 49, 57, 58, 62, 66–68, 71, 72, 74, 75, 77, 81, 84, 86–88, 90, 93, 94, 96, 101, 102, 107–12, 114, 117, 121, 151–55, 157, 163–64, 177, 181, 183, 196–99, 203–4, 209–11, 213, 222, 223, 230, 236, 239, 244–61, 265, 269; ocean escape to Hivaoa, 124, 126–30, 138, 140, 143, 148–49; Polynesian name for, 24

Hitler, Adolf, 79, 265

Hittites (ancient), statues of, 174

Hivaoa, island of, 28–29, 137, 151–83, 240; arrival on, 149; population, 152–53; Spanish discovery of, 221; trading schooner calls at, 151; types of visitors to, 151–52; valleys in, 160–81

Hivaoa stone monuments, 166–78; radiocarbon analysis of, 177

Humboldt Current, 146, 228

Husk tomatoes, 230–31, 240

Hutchinson, J. B., 241

I'a te kea (fish of stone), 68

Inca Empire, 168, 170, 174, 218–20, 232; mythology, 219–20

Introduction to Polynesian Anthropology, An (Buck), 234

Ioane (guide), 35–36, 39–41, 43, 50, 59–60, 73–74, 88, 128, 133–35, 143–45, 148, 152–54, 157, 161, 197, 267

Ipomoea batatas (sweet potato), 232–34

Isolationism, 242–43

Japan Current, 265

Jews, 79

Kaahua (legendary vessel), 217

Kao-kao fish, 126

Kapiri, 112

Kava (drink), 189

Kava-drinking custom, 245, 246

Keakea, 112

Kekela (missionary), 167, 174

Kiwi bird, 162

Kon-Tiki Expedition, The (Heyerdahl), 11

Kon-Tiki (raft), 22, 231, 267

Kon-Tiki (sun king), 174

Kroepelien, Bjarne, 9, 13, 15, 22, 72

Kumara (sweet potato) plant, 232–34, 240, 243

Lagenaria (plant), 232

Lake Titicaca, 170

Lapps, 7

Larsen (teacher), 20–21, 126

Leprosarium (Tahiti), 186

Leprosy, 73

Lie, Aletti, 165–68, 170–73, 176, 177

Lie, Henry, 153, 162, 164–65, 168, 169, 171, 174–78, 187, 217

Linden hibiscus (*maho, mao, hau*), 241–43, 249

Linton, Ralph, 52, 162, 174, 188, 226

Lothrop, Dr. S. K., 233

Magellan, Ferdinand, 218

Mai-mai (piglet), 248–54, 256

Maita (billy goat), 239, 249

Manuoo tribe, 235

Marquesan cuckoo, 45

Marquesaner und Ihre Kunst, Die (Steinen), 174

Marquesan fruit rat, 187
Marquesan Legends (Handy), 217, 235
Marquesan Somatology with Comparative Notes on Samoa and Tonga (Sullivan), 219
Marquesas Islands: population, 12; Spanish discovery of, 220–21; *Te-Fiti* (ancestral homeland), 217, 218
Mehren, Martin, 7–8
Melanesian pig, 94
Melville, Herman, 14
Mendaña, Admiral, 220–21
Mendaña expedition, 218, 232–33
Mendel, Gregor, 10
Merrill, E. D., 241, 242
Mesopotamia (ancient), 79, 266
Métraux, A., 175
Mexico, cotton agriculture in, 241
Mio trees, 208
Missionaries, 23, 80, 88, 109, 177, 207, 216, 229, 240
Mister Bob (shopkeeper), 152–57, 181, 182, 185, 200, 212, 238, 243, 244, 249
Moa bird, 162
Moana (schooner), 71, 185–87, 190
Moon goddess, 215
Moray eels, 65, 66, 257; danger from, 255–56
Mormons, 89
Mosquitoes, 127–28, 141, 197–99, 207; nocturnal types of, 131–32
Motane, island of, 146, 175, 193; barren landscape of, 188–92, 194–96, 212; marine life, 190; sheep on, 188–90, 196; Spanish discovery of, 221
Motaro, 179
Motu-nui (The Great Rock), 109

Naiki tribe, 162
Namana Mountains, 199
Nansen, Fridtjof, 3

Napoleon (islander), 246, 247, 249
Narrative of the Second Voyage of the Adelantado Álvaro de Mendaña (Fernández de Quiros), 220
Natahu Peak, 245
Native Culture in the Marquesas, The (Handy), 226
Negroid Melanesians, 83
Nordenskiöld, Erland, 232
Northwest Coast Indians, 265
Norwegian lemming, 65
Nuku-Hiva, island of, 27–28

Omoa Bay, 220
Omoa Valley, 30–31, 196, 203–4, 209, 240, 243, 245, 246, 252, 253, 258, 263
Origin of the Indian Civilizations in South America (Nordenskiöld), 232
Oslo National Theater, 8
Oslo University, 9, 131
Ouia Valley, 199–236, 243, 244, 248, 250–52; food in, 212–14, 227–29; tropical luxuriance, 212–13

Paa Jakt efter Paradiset (Heyerdahl), 11
Paepae (elevated stone platform), 52, 82, 232
Paho, 90, 92–93, 124, 125, 130, 200, 202–3
Pakeekee (parson), 23–24, 59–60, 71, 88–90, 95, 98, 99, 101, 121, 124, 134, 135, 137–38, 141, 154, 161, 199, 200, 242, 248, 253, 267
Panther (wild cat), 130
Papaya plants, 229, 240
Paracas, Peruvian tombs at, 232
Pavahina grass, 228
Peru, 264, 267; cotton agriculture in, 241; rafts from, 265
Petroglyphs, 69, 70
Philippine Sea, 265

Pineapple seedlings, 240
Pitcairn Island, 175
Pizarro, Francisco, 3, 168, 218
Pizarro, Pedro, 219
Plankton, functions of, 54
Poipoi (food staple), 82–83, 135, 138, 152, 213, 238, 244
Polo, Marco, 53
Polynesia: canoe boats, 70; contact with America, 70, 222–36, 240–43, 245–46, 265; culinary arts, 24; origins of, 79, 80, 171, 217–20; population, 188
Polynesian dog, 173
Polynesian language, 33–34, 42
Polynesian pig, 50
Polynesian Religion (Handy), 216
Polynesian triangle, length of, 167
Porter, Captain, 231–32
Poto (wild cat), 129–30, 197
Progress, defined, 260–62
Puamau Valley, 160–78, 217; cannibalism, 199–200; Norwegian cabin in, 164–65; stone monuments at, 166–78

Quechua Indians, 219, 232

Ra II (papyrus boat), 267
Raivavae Island, 175
Reed boats, 266
Relation of the Discovery and Conquest of the Kingdoms of Peru (Pizarro), 219
Religion, 24, 60–61, 216–17. *See also* Tiki (god)
Reports of the Norwegian Archaeological Expedition to Easter Island and the East Pacific, 166
Royal Anthropological Institute, 233

Sahara Desert, prehistoric cliff paintings, 191–92

San Agustín statues, 170–71, 173
Schurtz, H., 70
Sea food, gathering of, 213
Sea Routes to Polynesia (Heyerdahl), 219
Sharks, 119, 137
Silow, R. A., 241
Skulls (ancient), 79–81; trephined craniums, 226–27
Sling stones, use of, 172, 224
Society Islands, 226, 240
Solomon Islands, 220
Spanish Civil War, 136
Spider crabs, 115
Stalin, Joseph, 265
"Statues of the Oipona Me'ae, With a Comparative Analysis of Possibly Related Stone Monuments, The" (Heyerdahl), 166
Steinen, Karl von den, 52, 162, 173–74, 218
Stephens, S. G., 241
Stewart, C. S., 226
Sullivan, L. R., 219, 229–30, 241
Svenson, Calle, 20–21
Sweet potato, 241

Taboo ground, 101–21, 186; departure from, 111–21; devil beliefs about, 103; Hanavave Valley, 104–11; journey to, 101–4; rules respecting, 105–6; *Tiki* images, 108
Tahaoa beach, 61–68, 213, 254–55, 257–69; marine life, 63–67
Tahia-Momo, 199, 203, 205, 207, 209–11, 213, 223, 236–39, 243–46, 248, 250–51
Tahia-pitiani, 81–82, 243
Tahiti, 13–24, 87, 134, 226, 240, 248; daily wage rate, 42; national hymn of, 14; Spanish flu epidemic, 15, 72
Tahuata, island of, 137, 146, 188, 221

Taiohae Valley, 147
Taiokai Valley, 112, 118
Takapoto Atoll, 26
Takaroa Atoll, 26
Tane (god), 216, 221
Taoa Teke (Dr. Teke), 224–27
Tauaouoho Mountains, 37, 51, 68,
    196, 199, 200, 218, 227, 238, 249
Tehavahinenao (tunnel), 105
Teita grass, 124, 249, 250
Tei Tetua, 199–216, 219, 221–26,
    230–40, 243–47, 249, 252;
    cannibal ceremony, 223; religious
    beliefs of, 216–17
Terai (nurse), 156–57, 160–63,
    165, 171, 178, 181, 185, 208
Tereora (schooner), 23, 26–31,
    87–88, 90, 136, 144, 145, 156–59
Teriieroo, Chief, 9, 13, 15–20,
    22–24, 47, 53, 59–60, 72, 87, 136,
    156, 161, 208, 224
Théodore (trading master), 27, 29,
    30
Tiahuanaco, pre-Inca cult site
    of, 170, 174, 177, 218, 232
Tiare flowers, 117
Tiki (god), 69, 83, 108, 109, 140,
    141, 205, 216–17, 221, 235; Inca
    mythology and, 220; liturgical
    recitation of, 216; stone statues
    of, 236; weapon carvings of, 224
Tioti (sexton), 42, 60, 61, 64, 65,
    67–69, 72, 81, 88–90, 92, 95,
    101–12, 114, 117, 119–21, 124,
    126, 127, 130, 132, 137–38, 141,
    145, 161, 197, 199–201, 203, 204,
    207, 253–54, 255, 257, 258, 267
Tioti, Madame, 67
Toeva (finger-shaped rock), 171–72

Totora reed boats, 233
Trepanning operations (ancient),
    226–27
Triffe (gendarme), 152–54, 156,
    159, 181, 182
Tuberculosis, 73
Tubuai Islands, 165
Tuimata, Princess, 15
Tuiveta (stallion), 95–97
Tukopana (medicine men), 103
Tupac Yupanqui, 218–19

Uapou, island of, 25, 235
Uta (father of Tei-Tetua), 216,
    223
Uvea, island of, 227

Vai-Po (the Water-of-the-Night),
    112, 117–18
Venereal disease, 73, 221
Veo (hunter), 83–84, 88, 89, 95,
    126, 135, 199, 200, 226, 243–45
Victorin, Père, 60, 88–90, 98, 99,
    135–40, 154, 157, 242, 246
Vikings of the Sunrise (Buck),
    175, 234
Viracocha (god), 219
*Visit to the South Seas in the U.S.
    ship "Vincennes," During the
    Years 1829 and 1830, A*
    (Stewart), 226
Völkerkunde Museum (Berlin), 53,
    173

Water pollution, 267
Wölfel, D. J., 224
World War I, 4, 26, 136
World War II, 11

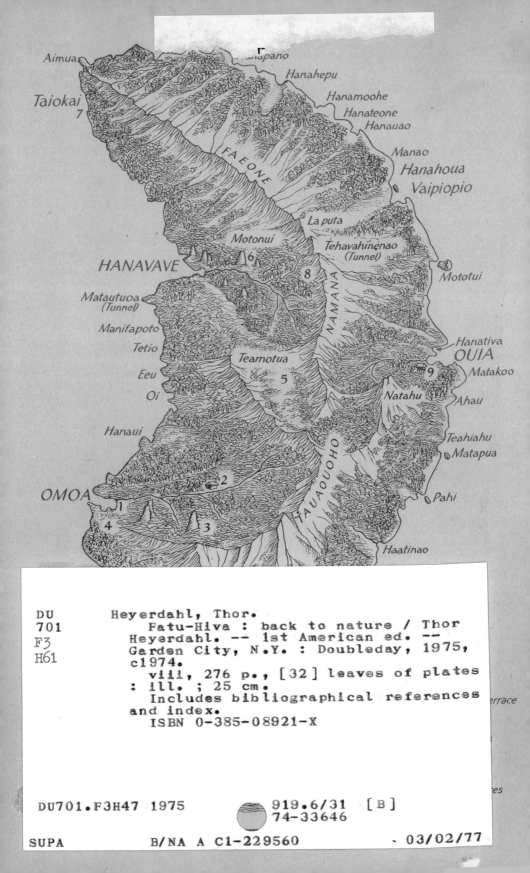